D1195412

Doings and Undoings

DOINGS *and* UNDOINGS

the fifties and after in American writing

Norman Podhoretz

New York FARRAR, STRAUS & COMPANY

Library of Congress catalog card number 64–12358

Published simultaneously in Canada by
Ambassador Books, Ltd., Toronto
Manufactured in the U.S.A. by
The Book Press, New York
Designed by Betty Crumley

Acknowledgment is made to the editors of Commentary, Harper's, The New
Leader, The New Yorker, Partisan Review, The Reporter and Show, in whose
pages these articles originally appeared. The essays, "Snopesishness," "Nathanael West," and "Gallipoli: Romance and Reality," were published in
The New Yorker in slightly different form.

New York FARRAR, STRAUS & COMPANY

FOR MY MOTHER AND FATHER

CONTENTS

III : THE WORLD OUT THERE

Doings and Undoings

Introduction

As I hope you will bear with me long enough to discover, I do not believe that a collection of essays ought to pretend that it is anything but a collection of essays. Permit me to announce, then, that what you have before you is a collection of occasional essays, written over a period of about ten years. It is not a unified collection, and it does not claim to be secretly exploring a single theme beneath all the apparent diversity. In a sense, indeed, it does not even claim to have been written by a single person. How many people wrote it, then? Two, I think, or possibly three. I am one of them. The others are comparative strangers to me now, but I have allowed them a place in my book because while I differ with them on many points of detail—and sometimes even on crucial questions—they had certain things to say that I am no longer capable of saying myself, but that are not necessarily the less relevant for that.

For in calling this a collection of occasional essays, I mean precisely that every one of them was written in hot response to a particular event and out of a highly specific context. Most often the event was the appearance of a new book that seemed to me to raise important issues of one kind or another; and almost always it was the issues rather than the book itself that I really cared about. Is that a damaging admission for a literary critic to make? I suppose in a way it is. A literary critic ought—or so they tell me —to regard literature as an end in itself; otherwise he has no business being a literary critic. For better or worse, however, I do not regard literature as an end in itself (and neither do those young men who are responsible for some of the earlier-dated pieces in this collection—which is one of the things, at least, I still have in common with them). And since I do not regard it as an end in itself, I have only very rarely considered that it was enough in discussing a book to pronounce judgment on its artistic merits. The judgment, of course, always has to be made: without it, literary discourse is nothing, it becomes pointless or merely subservient to fashion, and it never acquires an urgency or a grace of its own. Even a wrong or a stupid judgment is better than none, provided it emerges authentically out of the critic's experience. But if judgment is a necessary condition of the vitality of criticism, it is most emphatically not a sufficient one, exact perhaps in those cases where the critic is trying to correct what he considers to be an egregious error in the prevailing estimate of a book or a literary reputation. The reason we can make an exception in such cases is that they supply their own polemical edge: the context is already there and the issues are implicitly drawn. Where the context is not self-evidently given, it is up to the critic to supply it out of his own sense of what the relevant issues are—that is to say, out of his own view of the world around him, out of his own perception of its needs, out of his own apprehension of its problems.

What I mean, then, in saying that for me literature is not an end in itself is that I look upon it as a mode of public discourse that either illuminates or fails to illuminate the common ground on which we live. My attitude toward it, in other words, is agnostic rather than religious: I do not go to literature for the salvation of my soul, but only to enlarge or refine my understanding, and I do not expect it to redeem the age, but only to help the age become less chaotic and confused. The novel—let me restrict myself to that, since it is the literary form with which I have been most closely concerned—has its own history, its own rules, its own inherent possibilities and limits. These may all be of great interest to me as a student of literature, and they may be of some interest to me as an habitual reader. But they are of no interest to me as a man living in a particular place at a particular time and beset by problems of a particular kind. Most serious critics today write either as students or as passionate and habitual novel readers. I write as a participant observer of the culture for whom the novel is one form of discourse among many, and not necessarily the most valuable. I have lost my piety toward the form in its own right, which means that I do not feel an automatic sympathy for the enterprise of novel-writing. Indeed, nothing seems to me more ridiculous, or more damaging to cultural health, than the idea that novel-writing is the only "real" writing there is.

It would, however, be equally ridiculous to deny that the novel plays a unique, and uniquely valuable, part in the life of our age. More than anyone else, perhaps, the novelist acts out his attitudes in public, and since his attitudes are likely to reflect the prevailing ideas and aspirations of the culture, he more than anyone else tells us what these ideas and aspirations actually mean and finally come to. Often what he tells us is inadvertent; often it is even the opposite of what he wishes to tell us. When Blake said that Milton in *Paradise Lost* was really of the Devil's party, he was perceiving the kind of discrepancy between intention and true feeling that we find over and over again in works of fiction. For as Blake also said, conception may lie, but execution never: a failure of execution exposes the lie of conception. And just as Milton's inability to prevent the Devil from becoming the hero of *Paradise Lost* tells us something not only about Milton but about the nature of Puritanism and the realities of the Puritan temper, so the concrete results of a contemporary novelist's intentions can speak worlds about the spiritual contours of our own age. This is why judgment is only the beginning for a critic to whom literature is not an end in itself, but rather a wedge into matters beyond the confines of literary history proper. For such a critic, the question is what the strengths or weaknesses of the book under consideration mean. He wants to know what they suggest about the possibilities of life in his time.

Whatever you may say about this as an approach to literature in general, it is, I am convinced, the only approach a serious critic can take if he is to devote his attention to new writing at all usefully. Consider in this connection the case of F. R. Leavis, who is surely one of the few great critics in English literary history. Leavis is scholarly but very far from academic, and he is, to put it mildly, passionate about the state of contemporary literary culture. In England he was among the earliest partisans of the modernist movement and his critical "revaluations" of all the major English writers were very much determined by his sense of the needs of the present moment. Despite his lively involvement with the new, however, Leavis has not to my knowledge found a single novel or poem written in the last twenty years or so that could satisfy his critical standards—not a single one. Is it possible that Leavis is right? Is it conceivable that *nothing* of substantial merit has been produced since the end of World War II? Obviously it is inconceivable. And yet if you approach literature with the absolutistic expectations that Leavis brings to it, if you come to the new with a mind and a sensibility and a set of preconceptions formed by the best works of the past, and if you are imbued with a puritanical determination to make no charitable concessions at

all, the pickings of the last two decades are bound to seem pitifully lean.

On the other side, if you come to the new with a mind and a
sensibility and a set of preconceptions formed by the journalistic
culture of our day in America, you will probably find yourself
stumbling over a masterpiece with every step. You will discover
that at least five "good" or "interesting" or "serious" novels are
published every week of the year; and approximately once a
month you will happen upon a book that seems better than
"good" or "interesting," and so you will have no alternative but to
call it "extraordinary" or "overwhelming" or "brilliant." Everywhere you look you will see "promising" and "talented" new writers appearing, and to make sure that their promise is fulfilled and
their talent brought to fruition, you will immediately award them
grants and fellowships. Soon, if they are not paralyzed by all this
admiration, they will publish a second book (a collection of short
stories) and then another novel, at which point they will have
become important writers commanding the respectful attention
of all the reviewers. A few of them, with a third or fourth novel,
will suddenly "break through" and acquire chic, and they will
henceforth be known as the major writers of their generation. And
so it will go until the process starts up again, and then again, and
then again.

On the one side, then, we have an overly demanding critical
vocabulary, and on the other a debased journalistic vocabulary.
Somewhere in the middle there has to be a language in which it
is possible to talk sensibly and with due proportion about new
books. I am suggesting that this language can only be found by a
critic who is tough on the new, but who does not ask of it that it
should justify itself as a pure and perfect object of aesthetic contemplation—as, so to speak, a contribution to the realm of Being.
All he asks is that it should be a contribution to the realm of
Becoming, to the life of the here-and-now. He will be as exacting

in his critical judgments as he has the courage and the intelligence to be: he will try to discriminate between the genuine and the counterfeit, the authentic and the dishonest, the realized and the willed, the central and the peripheral. But at the same time he will know that he is making these judgments as a total relativist—he will know, in other words, that what he is measuring a new novel against is primarily itself and not the giants. He will know this because he looks upon the new novel before him as the acting out of a present possibility, as a struggle with the unique conditions of the here-and-now being waged by a man who is also uniquely of the here-and-now. And since he will understand himself to be no less uniquely of the here-and-now than the novelist is, he will recognize this struggle to be his own in a way that nothing in the past can ever quite be. That is why he chooses to be a critic of the contemporary rather than a browser among masterpieces or a reverent interpreter of the classics.

And that is also why he will read the established writers of the immediate past with a special suspicion—in our case, writers like Faulkner, Hemingway, and Fitzgerald. A pious mystique always surrounds such writers; they can no more be escaped than one's parents can be escaped. But like one's parents, they can be crippling unless they are seen in human scale, as people who had other battles to fight and other wisdoms to acquire. They too are unbearably taxed by being approached as though they were fixed for all eternity in the pantheon of the giants, as though their work transcended its own here-and-now, as though it were a species of Being rather than a record of yesterday's Becoming. We are much too close to these writers to judge them truly in any but the relativistic way that we can judge our own contemporaries. And when we judge them in that way, one of the things we find is that they have little to say to us that is not terribly misleading and terribly inhibiting to the development of the wisdoms that we must earn for ourselves. Being so close to us in time, they can fool us into thinking that their world, their here-and-now, is the world we still inhabit. It is not, things have changed too fast. We are, indeed, separated from the writers of the 1920's as Bernard Shaw once said the English were separated from the Americans—by the illusion of a common language.

To the extent that the essays which follow have a unifying preoccupation, it is to expose that illusion and to look at some of the consequences that flow from its exposure. The pieces grouped together in the first section all deal with established writers of the immediate past, most of whom were still writing in the 1950's and a few of whom are still writing today. Usually what concerned me was to examine the effect of the radically new conditions of the postwar period on the writer's special vision of the world, and more often than not I found myself trying to demonstrate that the effect was damaging—that the force of his work had been diminished by the growing irrelevance of the attitudes on which it had always depended. Needless to say, my own attitudes were— and are—far more time-bound and fragile than the formidable visions I was pitting them against, and so some of them already seem, after only a few years, to be showing the signs of premature senility. For example, although I still think Faulkner's *A Fable* is a very bad novel, and pretty much for the reasons I gave in the piece reprinted here, I would be inclined today to see the book as reflecting a sounder moral response to cold-war America than the somewhat complacent attitude implied by several of my formulations.

At the same time, however, I would not wish to repudiate those formulations altogether. It has become fashionable in certain quarters to dismiss the revisionist liberalism of the 50's—which is associated with names like Lionel Trilling, Sidney Hook, Daniel Bell, and Richard Hofstadter, and which exerted a considerable influence on the earliest pieces in this collection—as a species of conformist thinking developed by intellectuals who, motivated in part by a genuine horror of Stalinism and in part by an abject failure of critical nerve, took to celebrating the virtues of American society and the values of the middle-class spirit. I myself have come more and more to see revisionist liberalism as involving an abdication of the intellectual's proper role as a critic of society, and whatever documentary interest this book may have lies in the record it indirectly supplies of how the ideological climate has changed over the past ten years and how the changes have been expressed and reflected in the literary world. It is for the sake of that interest that I have refrained from the temptation to do any updating and from the effort to impose my present attitudes on every piece in this book—not that I really could have imposed them even if I had wanted to. But that is not the only reason. Revisionist liberalism had something important to say in the 50's, and because what it had to say is now being overlooked or distorted or misunderstood, it continues to need saying. There can be no bypassing it; we can only go beyond it by going through it—which, as is obvious from some of the pieces in Part II, is what I have been trying to do for the past few years.

Part II is mainly devoted to writers who have emerged since the 1940's. It does not give anything like a complete picture of what the postwar American novelists have been doing, but it does, I hope, indicate what the major directions have been and where the pitfalls have turned up. In general, the question that any serious critic looking at this period is bound to ask is why so much promise, so much devotion, and so much ambition have yielded so little in the way of substantial achievement. As you will notice, I have found different answers to that question at different times and in connection with different writers. And as you will also notice if you get as far as Part III, I have even on occasion toyed with the idea that we may be looking in the wrong place for the achievements of the creative literary imagination when we look for them only where they were last seen—in novels and poems and plays.

Accordingly, although many of the books discussed in Part III would not ordinarily be regarded as proper objects of a literary critic's attention, it was as a critic of the kind I was describing a moment ago that I invariably approached these books. And although most of the issues discussed in Part III would not ordinarily be regarded as falling within the competence of a literary critic, it was as a critic of public discourse and a highly interested party to the social and political and cultural disputes of the day that I presumed to speak on these issues.

We all inhabit the same world; it is the only world there is to inhabit. Those of us who write, if we are doing anything, are trying to make sense of that world, and our ways of trying are not nearly so different as we have been led to assume: in one form or another, we are all testing our beliefs and acting out our attitudes in public. Such, at any rate, is the belief being tested and the attitude being acted out in the pages that follow.

I

Traditions

Faulkner in the 50's

I. THE PROBLEM OF WAR

A *Fable* may not be William Faulkner's worst book; one would have to re-read *Pylon* to make a definitive judgment, and I personally could not face the ordeal. But whether or not it is his worst, this new novel is for the most part so dull, so tortured, so pretentious, that it forced me back to *Red Leaves* and *Spotted Horses*, *Light in August* and *The Sound and the Fury*, for reassurance. Perhaps Faulkner was always as bad as this; perhaps some obsolete piety has prevented us from seeing him truly. But the reassurance was there: those earlier works *are* wonderful, they *are* masterpieces. Nevertheless they struck me as the consummation of a minor, and not, as I once thought, a major talent. I found them narrower than I remembered, and what was more surprising, not in the least complex. Faulkner's prose style, perhaps, has fooled us into attributing complexity to his mind. It now seems obvious, however, that he really is what he always claims to be: a simple man. His warmest admirers have usually refused to take him at his word, insisting that the pettish autobiographical remarks he has made to interviewers were a pose, the great artist's secret revenge on the impertinent intruders who came south to pester him. Yet how much more impressive, after all, and how fitting, that it should be this way.

The narrowness I am speaking of is a narrowness of range. I am not suggesting that Faulkner's work exhibits just one mode of feeling or a single quality (it is often forgotten how funny this most solemn of writers can be), but rather that he deals best with only one kind of person acting in one kind of situation. Think of his greatest achievements: the transcription of how Issetibbeha's condemned Negro slave ran from his pursuers, never resting and finally eating a nest of ants to keep himself alive; or Lena Grove walking across two states with the patience of the stupid and the saintly, expecting to find the father of her unborn child; or the picture of Quentin Compson, crazed with a sense of honor so powerful that it drives him to suicide, buying a dirty little girl soggy cakes, only to be arrested for molesting her, and laughing when he is arrested; or the description of Lion, the great yellow hunting dog hurling himself time after time after time against a door he can never crash through and that he knows he can never crash through. These marvellous images share one overriding conception: a sense of all living things as possessed, fated, doomed—and the possessed are the simplest of creatures. They do and feel only as they must, and if they do what they must with dignity, beauty, and submission, Faulkner finds glory in their lives. "Come," his captors tell Issetibbeha's slave, "you ran well. Do not be ashamed." But the glory Faulkner attributes to the man is no different from the glory he sees in the dog—which tells us something about his view of reality.

Think also what is missing from his books. Perhaps it can be summed up by saying that as far as Yoknapatawpha is concerned,

the Enlightenment might just as well have never been. The qualities of reasonableness, moderation, compromise, tolerance, sober
choice—in short, the anti-apocalyptic style of life brought into the
modern world by the middle class—no more exists for Faulkner
than plain ordinary folks do (everyone is at least a demigod to
him). To a whimsical observer, indeed, his work might almost
seem a gigantic fantasy fulfilling the wish that the middle class
had never been brought forth onto this earth. He doesn't even
hate it accurately, as those great haters Flaubert and D. H. Lawrence did. In the very act of damning industrial, urban, middle-
class man, he reveals nothing more than an abstract conception of
what the type is like. Jason Compson, for example, is one of
Faulkner's supreme triumphs, but he hardly represents the cor-
rosive effects of the business ethos on a man's soul. For Jason is
really another variety of the possessed creature Faulkner always
writes about. There is nothing mean or diminutive—or middling,
for that matter—about him, except perhaps his objectives. He has
the same overwhelming compulsiveness, the same superhuman
drive exhibited by his characteristic adversary, Quentin Compson
—whereas the truth is that the middle class, if it stands for anything at all, supports the immediate exorcising of all known
demons. Its great cultural triumph is precisely that it brought
obsession into disrepute.

The view that takes Faulkner as a chronicler of the war between
pre-industrial civilization and the new world of the middle class
seems to me unfounded. I cannot discover a genuine sense of
history in the Yoknapatawpha series; unlike Stendhal, say, who saw
a new kind of personality emerging from major historical changes
and understood the drama and significance of its clash with a
moribund type, Faulkner has always taken refuge from historical
change in a vague sense of doom. We can speak without exaggeration of Julien Sorel's struggle with the de la Moles as the 19th
century versus the 18th—two different worlds quite literally meet

in *The Red and the Black*, two different temperaments, two different attitudes toward the self. Jason Compson, on the other hand, is merely Quentin Compson gone wrong. And who can blame him?

Faulkner's narrowness, then, has always stemmed partly from an unwillingness or an inability either to love or to hate the world of the 20th century enough to understand it. But it isn't contemporary reality alone that Faulkner has shied away from. The very effort to explain, to understand any living thing, seems to him sheer blasphemy. Moreover, he is utterly indifferent to subtlety and qualification. When he qualifies—and often he will do so at tiresome length—it is not with the Jamesian intent of suggesting how much the naked eye never sees. Nor does he wish to refine the gross perception and focus it on a delicate point. The fine points are a swarm of motes irritating to Faulkner's eyes; occasionally he can descend to a crude, surly tone in dismissing them as irrelevant:

"But tell me why—No, I know why. I know the reason. I know it's true: I just want to hear you say it, hear both of us say it so I'll know it's real"—already—or still—speaking, even through the other's single vicious obscene contemptuous epithet: "You could have surrendered the horse at any time and it could have stayed alive, but that was not it: not just to keep it alive, any more than for the few thousands or the few hundred thousands that people will always be convinced you won on it"—stopping then and even waiting, or anyway watching, exultant and calm while the prisoner cursed, nor toward him nor even just at him, but him, the ex-deputy, steadily and for perhaps a full minute, with harsh and obscene unimagination, then the ex-deputy speaking again, rapid and peaceful and soothing: "All right, all right. The reason was so that it could run, keep on losing races at least, finish races at least even if it did have to run them on three legs because it was a giant and didn't need even three legs to run them on but only one with a hoof at the end to qualify as a horse."

Is it fanciful to suggest that Faulkner's sympathies are with the obscene prisoner who thinks that the young man in quest of reasons is a fool and a monster? Faulkner frequently takes a kind of mischievous delight in tantalizing us with long passages which pretend to be explanations, but whose point is that no explanations are possible. These passages invariably consist of crude metaphysical assertions written with an ineptitude even translations of Hegel rarely match. He hurls his convoluted rhetoric and clumsy thought into the air like an educated version of his own prisoner cursing those of us who ask for a reason or two now and then. In any case, the notion that nothing can be explained is a half-truth which, in my opinion, has limited Faulkner's creative range. For let us be bold and admit it: a lack of ideas is no virtue in a novelist. I do not believe that Faulkner ever had ideas. Convictions, yes, and a terrifying energy behind them, but not ideas, not the wish to understand the world, only the wish to feel deeply and to transcribe what he felt and saw. (Compare him to Dostoyevsky and the difference between a demonic writer with ideas and one who has none becomes clear.) Heaven knows that what Faulkner did have was enough to make him one of the two or three first-rate writers in modern American literature. But it was not enough to make him a truly great writer.

It was also not enough to sustain his creative energy. For the paradox is that after a while the imagination of a novelist who has maintained merely an equivocal flirtation with ideas begins to flounder. At the very point when he needs more than his original enthusiasm about a subject to keep him going, he finds himself without resources. He may feel his subject as intensely as ever, but the convictions which once were enough to make him certain that it was a *significant* subject no longer appear self-evident. Eventually this loss of confidence will also affect his capacity to distinguish between emotion which refers to something outside and feeling which is created by the will to feel. (The rhetorical mode of *A Fable* seems to me evidence of Faulkner's present inability to recognize a self-generated paroxysm when he works his nerves into one.) And finally, it will betray the novelist into choosing subjects that he has no business dealing with.

The more explicitly Faulkner declares his "values"—as he has been doing lately—the more we suspect that he is terribly unsure of himself these days, unsure of the relevance of his way of looking at things. For what has the Glory celebrated in Yoknapatawpha got to do with the Korean War—that tiresome, drab, plodding, inconclusive war, from which not a single national hero emerged? What has become of Faulkner—or of us—when a speech like his Nobel Prize address affirming the nobility of man and his power to endure and to prevail despite atom bombs, falls on our ears with a sound dangerously like irrelevant cant? We do have our own kind of glory and our own kind of miraculousness, but Faulkner's vocabulary is somehow inadequate to describe them. And I think *A Fable* proves that he knows it and is trying to do something about it.

A Fable is Faulkner's version of the Passion of Jesus Christ. It is difficult not to see in it also his attempt to bring Yoknapatawpha up to date. The allegory is superimposed upon the story of a false armistice which takes place toward the end of World War I. Faulkner portrays the war as an endless, frustrating affair which seems meaningless to those caught in it, a war so devastating to the spirit that it doesn't even provide ambitious young men with their chance for glory: a war, in fact, rather like the one we have all been living through since 1948. Into this atmosphere, Faulkner introduces his extremely shadowy Christ figure, an illiterate corporal serving in the French army who inspires a whole regiment to mutiny. The mutiny frightens all the top brass of both sides so thoroughly that they suspend hostilities long enough to hold a conference for the purpose of forming a united front against this revolutionary move. People must never learn that they can end a war as simply as all that. But at least one man does learn. He is a former officer who has intentionally had himself degraded to the ranks and become a runner. When he hears of the mutiny, he experiences what can only be called a conversion, and though he has never met the corporal, he dedicates himself to spreading (among the "Gentiles") the new gospel, the secret that can transform the whole world:

> "Don't you see? If all of us, the whole battalion, at least one battalion, one unit out of the whole line to start it, to lead the way— leave the rifles and grenades and all behind us in the trench: simply climb barehanded out over the parapet and through the wire and then just walk on barehanded, not with our hands up for surrender but just open to show that we had nothing to hurt, harm anyone; not running, stumbling: just walking forward like free men—just one of us, one man; suppose just one man, then multiply him by a battalion; suppose a whole battalion of us, who want nothing except just to go home and get themselves into clean clothes and work and drink a little beer in the evening and talk and then lie down and sleep and not be afraid. And maybe, just maybe that many Germans who don't want anything more too, to put his or their rifles and grenades down and climb out too with their hands empty too not for surrender but just so every man could see there is nothing in them to hurt or harm either—"

That William Faulkner should be able to take such stuff not seriously but reverently, that he should see the trench mutiny as anything but a pathetic gesture of desperation! What are we to make of it?

Well, it is all done for the sake of an affirmation. Two years ago, in his Nobel Prize address, Faulkner "declined to accept the end of man." The passage in which he insisted most intensely on his faith is in A *Fable* also, spoken by the corporal's father, the Commander-in-Chief of Allied Forces in France, who acknowledges his (illegitimate) son in the act of condemning him to death:

> "I don't fear man. I do better: I respect and admire him. And pride: I am ten times prouder of that immortality which he does possess than ever he of that heavenly one of his delusion. Because man and his folly will endure. They will do more. They will prevail."

Heavenly immortality, then, is a "delusion"; man's true immortality lies in his glorious career on earth. There may or may not be a God (if the corporal is Christ, are we to take the Marshal of France as God the Father?), and he may or may not have actually given his son to save the world. For all we can tell from A *Fable*, it does not matter to Faulkner. Though Faulkner is a very religious writer, his work surely constitutes a paean to Man, not to God. He has turned to the Gospels as the source of his affirmation, not because he has suddenly discovered traditional Christianity, but because he rightly sees in the Gospels the greatest tribute to Man ever conceived: they tell how God became man and man became God for a brief moment, and it therefore presumably lies in man's power to become "God" again. Even today.

But it is an empty affirmation, for A *Fable* is another one of those proofs that an artist must either accept the religious view of the universe as a literal truth or leave its myths alone. The Gospel According to Matthew is a literary masterpiece because the author saw no contradiction in the idea of a man-God. He was not disturbed by qualities in the Messiah which many modern Christians would consider a blasphemy to attribute to the Son of God. The character of Jesus, as it appears in Matthew, Mark, and Luke, is not in the least monolithic: his Godliness is conveyed mainly through his ideas, thus never deteriorating into insipid virtue, while the plentiful evidences of his humanity are unabashedly displayed: we get glimpses of his arrogance, his impatience, his playfulness, his capacity to suffer. As for Faulkner's corporal, the trouble with him is not just that he is monolithic; he simply doesn't exist. Nor does the Olympian marshal. Nor do any of the characters who take part in the religious allegory. How could they exist when Faulkner doesn't seem to believe that they ever did? Under these conditions not all the biblical parallels in all the testaments ever compiled could give them life.

And there are parallels aplenty in *A Fable*. The corporal brings a complete biblical retinue along with him. Of the twelve men in his squad, one betrays him; he is "engaged" to a whore from Marseilles who he has said was really "a good girl"; he even has a virgin mother of sorts (his real mother had died in childbirth after having been cast off by her husband for committing adultery, so the corporal was raised by his sister who, being nine years old at his birth, could only be called his mother in a spiritual sense, I suppose). Many other analogies come to mind, including the traditional chronology of the Passion. The corporal is captured on a Wednesday, executed on a Friday, and "resurrected" on a Sunday. He is killed (at the age of 33) together with two other criminals, and though he is executed by means of a firing squad, Faulkner still contrives to have him die with a crown of "thorns" around his head:

> The corporal's post may have been flawed or even rotten because . . . the plunge of the post had jammed it and its burden too into a tangled mass of old barbed wire, a strand of which had looped up and around the top of the post and the man's head as though to assoil them both in one unbroken continuation of the fall, into the anonymity of the earth.

Before he dies, however, he performs miracles. The miracle at Cana is given a particularly "modern" naturalistic interpretation, where either Faulkner's sense of humor or his lack of reverence has got the better of his judgment. It seems that the corporal met a young American soldier who wanted to marry an orphan girl. Neither of them had any money and consequently could not prepare a wedding feast. To help them out of their predicament, the corporal walks into a crap game and calmly picks up the money lying on the floor, explaining to the soldiers (who are on the point of dealing with him as we might expect) that he needs it for one of their buddies. Miraculously, the soldiers experience a burst of sentimental enthusiasm and "adopt" the wedding, buying up all the wine in town, thus, I assume, turning water into wine. This sort of thing, embarrassingly silly as it is, can almost be compared to some of the details in D. H. Lawrence's version of Jesus' resurrection (*The Man Who Died*) which, in the monstrous reaches of its bad taste, strikes even an unbeliever as a blasphemy.

It would be dishonest to pretend that the occasional spurts of life in *A Fable* redeem the book. The story which Faulkner worked into the allegory about the wretched Cockney groom and the Negro preacher who steal a crippled race horse was written nine years ago, and though it is a good story, it certainly falls short of his best work on animals and men (for example, *The Bear*). As for the character of General Gragnon, the commander of the mutinied regiment who wants to execute all three thousand men, and would be prepared to execute a whole army for the sake of his reputation, he is Yoknapatawpha itself dressed in a French uniform. But Gragnon is buried in the allegoric mess; Faulkner never gives him the chance he deserves.

A Fable, then, is one of those disembodied, religiose affirmations that we have learned to regard as the typical literary symptom of a failure of nerve in difficult times. It can be read as a fantasy in quest of some optimistic statement on our present predicament. Faulkner offers us a "pure," primitivistic Christianity that we are meant to feel is nobler, more beautiful, somehow more effective than our worldly politics. For he can see nothing but silliness in the machinations of the political mind; his satiric chapter on the conference of the generals seems to me astonishingly simple-minded, a worthy foil to his conception of the Christian lesson for our time. We are confronted here with Faulkner's impulse to escape the complexity of a world he has no patience with, a world he cannot understand. He is saying to us: "I am tired and bored and bewildered by the way you go about things; I am sick of your conferences and your bickerings. They don't matter, they are little childish games. What matters is Love and Faith and Hope." Love of what? Faith in what? Faulkner never tells us. How could he, when he cannot realize that today as perhaps never before the question of man-and-his-destiny is inseparable from the hard, dull, wearisome details of EDC's and NATO's and Austrian Peace Treaties? Indeed, it is even possible that the committees and conferences and legalistic bickerings *are* the very question itself. The fact that this possibility is inconceivable to Faulkner may indicate that *A Fable* is something more than the usual product of social unrest.

I think this book marks conclusively, and as it were officially, the end of an era. The "modern" world of which Faulkner, Hemingway, and Dos Passos were the most penetrating interpreters, the world of the 20's and 30's whose articulate consciousness they were, froze to death in 1948. As I have suggested, Faulkner's point of view—and the same might be said of both Hemingway and Dos Passos—already has taken on that ever so slightly stilted, archaic look; the tint of brown begins to stain the photograph, the poses seem a little awkward and artificial. Even the best works of these writers, re-read today, induce nostalgia rather than the exhilaration of discovery. We are living now in a limbo that is neither war nor peace, yet it has given rise to a generation not "lost" but patient, acquiescent, careful rather than reckless, submissive rather than rebellious. We will recognize fully what a new world this is only when it finds a voice of its own. Meanwhile, however, the extent to which Faulkner has lost touch with contemporary experience—the way he has been bamboozled by irrelevant religiosity, while blinding himself to the real drama of salvation being played out before his very eyes—is enough to bring home the gap between his reality and ours. In the end, *A Fable* leaves us wondering whether the time will ever come again when a writer will be able to dismiss politics in favor of the Large Considerations without sounding like a chill echo from a dead world.

[1954]

II. SNOPESISHNESS

The Town is easier to read and more entertaining than anything William Faulkner has written in a long time. Compared with *A Fable*, indeed, it is a model of lucidity and of modest storytelling. But *The Town* differs less from *A Fable* than it seems to on the surface. Both books suffer from a profound discrepancy between what they present dramatically and concretely and what the presentation is supposed to mean. In each one, Faulkner is trying to say something that is in direct conflict with the realities he himself transcribes, and in each one this effort to force an unearned meaning out of his material leads to a distortion of the material and to the triumph of oratory over poetry.

The Town is mainly concerned with the further doings of the Snopes family, and particularly of their leading member, Flem, almost all of whom Faulkner first introduced us to at length many years ago, in *The Hamlet*. In the historical legend that runs through Faulkner's stories and novels about the imaginary Mississippi county of Yoknapatawpha, the Snopeses represent the class of poor whites who, after the Civil War, began ruthlessly using their talent for making money to take over social and economic power in the South. *The Hamlet* deals with the beginning of this process—the rise of Flem Snopes from "less than nowhere" to a position of prominence in rural Frenchman's Bend. By the end of the book, Flem has outsmarted nearly everyone—including Will Varner, the richest and most powerful man in the area, and V. K. Ratliff, the cleverest—in business deals, and has established relatives in jobs all over the village. He has also married Will Varner's daughter, Eula, a gloriously beautiful creature who happens to be pregnant with another man's child, and, of course, he has profited financially by the transaction. Having gone as far as he can in Frenchman's Bend, Flem sets out for nearby Jefferson in the last chapter of *The Hamlet*. *The Town*, picking up his story at that point, early in the 20th century, follows his progress from a partnership in a grubby little restaurant to the presidency of a Jefferson bank.

But if there are similarities between the two novels, there is also an immense difference. In *The Hamlet*, Faulkner defines the Snopeses in opposition to a world that is concretely characterized by the full-blooded virility of Will Varner, by the extravagantly lush, indolent beauty of Eula Varner, by the innocence and camaraderie of the farmers who sit around the village store, and especially by the rich personality of the itinerant sewing-machine agent, V. K. Ratliff. Ratliff is a superbly realized representative of the best and most valuable qualities the Old South has to offer, and because he has no formal education, his wonderfully civilized mind, his native delicacy of manner, his wit, and his humane curiosity are more fully the products of the society that nourished him. It is against this background that the Snopeses come into focus. After a while, their harshness, their coldness, their blindness to the concepts of honor and pride, nobility and heroism begin to seem not a mere deficiency of culture but a lack of the very qualities that differentiate the human from the bestial. The

Snopeses are funny in *The Hamlet,* but they are also terrifying—
just as an ape in the zoo is most amusing and most frightening
when it acts most like a human being. The laughter and the terror
both derive from the knowledge that only a thin line divides the
human from the bestial; we laugh because we understand the
absurdity of our pretentious attribution of uniqueness to humanity,
and we are terrified precisely because our resemblance to a mere
animal calls this uniqueness into question. *The Hamlet,* then, can
be described as a novel about what it means to be human. And
Faulkner sums it all up brilliantly in the famous section that has
been separately printed under the title "Spotted Horses": the wild
ponies Flem has brought into Frenchman's Bend from Texas are
a symbol of what barbarism has done to the Snopeses; like the
ponies, they are creatures of pure will, with no object beyond the
pure expression of will, rushing madly and blindly and senselessly
through the world, heaping destruction on the foolish innocents
who have been persuaded, against the evidence of their own eyes,
that these savage creatures are really gentle animals.

In *The Town,* which takes place mainly in the 1920's, Faulkner
insists a bit frantically (through no less than three narrators) that
the Snopeses are still as inhuman and dangerous as they seemed in
their earlier encounters with civilization. This insistence takes the
form of repeated, and explicit, comments on what he now calls the
"principle" of "Snopesishness." "They none of them seemed to
bear any specific kinship to one another; they were just Snopeses,
like colonies of rats or termites are just rats and termites." He also
tells us that they have "all federated unanimously to remove being
a Snopes from just a zoological category into a condition composed of success." Gavin Stevens, who does not appear in *The
Hamlet* but is one of the narrators in *The Town*—and the spokesman Faulkner usually employs when he is being most abstract and
wordy about the Old South—says to himself, upon hearing a
Snopes referred to as "that horse boy":

Horse boy, dog boy, cat boy, monkey boy, elephant boy: anything but Snopes boy. And then suppose, just suppose; suppose and tremble: . . . one generation more until that innocent and outrageous belief that courage and honor are practical has had time to fade and cool so that merely the habit of courage and honor remain; add to that then that generation's natural heritage of cold rapacity as instinctive as breathing, and tremble at that prospect: the habit of courage and honor compounded by rapacity or rapacity raised to the absolute *nth* by courage and honor: not horse boy but a lion or tiger boy: Genghis Khan or Tamerlane or Attila in the defenseless midst of indefensible Jefferson.

And in the last chapter Faulkner becomes altogether explicit about the bestiality of the Snopeses, bringing in four completely savage children who look like snakes, speak no language, and are quite indistinguishable from wild animals—"Byron Snopes's children out of a Jicarilla Apache squaw."

The trouble is that none of this is true either to the Snopeses as we see them in *The Town* or to the picture of Jefferson that Faulkner gives us here. The lions and tigers of which Gavin Stevens speaks are, in fact, surprisingly tame, and the things they do are almost prankish. Flem steals several tons of brass parts from the Jefferson power plant; years later, he uses his wife's infidelity to blackmail his father-in-law into making him president of the bank. Byron Snopes embezzles a small sum of money from the bank; Montgomery Ward Snopes is in the business of exhibiting pornographic pictures to respectable citizens of Jefferson; I. O. Snopes tries to force a widow into giving him a cut of her husband's insurance; an elderly Snopes (first name not specified) lures children into his watermelon patch so that he can have the pleasure of throwing stones at them. Hardly the kind of behavior we would associate with lions and tigers, Genghis Khans and Attilas, destroyers of civilization.

The humor of *The Town* lies almost wholly in such incidents, and there is also a good deal of horseplay around Gavin Stevens's successive infatuations with Eula and her teen-age daughter Linda. It is situation comedy without a hint of the terror that reverberates through the comedy of *The Hamlet*. But Snopeses like these could scarcely inspire the terror that comes from understanding the precariousness of our hold on humanity. Except, that is, in Gavin Stevens, the intellectual lawyer with a Ph.D. from the University of Heidelberg, who believes in the glories of the Old South. Yet even his hysterical reflections on the Snopeses are unconvincing; his tone sometimes suggests outraged gentility more than outraged humanity—as though it were the unfitness of Flem's rise in polite society that bothered him and not the invasion of "indefensible Jefferson" by a pack of wild animals.

At that, "indefensible Jefferson" is an infinitely less attractive place than Frenchman's Bend. The chivalry and honorableness of Gavin Stevens seem foolish and archaic and irrelevant; Major de Spain—Eula's lover and the president of the bank before Flem takes over—and the aristocratic Mallisons (not to mention Gavin Stevens himself) have none of the grandeur and vitality of their aristocratic counterparts in *The Hamlet* and other early works of Faulkner. V. K. Ratliff (another of the narrators) turns up in *The Town*, but now he is an avuncular gossip whose main occupation is to trade interpretations of the Snopeses with Gavin Stevens and to explain to Chick Mallison (the third narrator and a member of Jefferson's younger generation) why they are so dangerous. Worst of all, Eula Varner, the utterly female, utterly biological, utterly indolent, utterly silent Eula of *The Hamlet*, has become, in *The Town*, a matronly Southern lady who makes long speeches that sound exactly like the speeches of Gavin Stevens and not a little like the recent speeches of William Faulkner.

But the irony is that Faulkner knows all this. He knows that Gavin Stevens defending the honor of an adulteress in a back-alley brawl makes a silly spectacle; he knows that Ratliff and Eula and the other relics of the old order who once seemed so grandly heroic are diminished and paled; he knows that the Snopeses' teeth have been pulled by history. He cannot help recording at least that much of the truth about what has happened to the South, for he still retains the radical, uncompromising honesty of vision that belongs to his genius. He still has the honesty, but he no longer has the courage of his honesty. In *The Town*, Flem gets rid of all the other Snopeses he has brought into Jefferson, and begins to pursue —of all things—respectability. Faulkner tries hard to persuade us, and himself, that this makes Flem more dangerous than ever, but it is no use; he is fighting a losing battle against his own perception of the truth. And the truth is that time has dulled the conflict between the Snopeses and the Old South; to the extent that *The Town* is an honest book, it accurately reflects this development by showing Jefferson to be effete and the Snopeses domesticated. But Faulkner is not content with recording so undramatic a development; he must always be pretending—as in *A Fable*—that the reality he cannot prevent himself from seeing is some other reality, involving other, more impressive issues. Perhaps he is right in feeling that the truth of today is less interesting than the truth of an earlier time, and perhaps his tragedy is that the movement of history has robbed him of a contemporary subject equal to his passion. But as long as he refuses to surrender to the reality and the truth that he cannot help recording, he will continue to mount the stilts of oratory and to distort the things he sees. And the voice of the orator affirming his belief in the grandeur of life may yet completely drown out the voice of the artist, who knows perfectly well that there is no grandeur to be found in the life around him.

[1957]

Edmund Wilson: Then and Now

I. THE LAST PATRICIAN

It was during the 1870's and 1880's—when a fantastically rapid industrial expansion was changing the character of American life overnight—that the alienated intellectual first came into prominence on the American scene, notably among the old families of New York and New England. This was also the period when huge numbers of immigrants from southern and eastern Europe were pouring into the big cities and when ward politics, with its bosses and its colorful corruptions, began to emerge as an important force. "The men in the clubs of social pretension and the men of cultivated taste and easy life," as Theodore Roosevelt described the class from which he came, a class that had traditionally considered public service an honorable calling, were revolted and horrified by the coarseness and crudity of the Gilded Age. And their sons graduating from Harvard and Yale and Princeton in the 1870's and 1880's were hopelessly unprepared to cope with a world so different from the one into which they were born and in whose image they had been educated.

Not far below the surface of some of the high-sounding social criticism produced during the last thirty years of the 19th century we can detect a note of simple snobbery aroused by the "vulgar" upstarts who were beginning to dominate the country. (In our own day, a similar attitude has found expression in William Faulkner's chronicle of the displacement of the old aristocracy of the South by the rapacious Snopes clan.) But it was not only the complex of reckless commercialism, political corruption, and meanness of spirit that offended the young patrician intellectual of the 1870's and 1880's. There was also the fear of being swamped by the waves of new immigrants. "A New York boy who goes away to boarding school," wrote John Jay Chapman, "returns to a new world at each vacation. He finds perhaps on his return from boarding school, that the street where he and his companions used to play ball is given over to a migration of Teutons. When he returns from college, the Teutons have vanished and given place to Italians. When he reaches the Law school, behold no more Italians—Polish Jews to the horizon's verge." In the context, Chapman is using this description to make the point that New York is not a civilization but a "railway station," a "kaleidoscope," in which the present has completely obliterated the past—a situation he contrasts with the settled character of New England society, where the link with the classical European culture has never been broken and where "the influx of new blood and new idea has not overwhelmed the old blood and old idea." Although Chapman at this period of his life was not especially antagonistic to the Teutons and Italians and Jews who had been crowding into New York, his tendency to idealize the glories of an older American civilization which had its seat in New England led eventually, in his last years, to an astonishing outburst of xenophobia directed against "the Jesuit and the Jew." Nor was he alone in this: nativist attitudes which had once been the property of vulgar know-noth-ings were now emblazoned upon the banners of nervous patricians proclaiming the need to protect the salutary homogeneity of American culture.

By 1910, however, the situation looked much brighter. Time had both mitigated the excesses of the Gilded Age and equipped the men of cultivation with fresh resources for coping with the challenge to their values. The ideas of Shaw, Wells, Nietzsche, Ruskin, and Morris had filtered in, bringing to the young patrician intellectual a new way of conceiving his predicament and a new confidence in his ability to triumph over the "materialism" of American life. And these ideas joined with the work of the natural-ists and realists who had been active in American fiction since the 1880's to produce a demand for liberation from the "Puritan re-pressions" and the gentility that were the other side of the New England coin. A number of the younger dispossessed patricians called themselves "socialists" and "modernists" and rushed to participate in the exuberant movement (whose headquarters were divided between Greenwich Village and Chicago) to bring about the spiritual regeneration of America through art and craftsman-ship.

New voices begin to proclaim the birth of a new era and to clamor for a "revolutionary protest against whatever incubuses of crabbed age, paralysis, tyranny, stupidity, sloth, commercialism, lay most heavily upon the people's life." The quotation comes from Van Wyck Brooks, who was to lead a systematic assault on the ma-terialism and priggishness of the Gilded Age in two famous books that indicted America for crushing Mark Twain and for driving Henry James into exile, and who published in 1915 an enormously influential collection of essays called *America's Com-ing of Age.* Anyone who looks at these essays today is likely to be struck by their relative mildness, which is not a matter of rhetoric or tone but inherent in the argument itself. Though Brooks based a whole theory of American history on the traditional antagonism between "highbrow" and "lowbrow" (an antagonism he traces back to colonial times, taking Jonathan Edwards and Benjamin Franklin as the two opposing archetypes), he also urged a reconciliation between the poet and the professor on the one hand and the businessman and ward politician on the other. "Tammany has quite as much to teach Good Government as Good Government has to teach Tammany," said Brooks, and in saying so, he provided a good measure of the distance the patrician intellectual had traveled since the 1880's. We are a long way indeed from the Henry Adamses and the Henry Jameses and the "men in the clubs of social pretension."

The most distinguished member of this second generation of patrician intellectuals was Edmund Wilson. He was born in 1895 —about ten years after Brooks—and though he was not strictly of the patrician class, his ancestry (early American Dutch-English stock) and his education (the Hill School and Princeton) associate him firmly with the patrician ethos. One of his grandfathers was a Presbyterian minister and the other a doctor; further back there was a New York State assemblyman who was descended, according to family legend, from one of the Earls of Essex. Wilson's father, Edmund Senior, was a prominent New Jersey lawyer who, though a Republican, won the respect and admiration of Governor Woodrow Wilson by cleaning up the rackets in Atlantic City while serving a term as attorney general of the state.

In "The Author at Sixty," one of those superb autobiographical essays that are among the best things Wilson has written, he provides a good deal of illuminating information about his father's life and character. Edmund Senior was a brilliant and extremely neurotic man who suffered from severe hypochondria and spent all his later years in and out of sanitariums. Wilson ascribes these periodic breakdowns largely to a "fundamental lack of adjustment to the American life of the period." "The period after the Civil

War—both banal in a bourgeois way and fantastic with gigantic fortunes—was a difficult one for Americans brought up in the old tradition: the generation of my father and uncles. They had been educated at Exeter and Andover and at eighteenth-century Princeton, and had afterwards been trained, like their fathers, for what had once been called the learned professions; but they had then had to deal with a world in which this kind of education and the kind of ideals it served no longer really counted for much. . . . Of my father's close friends at college, but a single one was left by the time he was in his thirties: all the rest were dead—some had committed suicide. . . . Like many Americans who studied law, [my father] had in his youth aimed at public life. . . . But the political career he had hoped for was conceived in the classical republican terms . . . [and] he could not . . . be induced to take any active part in the kind of political life that he knew at the end of the century."

Though Wilson when he entered college may have imagined himself a rebel against his "reactionary" parent, he was in fact enlisting in the battle to make the values represented by his father's character prevail in American life. The story of his literary career is the story of how he managed to continue waging the fight even after so many of his fellows in arms had either been consumed by fire or had deserted the cause to pursue some other end. Wilson's work cannot be fully understood unless we remember that his voice has always been the voice of the old Anglo-Saxon America, even when it was insisting on the greatness of Joyce and Proust and Valéry, and even when it was declaring its intense admiration of Marx and Lenin. In Wilson, as in no other writer of the past fifty years, we can see how the old American mind, having recovered itself from the first shock of the post-Civil War days, went on to cope with an America that it passionately felt to be its very own but which became more and more alien to it with the passage of the years.

The young writers of the 1920's were fond of thinking that the great boom was another Gilded Age and that they were its victims just as Mark Twain and Henry James and Herman Melville had been victims of the same forces in an earlier day. The truth was, of course, that thirty years of literary and social protest had done a great deal to establish a favorable climate for the new standards in art and morals, with the result that a good many Babbitts were numbered among the admirers of Mencken and Sinclair Lewis and Sherwood Anderson. *Sister Carrie* had been suppressed in 1900, but in the 1920's Dreiser was an American classic; Henry Adams's *Education* amazed the Massachusetts Historical Society by becoming a best-seller after its release to the general public in 1918; and the leader of the "rebellious" younger generation, F. Scott Fitzgerald, was earning huge royalties for his novels and fantastic fees for his stories.

In fact, what seems most enviable today in the writing of the 1920's is its radiant confidence in its own importance, a confidence that owed little or nothing to commercial success and everything to the feeling these writers had of belonging to a community devotedly absorbed in the practice of letters and able to make contact with a responsive audience. Wilson's early journalistic pieces (collected in *The Shores of Light* and *The American Earthquake*) exhibit both this confidence and this sense of community. His attitude toward the new novels and poems he was reviewing from week to week—an attitude that can be characterized as receptive, sympathetic, and rigorous all at once—flows directly out of his calm belief that the Republic of Letters has an existence at least as palpable and concrete as the Republic of France.

No doubt the fact the literary people in the 1920's were always so aggressive in asserting the superiority of their values indicates that this belief was less assured than it may appear. Nevertheless there is a difference between losing the luxury of being able to take something for granted and being unable to believe it at all without an unremitting effort of will. (And in that distinction, one may say, lies the difference between the culture of the 1920's and the intellectual life of the 1950's.) The 1920's were still close enough to an age in which the reality of the things of the spirit would no more have been questioned than the reality of the rocks and stones and trees, so that men like Brooks and Wilson, brought up in "the old tradition" and educated as a matter of course in the humane disciplines, might under assault lose their right to an automatic assumption of the importance of the arts and all that the arts implied, but they would never lose their natural, comfortable, easy relation to the world of books, ideas, and ideals. Nor would they lose the perspective that always accompanies such a relation—the historical point of view, the sense of a perpetually ongoing cultural enterprise from one generation to the next, the feeling that thinkers and writers and artists of all periods are bound together in a common fraternity, and that a new writer who produces a good book is immediately absorbed into the stream of the national literature.

Wilson's early journalistic pieces breathe a natural and easy relation not only to the "fine arts" but to the whole cultural life of his age. He will deal with everything from literature, music, painting, and theater to movies, burlesque shows, vaudeville, murder trials, the character of New York neighborhoods; and whatever the subject, he brings to it the same active intelligence, the same learned interest, the same degree of intellectual seriousness—in short, the same personal identity. The critic who in his book reviews is sufficiently at home in the Republic of Letters to discuss Dante and Catullus and Verlaine without standing on tiptoe, and who analyzes the work of his contemporaries in the same upright posture, is also the man who can without stooping produce an article on Farfariello, who was doing impersonations in Italian at the Fugazy Theater on Houston Street in New York's lower East Side during the month of October, 1925. The assumption that made this feat possible was that all forms of human expression on all levels of literacy exist in a tangible continuum—an assumption that those who came to maturity in the 1930's, 1940's, and 1950's would find it increasingly difficult to make.

Though Wilson returned from the Army in 1919 "full of Wells and Shaw and Barbusse and the Russian Revolution," he did not become deeply involved in political questions until the stock-market crash had justified the worst prophecies of the criers of capitalist doom. Throughout the 1920's he concentrated mainly on cultural matters. He also wrote poetry and fiction and had a play produced by the Provincetown Players, the ancestors of the off-Broadway movement. Wilson's non-discursive writing has always rightly been considered inferior to his essays, and it may be that the key to that inferiority lies in the discrepancy one can detect between his character, which seems essentially rigid and closed, and his mind, which is open and unstintedly generous. His poetry, for example, has a curiously old-fashioned quality that contrasts sharply with the attempt to be modernist in the use of homely images and harsh speech rhythms. His criticism, on the other hand, is almost always marked by a marvelously effective balance in which his character operates to set limits to the infinite receptiveness of his intelligence.

A striking illustration of how this balance functions can be found in *Axel's Castle* (1931), where Wilson's intense excitement over a group of writers he was trying to sell to a reluctant public never for a moment clouded the grounds of his resistance to certain elements of their work. Not the least interesting aspect of *Axel's Castle*—and the one that makes this great critical study of the symbolist movement a work of literature in its own right— is the spectacle it presents of a stubbornly rationalistic temperament, a temperament almost aggressive in its secularism, in its friendliness toward science, in its conviction of the possibility of progress through the efforts of human will, successfully grappling with a literary school most of whose members would have identified his point of view with the very forces they were condemning and who would have drawn from their own artistic achievements the very opposite moral.

Thus, for example, instead of agreeing with Valéry that the obscurity and extreme subjectivism of modern literature constitute the first stage in a process that will end with the transformation of poetry into a sort of harmless esoteric game for connoisseurs, Wilson asserts that on the contrary symbolist literature might prove to be an immensely important step in the orientation of modern man toward a view of reality that would re-establish the power of ideas and ideals in everyday life. He sees in the new forms developed by the symbolists "a revolution analogous to that which has taken place in science and philosophy: they have broken out of the old mechanistic routine, they have disintegrated the old materialism, and they have revealed to the imagination a new flexibility and freedom." T. S. Eliot's religiosity, Yeats's magic, Valéry's rarefied speculations, Proust's "fretting self-centered prolixities," Joyce's over-intellectuality—all are permitted by Wilson to derive no authority whatever from the great works of art which these writers succeeded in producing. Indeed, he regards the qualities and ideas that repel him as products of the dying era that the symbolists have been helping to kill—the tax, as it were, imposed on the service they have performed for a humanity bent on marching toward "the hope and exaltation of the untried, unsuspected possibilities of human thought and art." Here speaks the Puritan tradition, with its belief in independence, self-reliance, steadfastness, and hard work, thundering approval of men who might so easily have been written off by a mere Puritan as whiners and idle dreamers.

The moral of the whole story, at any rate, is early-American to the bone. The world, Wilson says, has changed a great deal since

1920, especially as a result of the Russian Revolution, and "the question begins to press us again as to whether it is possible to make a practical success of human society, and whether, if we continue to fail, a few masterpieces, however profound or noble, will be able to make life worth living even for the few people in a position to enjoy them." A book celebrating symbolist literature that ends with the determination to "make a practical success of human society" surely could never have been written by a man who was a thoroughgoing avant-gardist, any more than the extraordinarily sympathetic and lucid exposition of the difficult novels and poems discussed in *Axel's Castle* could have been done by an old-fashioned American rationalist alone.

Many followers of the New Criticism—the school that grew directly out of the aesthetic theories on which symbolist literature was based, and which rose to dominance in the universities and the quarterlies on the shoulders of the new wave of enthusiasm for Eliot and Joyce and Yeats and Proust that developed in the years following the Second World War—have come to consider *Axel's Castle* a work of "mere" popularization. This judgment not only overlooks the high distinction of the book but also serves to register the great distance between the literary life of the 1920's and that of the 1940's and 1950's. Wilson could still believe in the existence of a general reading public literate enough to understand a complicated exposition and willing to take the trouble to grapple with what must have seemed hopelessly obscure texts; and the New Critics could not. Indeed, the increasing specialization and narrowing of focus within American intellectual life since the end of the 1920's, particularly in the last fifteen years, itself grows out of the disappearance of such a public.

Or is it something else that has disappeared? For it may be that the "common reader" is as much—or as little—a reality today as he was thirty years ago, and that Wilson and others like him were able to assume the existence of an interested general audience only because they believed so strongly in the relevance to all men of the things they were writing about. And it may also be that this belief derived from their stubborn refusal to admit—as the New Critics, and not they alone, implicitly admit—the doom of the arts in our time. That "popularizations" as good as *Axel's Castle* are no longer produced, in other words, may be another sign of the loss of confidence by writers in the value of their own vocation.

In *Axel's Castle*, then, we see a Wilson who has decided that the various forms of retreat from contemporary society practiced by writers throughout the 20's could no longer serve the purposes of either life or literature. In 1929 (the year *Axel's Castle* was begun), he turned out article after article emphasizing this point. A review of the diary of Dostoevsky's wife becomes a kind of warning to expatriate American writers of the dangers of cutting themselves off from "the realities of our contemporary life"; he urges Thornton Wilder to try his hand at a novel set in modern America instead of in exotic locales; he attacks Mencken for making it "the fashion to speak of politics as an obscene farce." What was bothering Wilson in the months immediately preceding the stock-market crash of October 1929, was the feeling that the indifference to politics and social questions shared by most American writers in the 20's amounted to a complacent acquiescence in the triumph of the businessman. A short time after the crash, he pounced on the idea that the depression might be the first great turning point in American history since the Civil War, marking the final collapse of all Gilded Ages, and that it therefore offered an opportunity to right both the social and cultural evils of the era born in the 1870's. Thus, when he looked to the Soviet Union and Marxist literature for guidance, it was still as an American fighting the same old fight and defending the same values.

Like Van Wyck Brooks, who now abandoned his campaign against American materialism and priggishness and turned to search for a "useable past" in what he had once called the "dry Yankee stalk" of 19th-century New England, Wilson too was affected by nationalist sentiments in the 30's, but they were not in the least of the nostalgic variety. He brought back with him from a visit to the Soviet Union in 1935 "the feeling that being an American did mean something unique, that Americanism was a solid social entity which stood quite apart from Europe, belonging to a separate category rather than merely differing from it as the characters of the various European peoples differed from one another; something that, in fundamental ways, was just as unlike what one finds in Russia as what one finds in the Western European nations." He had at first been struck by how much Americans and Russians had in common as against all Europeans, and this he attributed to the fact that the United States and the Soviet Union had both done away with rigid class systems. (In reprinting these observations in 1956, Wilson admitted that his one dishonesty had been to soft-pedal the already observable phenomenon of a new class system in the U.S.S.R.) The defects of Soviet Communism he ascribed to the special historical circumstances of Russia; his faith in socialism remained as unshaken by his Russian experience as his faith in democracy was unshaken by the crash. And he was now sure that "the socialist ideal is more natural to us than to the Russians."

Having learned some Russian during his Soviet trip, Wilson now began to apply himself with characteristic industry and thoroughness to a study of the intellectual background of the Russian Revolution. He spent six years writing *To the Finland Station*, his most ambitious work and the only one, apart from *Axel's Castle*, that really constitutes an organic whole rather than a collection of more or less closely related pieces. Wilson's talents as a biographer, his extraordinary skill at summing up the contents of a book, his ability to digest an immense volume of material, his gift of elucidation, and his keen critical powers are all brought

into play in this account of the development of socialism from
the Utopians through Marx and Engels and finally to the im-
plementation of Marxism by Lenin and Trotsky in the Russian
Revolution. The method he employs is to concentrate on men
rather than doctrines—or rather, his detailed exposition of doctrine is woven so closely into the biographical framework in each
case that we are left with the very Emersonian and rather un-
Marxist feeling that it is individuals who count in the last resort,
that history is made by men out of their determination, their passion, their steadfastness, their willingness to sacrifice themselves
to ideals—even when, like Trotsky, they imagine themselves to be
nothing more than the passive agents of history.

The main weakness of *To the Finland Station* lies in its account
of Marxist theory and its portrayal of the character of Lenin. Wilson was very eager to believe that the ideals of Marxism and of
the Russian Revolution were continuous with the ideals of the
Enlightenment and the American Revolution, and he was therefore forced into writing off all those elements in Marx that conflict with this image as Germanic "myths" and imperfectly secularized religious ideas. Similarly with Lenin, who emerges from
this book as a saint of progress, a kind of enlightened and nobler
Oliver Cromwell. Just as Wilson had tried to ascribe the defects
of Soviet Communism in 1935 to the peculiarities of the Russian
character, so here he ascribes the weaknesses and inconsistencies of
Marxism to "religion" and "utopianism," and explains away
Lenin's ruthlessness and cruelty as political necessities of the moment.

To the Finland Station supplied the final term in Wilson's shift
from liberalism to radicalism. The Russian Revolution, one might
say, figured for him as the political aspect of the revolution in
sensibility effected by the symbolists. Joyce, Proust, Yeats, and
Eliot had opened up new possibilities for humanity by pointing
to a way out of the dilemmas of mechanism, while Marx and

Engels and Trotsky and Lenin had traced a path out of the cruel social system in which mechanism flourished. But both the symbolists and the Marxists had paid the price of pioneers in error and inconsistency, departing from the road of pure reason that leads to human fulfillment on earth, and it was up to us in America, where conditions were so much more propitious, to benefit from their achievements and their mistakes and to push forward to the goal of making "a practical success of human society."

Though Wilson's radicalism kept him in tune with the times, he gradually came to feel increasingly estranged from the intellectual temper of the 30's. The suspicion may have been stirring within him that his socialism had a different source, a different tone, and a wholly different emphasis from the Marxism of most literary intellectuals of the day, very few of whom were thinking in such strongly American terms. But whether or not some such perception was at work in Wilson toward the end of the 30's, his uneasiness at the attitudes toward literature prevalent in left-wing circles was certainly powerful. He was disturbed by the lack of enthusiasm among the young for books, and suggested that the obsessive hunt for "social significance" was destroying their pleasure in reading; and he spoke out repeatedly against the tendency to judge a work of literature by its ideological content. The job of a writer, he kept saying, was to write as well and as truthfully as he could, and he would best serve the purposes of socialism by devoting himself to his craft while refusing to subordinate the requirements of craft to the discipline of politics or any other external consideration.

Wilson's growing disaffection with the 30's expressed itself at first in a nostalgia for the 20's that became more and more poignant as time went on. In a play called *This Room and This Gin and These Sandwiches* written in 1937, he portrays the disintegration at the end of the 20's of a passionate little-theater group in Greenwich Village which breaks up as a result of economic pressures without and silliness and confusion within. But there is an elegiac tone to the play, which is really an obituary for the intransigent spirit that once lived in the Village and that seemed to exist there no more. One of the themes of *This Room* is that people who keep the reality of the spirit (i.e., civilization) alive by dedicating themselves entirely to its demands often must do so at the expense of self-mutilation and the sacrifice of "repose"—a point he kept harping on in his critical essays of the 30's. He published (in *The Triple Thinkers*) a long piece on John Jay Chapman, whom he represents as having heroically inflicted "permanent psychological damage" on himself "by beating his head against the gilt of the Gilded Age," and whom he clearly admires for having carried his "Thoreauvian intransigence" into society instead of solitude. In the same volume, he quotes again one of his favorite passages in all literature, Proust's remark about the moral obligations imposed on us which are "invisible only to fools —and are they really to them?" and declares that Proust was speaking "for every moral, esthetic or intellectual passion which holds the expediencies of the world in contempt."

This continual assertion, both in his studies of Marxism and in his literary criticism, that civilization rests on the individual's "affirmation of the power of the spirit in indifference to, if not in defiance of, what may be called the worldly situation—that is, of the *mise en scène*, the conditions of life, the amenities," indicates how deeply the secularized Puritanism of Thoreau and Emerson had penetrated Wilson's thinking, and how little his absorption in 20th-century revolutionary ideas had been able to touch the "early American" core of his character—how, indeed, they had only served to reinforce it. ("The world," wrote Emerson in an essay that Wilson once said supplied the text of which Thoreau's life and work were an exemplification, "is nothing, the man is all; in yourself is the law of all nature . . .; in yourself slumbers the whole of reason; it is for you to know all; it is for you to dare all.") And we can also see that Wilson's orientation toward the world continued to be determined even at this period of his life by the memory of what had befallen his father's generation, which, he says in the Chapman essay, had to contend with a society that drove the best of them to insanity and suicide.

Some time during the 30's Wilson himself suffered a breakdown, and this experience probably lay behind the concern with neurosis in relation to art that informs the essays collected in *The Wound and the Bow*. But another factor must have operated to produce this new preoccupation—his brooding over the failure of the 20's to accomplish what they had set out to do, over the dimming of so many shining stars, and over the very different failure of the 30's, which began with such glorious hopes and were now ending in a worse demoralization than the decade before; demoralization and war.

From about 1941 on, we have to deal with a new Wilson, a Wilson whose estrangement from the intellectual world around him was aggravated by the passage of the years until he finally washed his hands of it altogether and retreated into a special "pocket of the past." Like several other liberals who still vividly remembered the last war and its outcome, he had opposed America's entry into the Second World War, and he seems to have considered British imperialism as great a menace to civilization as Nazism. After he had resigned in a fury from the staff of the *New Republic* when its then owner forced a change in policy from isolationism to intervention, his bitterness against the British mounted, and he fell into the habit of speaking of them in an accent that combined the snarl of America Firstism with the moral indignation of a New Englander who still cherishes memories of the hated redcoats at Lexington and Concord and Bunker Hill.

This astonishing Anglophobia erupted all over the pages of

Europe Without Baedeker, a book written just at the end of the war in the form of "sketches among the ruins of Italy, Greece, and England." Here, in his remarks about the British, we get our first glimpse of what the "early American" component of Wilson looks like when it dissociates itself from his "avant-garde" side; it is rather a startling spectacle. Gone (or at least largely gone) is the poise, the judiciousness that always characterizes his literary criticism; gone is the marvelous balance of stern, unyielding principle and unlimited imaginative sympathy that makes his best work so immensely impressive. And in their place come crankiness, irascibility, intolerance, self-righteousness, and a complete relapse into the old myth of American innocence and moral purity caught in the corruptions of Europe.

The cultural sterility of the early 40's bothered him as much as the political atmosphere, and he went so far as to draw a connection between the two, blaming the loss of creative energy on the fact that writers had given themselves over whole hog to the war. In 1943, he expressed the hope that the end of the war would release a demand for better work in the arts, just as 1918 had done, but when nothing of the sort came to pass, he apparently found himself bewildered. Wilson's book reviews of the 40's (collected in *Classics and Commercials*), valuable as they are in many important respects, present a picture of the patrician American mind that had triumphantly coped with the whole rapidly shifting world of the period between the two wars floundering before the radically new situation of the war and postwar years.

One aspect of this confusion shows itself very clearly in *The Boys in the Back Room,* a series of short pieces on some of the young novelists who came up in the 30's and who all derived from Hemingway (John O'Hara, James M. Cain, William Saroyan, John Steinbeck, and a few others). Wilson was bothered by the element of "trashiness" (his favorite pejorative word in this period) that seemed to mingle in strange juxtaposition with artistic seriousness in their books, and particularly in the work of Steinbeck. His explanation of this anomaly is the influence of Hollywood—all these writers are unconsciously trying to produce novels that can be translated to the screen with a minimum of difficulty. But if this were the case, why would they not simply turn out pure trash? Wilson's rather lazy-minded attempt to refer the problem, in good 20's style, to the lure of filthy lucre constitutes a failure on his part to recognize the existence of a crucially important new phenomenon in American culture: the middlebrow writer. The fact is that Steinbeck and the other boys in the back room were writing as well as they could, and that something had gone wrong with their relation to their own experience—and therefore to the means they used of interpreting this experience to themselves— that rendered them incapable of perceiving the difference between the serious and the "trashy."

Having lost a sense of vital connection with the contemporary cultural situation in America, Wilson began taking periodic leaves of absence. In 1947 he went off to describe the Shalako festival of the Zuñi Indians, and in 1949 he produced a long account of life and literature in Haiti. A few years later he astonished everyone by publishing an essay called "On First Reading Genesis," in which he announced that he had been studying Hebrew (he already knew Greek, Latin, and Russian, and was fluent in most of the modern European languages) and that he had looked carefully into the Old Testament for the first time in his life. Subsequently he visited Israel, and soon thereafter plunged deep into the issues raised by the discovery of the Dead Sea Scrolls, mastering an incredible volume of highly technical scholarly detail along the way. Though his interest in the Jews and especially in the Scrolls seemed on the surface only an extension of the freethinker's irrepressible urge to discredit the supernatural claims of religion (the urge that also drew him to Zuñi and Haiti), in reality a much deeper impulse was being served here. This excursion into the Old

Testament was one of the two paths Wilson was taking back into his own origins, for what mainly concerned him was the deep affinities he discovered between the Jews and the American Puritans from whom he himself derived ("The Puritanism of New England was a kind of new Judaism, a Judaism transposed into Anglo-Saxon terms"). The other path was a series of biographical studies of important Americans of the past century—Lincoln, Theodore Roosevelt, Oliver Wendell Holmes, and a whole host of Civil War personalities.

Like everyone else in this period, then, Wilson has become extremely self-conscious about his relation to the national past. But it is a feeling of isolation from the present, not of being cut off from the past, that accounts for his current preoccupation with the Presidents and generals and obscure novelists of the second half of the 19th century. We get the impression in reading Wilson on Lincoln and Teddy Roosevelt and Oliver Wendell Holmes and General Sherman that the real purpose of these essays is not an impersonal investigation of the particular subjects under discussion so much as his attempt to contruct an image of the American character that will show him to be the truest living representative of its most fundamental qualities and its deepest aspirations. And when he says in *A Piece of My Mind* that he fears he may be an "exceptional case" living in a "pocket of the past," we suspect a certain disingenuousness—we suspect him of meaning us to understand that he alone is actually living in the "real" America and that he is an exceptional case by virtue of that fact.

One guesses that Wilson's self-image is of an American who has combined the "internationalist" ideal of Henry James with the "republican patriotism" of Lincoln; and indeed, we have seen how hard he has worked to assimilate the symbolists, Marx and Lenin, Freud, and finally the Jews (whom he calls the founders of "international thinking") to the concept of Americanism to which he has always been loyal: the readiness to explore new possibilities of human development, the refusal to accept individual frustration or social misery as given in the nature of things, the faith in the human imagination as the source of all values and in the human will as the agent of progress. And one guesses that Wilson, now in his sixties, will spend the rest of his days elaborating a theory of American history in which periods of "republican patriotism" will be shown to alternate with fallings-off into careerism and baseness. The Republic, which has "had to be saved over and over again, and . . . continues to have to be saved," will moreover be shown to depend for redemption on a recurrent outburst of "the traditional American idealism" that he himself has so magnificently embodied.

So with "old-fogeyism comfortably closing in" on him, Edmund Wilson now sits in the old stone house at Talcottville in the western part of upper New York State, where his mother's family came to live from New England over a century ago when Talcottvile was still a frontier town, and where he feels himself in touch with an older, cruder, simpler America that has somehow managed to survive there in an isolated pocket. He reflects that his generation, while not having had so difficult a time as his father's, piled up enough casualties of its own in the new America. "Too many of my friends are insane or dead or Roman Catholic converts—and some of these among the most gifted; two have committed suicide." But he continues to work, probing into the American past, and also finding the time to write essays (like the long pieces on Turgenev and T. S. Eliot in the *New Yorker*) on literary subjects that happen to interest him and that he simply wants to explore for their own sake. When he speaks out directly these days, giving us a piece of his mind, we can feel his relish at abandoning himself to the role of an old American crank who can express without qualification or fancy embroidery anything he damned well happens to feel like saying ("The word God is now archaic, and it ought to be dropped by those who do not need it for moral support").

He is *the* American, relegating himself willingly and proudly to the semi-posthumous position that he had protested against in 1943 when the Princeton Library asked him for a bibliography of his work. At that time he had said that the literary worker of the 20's seemed to the teachers of English and the young writers who grew up in the 30's "the distant inhabitant of another intellectual world" who belonged "to a professional group, now becoming extinct and a legend, in which the practice of letters was a common craft and the belief in its value a common motivation." Today, when the process has gone much further, Wilson—and the group of which he is the best and most impressive representative —seems more distant than ever, and the two possible ways of dealing with him, now as then, are apparently either to make him an object of veneration or to ignore him altogether. But these are not really the only alternatives. We can recognize the element of myth and simplification in his sense of America, in his Whiggish interpretation of the nation's history, and in his image of himself without thereby denying that what he stands for—faith in the importance of the things of the spirit and the responsibility that rests with writers and thinkers to maintain that faith—is the only principle on which, in the long run, civilization can be maintained, or by which intellectuals can be immunized against a sense of futility.

[1958]

II. MR. WILSON AND THE KINGDOM OF HEAVEN

The first thing that strikes you in reading Edmund Wilson's new book, *Patriotic Gore,* is amazement at the size and scope of it, the labor and patience that must have gone into it, the energy of mind and spirit that infuses it—in short, the immense intellectual vitality that Wilson still commands, at the age of sixty-seven and after a career that has already earned him a secure place as one of the greatest men of letters this country has ever produced. "Life in the United States," he himself once observed, "is much subject to disruptions and frustrations, catastrophic collapses and gradual peterings-out"; or, as his friend and contemporary F. Scott Fitzgerald liked to put it, "There are no second acts in American lives." Yet Wilson ran through his second act a long time ago, and his third, and fourth, and how many more? What number would we give to the act he is playing now? Whatever the number, there can be no question of the richness of the plot and the settings, for *Patriotic Gore* is certainly the most ambitious thing Wilson has done since *To the Finland Station* appeared in 1941.

Rather disingenuously subtitled "Studies in the Literature of the American Civil War," *Patriotic Gore* could more properly be described as a study in the spiritual history of American civilization. Wilson begins with a long chapter on Harriet Beecher Stowe, in whose novels he traces the effects of the crisis in Calvinist theology on social life and morals in 19th-century New England; he ends with an even longer chapter (and a particularly brilliant one) on Justice Oliver Wendell Holmes, who is presented as the only gifted survivor of the Civil War never to have been corrupted, discouraged, or broken by "the alien conditions that the war had prepared," and whose escape from "the democratic erosion" Wilson relates to the Calvinistic habits of mind that persisted in Holmes even after the theology of Calvinism had lost its hold on him. Between Harriet Beecher Stowe, experiencing the first symptoms of the collapse of Calvinist doctrine, and Oliver Wendell Holmes, saving his soul with the help of the Calvinist heritage, falls the terrible shadow of the Civil War, which Wilson portrays and analyzes through a series of essays based on various diaries, memoirs, and journalistic reports of the period. This takes him about half-way through the book (which runs in all to more than eight hundred pages). In the remaining chapters, he concentrates largely on the minor novelists and poets of the latter half of the 19th century, the idea being to describe the new kind of America that came into existence after the war was over and that we all (presumably) still inhabit today.

In the introduction to *Patriotic* Gore—a wonderfully irascible assault on the self-righteousness of the American mind in politics —Wilson tells us that having lived through two world wars and having read "a certain amount of history," he is no longer disposed "to take very seriously the professions of 'war aims' that nations make." Wars, he says, are fought out of the same instincts that drive animals to "prey on some form of life that they can capture"; in other words, wars are the consequence of an irrepressible "appetite for expansion" that all nations have in common and that they will all act upon whenever they feel strong enough to dare. The "self-assertive sounds" that man utters "when he is fighting and swallowing others . . . rarely have any meaning," even though they may "at first express a real exaltation on the part of some social group" which hopes (and usually in vain) that the war will bring about the creation of a freer and happier society. All this, Wilson informs us, makes up the general point of view from which his picture of the Civil War has taken shape. Like every other country in the world, the United States always has been (and still is) an expansionist power. The process of expansion began the moment we expelled the British, but except for our struggles with the Indians and our imperialistic war against Mexico, it was largely a peaceable process until the Southern states tried to secede and set up a republic of their own. "The slave-owning Southern states and the rapidly industrializing North had by this time become so distinct from one another that they were virtually two different nations; they were as much two contending power units—each of which was trying to expand at the other's expense—as any two European countries." The action of "the Washington government" in preventing secession was motivated neither by the wish to free the slaves nor by the conviction that secession was wicked; these were "rabble-rousing" and "pseudo-moral" issues. The truth is that the "North's determination to preserve the Union was simply the form that the power drive now took," and Lincoln was simply the agent of a typical 19th-century impulse toward the unification of "hitherto loosely coordinated peoples."

Now, views like these—whatever else we may say about them—are not exactly calculated to encourage a sympathetic understanding of how the people who made and fought the Civil War actually saw themselves and the conflict in which they were engaged. Yet such an understanding is precisely what Wilson manages to achieve in the first half of *Patriotic Gore*. How can we account for this? The answer is that Wilson is always at his best—as in *Axel's Castle*, as in parts of *To the Finland Station*, and as in the marvellous chapters on Lincoln, Grant, and Sherman here—when he is pitting himself against a writer or a figure whose temperament and cast of mind are essentially alien to his own (Kafka is an exception). Wilson is a very stubborn man, so stubborn that no writer has ever really been able to shake any of the attitudes or prejudices with which he began his career as a critic more than forty years ago. But it is a peculiar form of stubbornness, going along as it does with an almost incredibly large curiosity about what the other side has to say for itself and a commensurate willingness to follow it patiently, to sort it out, to turn it over, to get it right, to take from it what can comfortably be assimilated into his own sense of things, and then to reaffirm with greater confidence than ever his original resistance to the whole sorry business. Thus he listens to Harriet Beecher Stowe when she tells him that God was the author of *Uncle Tom's Cabin*; he listens, he considers a moment, and he says (he who believes, as he declared only a short time ago, that "The word God is now archaic, and . . . ought to be dropped by those who do not need it for moral support"): "This is actually a little the impression that the novel makes on the reader." Not that this is in the least permitted to affect his conviction that slavery was only a "pseudo-moral" issue in the Civil War, any more than his moving account of Grant's memoirs (whose "purified fervor and force," he is ready to admit, exhilarate and fill him with moral pride) lead to any serious modification of his idea that the war was a hideous acting out of predatory lusts and that its main consequence was to unleash "the money-grabbing interests" and permit them to take over the country. Lincoln, on the other hand, so fascinates Wilson that he is almost seduced into accepting the religious vision of the war that "imposed itself" upon Lincoln and that he then imposed upon the world. But with the help of Charles A. Beard's *The Rise of American Civilization* (a book he remembers from his youth and that he drags in with what seems to me a certain desperation), Wilson manages to recover himself sufficiently to assert that Lincoln, too, unwittingly served the purposes of the wicked industrialists and businessmen who were soon to transform America into a place that men of ideals, cultivation, taste, and intellect would find it murderously difficult to survive in.

This new America is the scene of the second half of *Patriotic Gore*, and in order to describe what it did to talent and intellect Wilson parades a host of minor novelists and poets before us, dealing tenderly and at interminable length with half-forgotten writers like Sidney Lanier, Ambrose Bierce, and George W. Cable, and even more lovingly with completely forgotten ones like Albion W. Tourgée, Thomas Nelson Page, Kate Chopin, and Frederick W. Tuckerman. Though some of this is intermittently interesting, for the most part it rambles along at what can only be called a self-indulgent pace, following where Wilson's idle curiosities and momentary enthusiasms happen to lead. And if they happen to lead into seventy pages (seventy pages!) on an obscure novelist from New Haven named John W. DeForest—why, then, so they do.

All this, of course, can be taken—and to some extent should be taken—as yet another demonstration of Wilson's famous independence, his simple refusal to go anyone's way but his own, his beautiful assurance that anything *he* finds interesting must in fact *be* interesting. Nevertheless, I can't help feeling that there is more than a touch of the tendentious in Wilson's disproportionate concern with writers like DeForest, Tourgée, and the others. He is out to show that the "triumph of the businessman"—whom he sees as the real victor in the Civil War—created an environment in which it was almost impossible for literary or intellectual talent that was less than major to come to anything very much, and that is why he places his emphasis on the minor writers of the period and pays so little attention to Whitman, Mark Twain, or Henry James. But he is also out to define the possibilities for the flowering of talent in an age of commercialism, materialism, and centralization, and that is why he ends the book with a long essay on Justice Oliver Wendell Holmes, the only member of the Civil War generation (according to Wilson) who retained the ability "to function as a first-rate intellect" throughout "the whole turbid blatant period that followed."

How did Holmes do it? Partly through the self-confidence that came of being a Boston Brahmin, partly through a "philosophic temper of mind," but chiefly through a "high-minded egoism" that took the form of an ideal he liked to call "touching the superlative." Discussing this ideal, Wilson remarks that "in his grandfather Abiel Holmes's time [it] would have been called being chosen for salvation." It would indeed, and Wilson is surely right to stress the element of Calvinism in Holmes's single-minded dedication to his work. But there is more to Calvinism than the idea of personal election; there is also the duty it enjoins to struggle for the realization of the Kingdom of God on earth. It was out of an obedience to this duty that so many Northerners enlisted in the fight against slavery, and it was through a rejection of the same duty that Holmes (whose "high hopes of the Northern crusade" were dashed by his experience of the war) could feel free to forget about the aim of "transforming human society," cut himself off from the problems that were bothering his contemporaries, and concentrate entirely on demonstrating his own "eligibility to be counted among the Elect" by striving to touch the superlative in the performance of his job.

Is this also what Edmund Wilson is now doing? Certainly the act of writing a book on a subject as remote from the pressing concerns of the moment as the literature of the Civil War and giving his best to the job, even when the job requires spending an enormous amount of energy on the likes of John W. DeForest —much as Holmes had to spend his energy on the trivial details of taxes and railroads—seems to indicate that Wilson has now opted for the same kind of isolation that Holmes achieved and is pursuing the same kind of private salvation that Holmes sought in solitary dedication to his work. But whatever Wilson himself may be doing, I don't think there is any question that he means us to see a parallel between the situation over which Holmes triumphed and our own situation today. Nor is there much doubt that he is counselling writers and intellectuals to follow the example of Holmes by reaching for the superlative in their work "without trying to improve the world or make a public impression." He knows, of course, that this entails a price, just as he knows that becoming what Holmes called a "jobbist" also involves an implicit acquiescence in "the dominant will of the society." But the "jobbist" will at least hold out against the debasement of standards, and he will have his integrity to keep him warm while living alone with his work. If this seems a chilly prospect, the "jobbist" can comfort himself with the reflection that the only alternatives to it are corruption or quixotic activism, for the world is even more intractable today than it was in Holmes's time—more intractable, more vicious, less civilized, and even more destructive of independence and integrity (see the introduction to *Patriotic Gore*).

Now I have to say in reaction to all this that I find myself a little resentful at being told by Edmund Wilson, of all people, that there is no longer any point in trying to change the world and that we might as well settle down to the business of pursuing a private salvation. The America of the Gilded Age may have been everything Wilson says it was, but the America of today is a very different place, and the attitudes of the alienated patricians of the Gilded Age which Wilson is now urging upon us are not, in my opinion, particularly relevant to the situation we are presently confronted with. Certainly this is a bad and difficult time, but it will not be through "jobbism" or withdrawal that we survive (if we ever do), let alone triumph (if we should ever be so blessed). We have all learned the lesson of withdrawal only too well in the past ten years, and surely what we need now more desperately than ever is a new sense of our power to affect the course of history through determination, intelligence, and involvement. It was precisely this sense that Wilson—rebelling against the hysteria and defeatist self-pity that overcame his own patrician elders when in the 70's and 80's they first saw themselves being dislodged as the dominant class in America—strove to arouse in his contemporaries during the 20's and 30's. Throughout that period, he was repeatedly insisting that the production of literary masterpieces was not enough, that writers and intellectuals who turned their backs on the problems of contemporary society were in effect acquiescing passively in "the triumph of the businessman," that citizens of the Republic of Letters were also citizens of a human society that had gone wrong but could also be righted, and that they bore a great responsibility for working to make it right.

Like Holmes, then, Wilson has retained the ability to function as a first-rate intellect in a period when so many others have been discouraged or broken. Unlike Holmes, however, Wilson was always able to operate at the top of his bent without having to cut himself off and without leaning on the crutch of an arbitrary skepticism about human nature and history. If the energy and vitality of *Patriotic Gore* show that Wilson is still functioning as a first-rate intellect, the book also unfortunately indicates that he is no longer able to do so without the help of isolation and pessimism. From now on, it seems, we shall have to look elsewhere for the kind of guidance that it was once his particular glory to give.

[1962]

Fitzgerald in Perspective

The recent publication of Andrew Turnbull's *Scott Fitzgerald*—a carefully researched and quietly reverential biography—is almost certain to stimulate yet another rash of articles attempting to explain why Fitzgerald "failed." The blame will be put on the 20's or the 30's or both; on Zelda, alcoholism, and the Ritz Bar; on St. Paul, Princeton, and the Riviera; on psychology, sociology, and history. But the most prominent villain of the piece will be America—American innocence, or American idealism, or American corruptibility, or all three. Once again we shall be hearing that there are no second acts in American lives, and that in a real dark night of the soul it is always three o'clock in the morning. Once again we shall be told that the really rich are really different from us, but that Scott really hated the really rich, no matter what Ernest Hemingway thought. We shall be treated to digressions on the deep difficulties that beset the novelist of manners in America, there will be hymns of lamentation by some on the disappearance of class distinctions and righteous attacks by others on the evils of snobbism. There will be nostalgia for midnight dips in the Plaza fountain and sighs for Riviera summers before the vulgar hordes invaded.

Of course, it may be that everyone is as bored as I am with the fuss that has been made over Fitzgerald in the past ten years or so, in which case there will either be silence or a flood of articles asking whether the left-wing critics of the 30's may perhaps not have had a point when they said good riddance to Fitzgerald and the whole frivolous decade he represented, and/or symbolized, and/or spoke for, and/or embodied, and/or chronicled. (When *Tender is the Night* came out in 1934 at the height of the Depression, one such critic, offended by the great to-do he believed Fitzgerald to be making over a bunch of neurotic expatriate parasites, began his review with the remark, "Dear Mr. Fitzgerald, you can't hide from a hurricane under an umbrella.") But it would be a pity if everyone suddenly decided to turn on Fitzgerald, for then the way would be left open for yet a third revaluation ten years from now, and off we would go again. How can we get Fitzgerald into a sane perspective?

I would suggest that the best way to start is by giving up the idea that he was a genius who tragically failed to fulfill his immense promise. Since this idea lies at the basis of the Fitzgerald legend, there would be a certain sly justification for giving it up even if it were true—which, fortunately, it is not. On what does the notion of Fitzgerald as a genius rest? Having just spent several days investigating what some of his more extravagant admirers have to say about him, I can report that it rests on nothing more substantial than the sense one gets in reading Fitzgerald of the ease and the fluency, the energy and the grace that are the unmistakable qualities of the natural writer. But if Fitzgerald was a natural, he was also incapable, except at rare moments (and even then only imperfectly), of the profound self-awareness that more than anything else marks the really great writer, the writer of genius.

His first two novels, *This Side of Paradise* and *The Beautiful and Damned*, are so far beneath the level of his later work that it seems unfair to bring them into the argument, but I simply want to note in this connection that their badness comes from the fact of their having been written with an uncanny, almost monstrous, lack of self-consciousness. By the time Fitzgerald completed *This Side of Paradise*, at the age of 22, he had spent three years at Princeton, read many books, served a stint in the army as an officer, and worked at a grubby job in an advertising agency. Yet he knew less about himself and was as little capable of detachment from his adolescent fantasies as a boy of sixteen. Two years later—after getting married and becoming a celebrity—he published *The Beautiful and Damned*, which still shows only the faintest glimmerings of insight into himself and still exhibits the bright sophomore's idea of life.

This, of course, makes *The Great Gatsby* all the more astonishing. In the three years between *The Beautiful and Damned* and *Gatsby*, Fitzgerald had somehow managed to grow up. But that puts the matter far too weakly: what he had in fact accomplished was one of the most dramatic leaps in the history of literature. Suddenly, and from nowhere, had come the ability to see himself (almost) as he really was, to understand his relation to the world, and to pass a complex judgment on the nature and quality of that relationship. In the figure of Gatsby he found a means of acknowledging that the dreams and ambitions by which he had always been driven were attached to something meretricious and finally cheap, for all its apparent beauty and richness and charm. In Daisy (she of the famous voice that is "full of money") and her viciously stupid millionaire husband Tom Buchanan, he told, not without a touch of spite, what he must always have known in his soul about the rich and never dared to say for fear of having to surrender the "colossal vitality of his illusion," the illusion into which he had thrown himself, like Gatsby, "with a creative passion, adding to it all the time, decking it out with every bright feather that drifted his way": he told that the leisure class in America was not the aristocracy of style and grace and daring that he had for so long pretended to himself that it was. Such aristocracy as exists in the world belongs to Gatsby, with his talent for gorgeous gesture and his magnificently romantic readiness before life. He is, of course, deceived and cheated and then destroyed, but this becomes as much a judgment on life, and on life in America, as on Gatsby's foolishness and ignorance. It was a manfully proud judgment for Fitzgerald to make in the teeth of his new self-awareness (how easily he might have yielded to pathos and self-pity instead), and it seems even more impressive when we remember how acquiescent a man he was at bottom, and how little inclined by nature to attack or denounce the things he yearned for simply because they were out of his reach.

Good as *Gatsby* is, however, and far as Fitzgerald had come in writing it, it still falls short of being a work of genius. If in the character of Gatsby Fitzgerald expressed a deeper understanding of his own predicament than he had ever achieved before, the shadowy abstractness with which Gatsby is drawn also indicates that there were severe limits to this new self-awareness. It is almost as though Fitzgerald, in failing to endow Gatsby with flesh and blood, were failing to admit that *he* was Gatsby, that all this was happening to *him*; it is as though he could only go as far as he did in confronting himself by shrinking deliberately from the ultimate act of self-confrontation toward which the writing of this novel was pulling him.

Nine years elapsed between the publication of *Gatsby* and the appearance of *Tender is the Night*. They were bad years for Fitzgerald. His wife had a series of breakdowns, he was drinking too much, he had serious financial problems, he was saddled with complete responsibility for his young daughter, and he felt increasingly out of touch with the kind of world that came into being with the Depression. The wonder is not that it took him so long to write *Tender*, but that he managed to write it at all. (One of the many things about Fitzgerald that the legend characteristically omits is his stamina and his ability to work under the most impossible conditions—including drunkenness. Of course the legend casts him in the role of the doomed romantic poet, and doomed romantic poets are not supposed to be strong.)

Tender is brilliantly written, perhaps too brilliantly written, and is a more ambitious effort than *Gatsby*, but it fails to come alive—largely, I think, because Fitzgerald was less than completely honest with himself in conceiving Dick Diver's tragedy. What he tried to get into Dick Diver was his feeling of having been damaged by his marriage to Zelda (Nicole in the novel) and by his weakness for the life of luxurious aristocratic ease. But there is nothing in the character of Dick Diver to account for his deterioration—he comes through as purely the victim of forces outside himself, when he should have been presented as a different kind of victim of the same illusions that destroyed Gatsby. Here again, then, we can see Fitzgerald shrinking from the ultimate act of self-confrontation that a really great writer—a genius—would have the courage to perform.

He is also less than completely honest with himself in the three essays he published in *Esquire* about his famous crack-up in 1936-7. Why had he cracked up? Because he had squandered his resources, both physical and spiritual, in pursuing the dream of "being an entire man in the Goethe-Byron-Shaw tradition, with an opulent American touch, a sort of combination of J. P. Morgan, Topham Beauclerk and St. Francis of Assisi." Not a word, scarcely even a hint, of the effect the indifferent reception of *Tender* must have had on him, of the torture he must have suffered from the general opinion that he was washed up as a writer, of the terrible difficulty he must have had in trying to carry on without the admiration of the world to sustain him. In short, there is not a word about his greatest weakness as a man, the weakness that lay behind his eternal preoccupation with the rich and the glamorous: the desperate need for Success. If Fitzgerald is an exemplary American figure, as so many critics have told us he is, it is not because he was an "innocent" or a romantic with a head full of Hollywood-style dreams; it is because he wanted Success more than he wanted anything else. And if he is a hero, it is not because he bore misfortune bravely or because he acted out a great tragic drama; it is because, dependent as any movie star on popularity and acclaim and lacking the commitment to a cause or an idea or a vision that gives some people the resources to protect themselves from the ravages of worldly failure, he was yet capable of making himself into a serious writer.

"I have now at last become a writer only," he announced with a mixture of bravado and bitterness in one of the "Crack-Up" essays. A little over four years later he was dead, but not before he had demonstrated with the first half of The Last Tycoon (which is all he ever got to write of it) that he was not only far from being washed up but that he had not altogether lost the power he had begun to show in Gatsby of dealing in a complicated, intelligent, and critical way with his own sorry predicament. The Last Tycoon would probably have been even better than Gatsby if Fitzgerald had lived to finish it, for in the figure of the great Hollywood producer Monroe Stahr he found for the first time a way of objectifying and dramatizing and judging, more truly and vividly and concretely than in the vague character of Gatsby, the meaning of his own special relation to the world: Stahr, the creator and merchant of the fantasies and dreams of all America, who knows that they are fantasies and dreams and yet half believes in them and only half sees how cheap they are, who deals in the meretricious and the fake and is yet a profoundly dedicated man and a master of his craft. A writer who is being as straight with himself as he can possibly be will always write with assurance, authority, and economy, and so it is that the style of *The Last Tycoon* is closer to the superb style of *Gatsby* than to the elegantly baroque prose of *Tender* which so often reveals the strain of self-deception and defensiveness that went into its composition.

Fitzgerald, then, was not a genius: he was a highly gifted natural whose intelligence was not always equal to his talent, and the first step in ridding ourselves of the tiresome legend that surrounds his name is to recognize him as a minor novelist with only one enduring achievement to his credit. The second step is to bury the idea that he failed to fulfill his promise, for what do we see when we look coolly at his career? We see a writer whose first two novels are phenomenally immature and callow, but who suddenly comes forward at the age of 29 with a book so far superior to anything he had ever done and so unexpected in the light of his earlier work that one is hard put to explain where it came from. That this was followed by a failure is of no particular significance: *Tender* is a perfectly respectable failure, and anyway, who ever said that a writer is supposed to develop in a straight line? For all its faults, *Tender* can in no sense be taken as a sign that Fitzgerald's powers were on the wane or that he was not progressing in maturity and skill. It is a novel that comes directly out of a difficult personal crisis, and times of crisis are not notable for promoting balanced self-assessments in those who are doing the suffering. In any event, even if *Tender* could be thought of as a catastrophic regression from *Gatsby*, *The Last Tycoon* would still be there to show that Fitzgerald, damaged though his personal life and his health most assuredly were, was not severely damaged as a writer.

Fitzgerald was destroyed, but it was death that destroyed him, not America. And let us remind ourselves when we talk of how he developed or failed to develop, that he was only 44 years old when he died.

[1962]

Nathanael West: A Particular Kind of Joking

The Complete Works of Nathanael West comprises four short novels amounting to only four hundred and twenty-one pages—West was killed in an automobile accident in 1940, at the age of thirty-seven—but it contains some of the best writing that has been produced by an American in this century. During the 30's, West earned the admiration of several important critics, and his two most impressive novels, *Miss Lonelyhearts* and *The Day of the Locust,* are still widely circulated and praised; the others, *The Dream Life of Balso Snell* and *A Cool Million,* have only now been rescued, by the publication of this collected volume, from virtual oblivion. But though West has not exactly been ignored, neither has he been given the close attention he deserves. His name seldom comes up in discussions of modern American literature, and even now it is not clearly realized that, for all the "bitterness" and "savagery" people find in his work, he was first and last a writer of comedy. A year before his death, West complained that his novels were disliked because they fell "between the different schools of writing." He considered himself, he said, on the side of the "radical press," but the radicals objected to his "particular kind of joking," and the "highbrow press" accused him of avoiding the "big, significant things." It is difficult to imagine what the "highbrows" (whoever they were) could have meant; the big, significant things are precisely what West pursued, to greater effect, in my opinion, than Fitzgerald, who lacked West's capacity for intelligent self-criticism, or even Hemingway, whose view of life seems to me rather more limited than West's. But the "radical press" was right in being disturbed by West. Nothing could be further from the spirit of his work than a faith in the power of new social arrangements or economic systems to alleviate the misery of the human condition. West was one of the few novelists of the 30's who succeeded in generalizing the horrors of the depression into a universal image of human suffering. His "particular kind of joking" has profoundly unpolitical implications; it is a way of saying that the universe is always rigged against us and that our efforts to contend with it invariably lead to absurdity. This sort of laughter—which, paradoxically, has the most intimate connection with compassion—is rarely heard in American literature, for it is not only anti-"radical" but almost un-American in its refusal to admit the possibility of improvement, amelioration, or cure.

Yet West was also capable of lesser kinds of joking. His first novel, *The Dream Life of Balso Snell*—written mainly during a two-year stay in Paris, when he was in his early twenties, but not published until 1931—is a brilliantly insane surrealist fantasy that tries very hard to mock Western culture out of existence. Balso, who seems sometimes to represent the naïve romantic poet and sometimes the philistine American, comes upon the Trojan horse while wandering on the plains of Troy and literally gets inside Western culture by entering the horse (which is, of course, a symbol of that culture) through "the posterior opening of the alimentary canal." He meets a series of strange characters who inhabit the horse's innards, and each encounter is an occasion for West to deride art, religion, or civilization itself in the most shocking terms he can think of. There is, for example, Maloney the Areopagite, "naked except for a derby in which thorns were sticking" and "attempting to crucify himself with thumb tacks." Maloney, a mystic, is compiling a biography of St. Puce, "a flea who was born, lived, and died beneath the arm of our Lord." This trick of associating a pious idea with physical images evoking disgust is used generously throughout the novel, which overflows with references to diseased internal organs, mucus, and the like.

But it is all done much too innocently and exuberantly to be as offensive as West seemed to want it to be, and in any case the effort to *épater le bourgeois* is by no means the main purpose of *Balso Snell*. West incorporates into the novel several self-contained short stories that he obviously composed with intense seriousness. The most interesting—the confession of an insane intellectual who has murdered an idiot for what he calls purely "literary" reasons—is a precociously accomplished imitation of Dostoyevsky, and West might well have regarded its extravagant relish of the grotesque and the diseased as a form of deep spiritual insight. Instead, he attributes the story to a twelve-year-old brat named John Raskolnikov Gilson, who informs Balso that he wrote it to seduce his eighth-grade teacher, Miss McGeeney, a great reader of Russian novels. Mocking his own work in this fashion was West's way of telling himself that merely to indulge his feeling for the grotesque and the diseased was morbid sentimentality, that he had to do more with this feeling than take it at face value if he was going to produce mature fiction. The assault on culture in *Balso Snell* is really part of West's assault on himself; he is sneering not so much at Western civilization as at his own ambition to become a part of it. This novel, then, is a battleground on which West the sentimentalist is pitted against West the cynic, each party asserting his claim to superior wisdom and refusing to concede any value to the other. Though the battle ends in a draw, the fighting of it must have helped West achieve the astonishing control over his feelings that makes his second novel, *Miss Lonelyhearts*, one of the masterpieces of modern literature.

Miss Lonelyhearts (West never gives him any other name) is a young newspaperman who conducts a column of advice to the unhappy and confused. At first, his job had seemed a great joke, but after several months—the point at which the novel begins— the letters from his readers begin to trouble him deeply. Brooding over his inability to help the wretched people who turn to him for advice, he decides that love is the only answer; he must bring Christ to them. His colleagues, and particularly the feature editor, Shrike, have a fine time ridiculing this "Christ complex," and his fiancée, Betty, insists on driving him out to the country to cure what she believes is an urban malaise. He himself tries to escape from "the Christ business" through several mechanical ventures into sex and cruelty, but the complex only gets worse. In the end, driven almost insane by his sense of religious mission, he is murdered by one of his correspondents, a cripple whom he had first cuckolded and then attempted to "save."

The letters are the focal point of the book, and a terrifyingly authentic expression of the misery that can be neither cured nor explained away:

> I am 15 years old and [my sister] Gracie is 13 and we live in Brooklyn. Gracie is deaf and dumb and biger than me but not very smart on account of being deaf and dumb. . . . Mother makes her play on the roof because we dont want her to get run over as she aint very smart. Last week a man come on the roof and did something dirty to her. She told me about it and I dont know what to do. . . . If I tell mother she will beat Gracie up awfull because I am the only one who loves her and last time when she tore her

dress they loked her in the closet for 2 days and if the boys on the blok hear about it they will say dirty things like they did on Peewee Conors sister the time she got caught in the lots.

The letters make the fact of evil a concrete presence in the novel, and it is in relation to this fact that West forces us to measure the responses of his characters. What we learn is that Miss Lonelyhearts' sentimental spiritualism is no more adequate than Shrike's intellectual cynicism or Betty's naïve unconcern; all three attitudes are equally valid and equally futile, and they constitute, for West, the three possibilities of life in a world whose one ineluctable reality is the letters. And when, in the last chapter, Miss Lonelyhearts rushes feverishly to embrace the cripple who has come to kill him but who he imagines is crying out for salvation, we realize that Miss Lonelyhearts, like Shrike and Betty, suffers in the same degree as "Desperate," "Harold S.," "Catholic-mother," "Broken-hearted," "Broad-shoulders," "Sick-of-it-all," "Disillusioned-with-tubercular-husband." That is West's profoundest joke, and it incorporates all the other jokes of the novel.

The formal perfection of *Miss Lonelyhearts*—the spareness and clarity of the style, the tight coherence of the conception, the delicate balance between opposing points of view—is an aesthetic reflection of the harmony that West had established, in the years since the completion of *Balso Snell*, between the conflicting elements of his own character. The tone never falters in *Miss Lonelyhearts*, because the strong-minded, intelligent compassion that emerged from this harmony and that was West's special and most precious quality as a writer gave him a firm perspective from which to judge experience. The impulse toward cynicism that ran wild in *Balso Snell* gets some play in Shrike, but it is now put into its proper place in a comprehensive and complex scheme of things. West regards Shrike's cynicism as a stunted form of wisdom, deriving from the recognition that all talk of salvation through love is irrelevant cant beside the reality of the letters, but he also perceives that the price of hiding behind a jeer is an inability to communicate with others—Shrike can neither give nor accept love. By contrast, Miss Lonelyhearts, the embodiment of the morbid sentimentalist in West, does have the power to reach out to others, but West knows that Miss Lonelyhearts' spiritualism also involves a failure of intelligence that drives him to foolishness and ultimately to insanity and death. And the portrait of Betty, whose refusal to be bothered by the letters leads to the frustration of her ambitions for a normal domestic life, can be understood as an assertion by West that his preoccupation with the halt and the sick is not the sign of a decadent or an immature sensibility but a necessary concern with the problem of evil.

Having accomplished that much, West had earned a vacation. *A Cool Million*, published in 1934, a year after *Miss Lonelyhearts*, seems to me the sort of venture that a novelist who has achieved confidence in his powers feels he can afford to play around with. There are many amusing things in the story of Lemuel Pitkin, who leaves Rat River, Vermont, to make his fortune in another part of the land of opportunity and is dismantled step by step, losing all his teeth, one of his eyes, a leg, even his scalp, and then winds up as the martyred saint of an American fascist movement. But this obvious satire on the Horatio Alger myth, done in mock-heroic prose, must have come right off the top of West's head. And I suspect that he may even have been trying to satisfy the prevailing left-wing *Zeitgeist*, which demanded that a novelist be explicitly political. But that was a mistake for West; what he had to say about Fascism he said much better in *The Day of the Locust*, his very unpolitical last novel.

The Day of the Locust—written while West was doing screenplays in Hollywood and published in 1939, nineteen months before his death—is a difficult book to get one's bearings in. It lumbers along at a queerly uneven pace, and one is never sure what West is up to. There is also an ambiguity in the treatment of locale and characters, both of which he portrays with meticulous regard for realistic detail while contriving to make them seem unnaturally grotesque. But once we understand that *The Day of the Locust* is intended as high comedy, and once we see that the slight touch of unreality in the narrative is West's method of trying to convey the feel of Hollywood, this apparently weird, disjointed book begins to assume meaningful shape.

A young painter, Tod Hackett, has taken a job at one of the studios as a set and costume designer. Hollywood fascinates him, but not the Hollywood of the big stars and the important producers; he is obsessed with the people on the streets who "loitered on the corners or stood with their backs to the shop windows and stared at everyone who passed. When their stare was returned, their eyes filled with hatred." The only thing Tod knows about these people is that they have "come to California to die." Later, he learns that

All their lives they had slaved at some kind of dull, heavy labor, behind desks and counters, in the fields and at tedious machines of all sorts, saving their pennies and dreaming of the leisure that would be theirs when they had enough. Finally that day came. . . . Where else should they go but California, the land of sunshine and oranges?

Once there, they discover that sunshine isn't enough. . . . Nothing happens. They don't know what to do with their time. . . . Their boredom becomes more and more terrible. They realize that they've been tricked and burn with resentment. . . . Nothing can ever be violent enough to make taut their slack minds and bodies. They have been cheated and betrayed. They have slaved and slaved for nothing.

These living dead—together with the religious crackpots who worship in all manner of insane churches, venting their rage at the betrayal of their dreams in mad apocalyptic rhetoric—are the people Tod wants to paint. He is planning a painting to be called "The Burning of Los Angeles," in which—anticipating similar fascist outbreaks throughout the country—they gather, like "a holiday crowd," to set the city afire. "He would not satirize them as Hogarth or Daumier might, nor would he pity them. He would paint their fury with respect, appreciating its awful, anarchic power and aware that they had it in them to destroy civilization." And so, indeed, West paints them in *The Day of the Locust*.

So, too, he paints the still living creatures who inhabit Hollywood. The living are tyrannized by dreams, possessed of the same "need for beauty and romance" that once animated the cheated people now waiting for death, but they have not yet acknowledged the futility of their dreams, the inexorability of their betrayal. In another of a series of pictures he calls "The Dancers," they are driven by the stares of the cheated ones "to spin crazily and leap into the air with twisted backs like hooked trout." This is a precise description of the way they look in the novel. Their bodies move uncontrollably, in jerks and spasms, as though refusing to coöperate in their struggle to achieve grace and dignity. They are "hooked" to the most elaborate, most awkward, most obvious of pretenses. Harry Greener, the broken-down old clown whose gestures all come out of an unfunny vaudeville act; his daughter Faye, who wants to be a star but whose affectations are "so completely artificial" that to be with her "was like being backstage during an amateurish, ridiculous play"; Earle Shoop, the cowboy from Arizona, who goes through life giving an unconvincing, incredibly stiff performance of the strong, silent Western hero; Abe Kusich, a pugnacious dwarf who tries to appear big and tough—these sad creatures make up the living populace of Hollywood. Tod, the artist, associates with them, implicated in their antics (he is in love with Faye), aware of their pretenses, but eager to see value and meaning in their grotesque dance of life.

West's Hollywood is a world in which the alternatives are the bitterness of a living death that is consummated in an orgy of destruction, and a convulsive reaching after nobility and grace that culminates in absurdity. There is no escape from these alternatives: Homer Simpson, the bookkeeper from the Midwest to whom nothing has ever happened, whose dreams are suppressed even in sleep, who has been reduced to a subhuman, almost vegetable condition, is finally "hooked" by the dream of love. In the last scene, Homer, maddened by the cruelty and infidelity of Faye, attacks a child who has annoyed him on the street and is mobbed by a crowd waiting outside a theater at a movie première. It is this incident which sets off a riot that finally unleashes the "awful, anarchic power" of the cheated and betrayed of Hollywood.

The Day of the Locust was West's first attempt to explore the implications of the compassionate view of life he had arrived at in *Miss Lonelyhearts*. Gloomy as it seems, this view of life provided a sound basis for writing comedy. *Miss Lonelyhearts* and *The Day of the Locust* are comic novels, not simply because they contain funny passages but because they are about the inability of human beings to be more than human, the absurdity of the human pretense to greatness and nobility. The fact that West has enormous respect for the fury and the hunger behind these pretensions, the fact that he does not demand of people that they surrender their dreams, the fact that he responds to the pathos of their predicament—none of this compromises the comedy. "It is hard," West tells us in *The Day of the Locust*, "to laugh at the need for beauty and romance, no matter how tasteless, even horrible, the results of that need are. But it is easy to sigh. Few things are sadder than the truly monstrous." This is one of the lessons that comedy teaches—neither to laugh at the need nor to be taken in by the results. It is also the animating principle of true sympathy, which is why West's "particular kind of joking" has so deep a kinship with the particular kind of compassion that is allied to intelligence and is therefore proof against the assaults of both sentimentality and cynicism.

[1957]

John O'Hara and Mary McCarthy

I. GIBBSVILLE AND NEW LEEDS

Mary McCarthy and John O'Hara are two of the most consistently interesting and provocative writers in America. They are so different that it takes the accident of the publication dates of *A Charmed Life* and *Ten North Frederick* to bring them together for discussion. Yet once having placed them side by side, it is difficult not to see a certain significance in their very opposition. Each navigates his own course, but both discover the same America.

O'Hara is a realist; that is, he considers his principal duty to be the creation of a plausible likeness of the world. His care and skill in achieving accuracy of detail are truly astonishing, so much so that if a vivid surface were all that mattered O'Hara would be a very great novelist. But his details are more than merely accurate. He is endowed with the kind of shrewdness that can derive the world from a brand label, and the whole universe from a fraternity pin.

Sharing O'Hara's angle of vision, one begins to believe that to learn where a man was born, educated, and buys his clothes is to know virtually all there is to know about him.

The brilliant surface makes O'Hara's world immediately recognizable. The moment you step into it, you feel at home and at the same time excited by all the bustle around you. O'Hara's prose style, casual and tweedy in texture, contributes to the relaxed, informal atmosphere of the visit. Only after you have been there for a while, when you pause and reflect, do you realize what a strange place you have come to.

The name of the place is often Gibbsville, Pennsylvania, though at times it has been New York or Hollywood or another Pennsylvania town. It is a place in which the social has superseded all other considerations. The nature of Gibbsville was most purely bodied forth in O'Hara's first novel, *Appointment in Samarra,* a book which seems to me a minor classic of our time. Julian English, the hero, in a fit of drunken petulance throws a highball into the face of an influential Gibbsvillian, and the insult sets off a chain of events that leads within three days to the break-up of Julian's marriage and his suicide. It speaks for O'Hara's integrity of conception that he makes this fantastically disproportionate sequence credible, convincing, and even inevitable. And fantastic the story is: no other word will do. A breach of the peace at a country club followed by a few tactless moves (most crucial of which is Julian's flirtation with another woman)—and an apparently happy life is cut off.

Of course there is a history behind Julian's disaster. Though he is of good family, a perfectly respectable businessman, and a member of the best circles in town, he has always been a "bad boy." But all this seems to mean is that he committed a few harmless pranks as a child, and as a young man proved unable to behave himself quite properly when drinking. The fact remains that in Gibbsville tactlessness is deemed a mortal offense: the real horror

of Julian's death is that no one complains of its madness. In Gibbsville, people would no more question the supremacy of the social
values than most us would question the laws of gravity. The social
values are all they have. With no inner resources to sustain them
against the decrees of the country club, an infringement of the
rules leaves them helpless and submissive, meekly awaiting punishment, and convinced that they deserve whatever they get.

To put all this another way, O'Hara appears to conceive that a
man is exhaustively defined by his observable behavior—by what
is usually called his manners—and beyond that, by his sexual
habits. There is nothing else, either implied or specified. But it
must be understood that O'Hara is not a "novelist of manners" in
the sense in which literary critics have used that term. Manners in
O'Hara refer to nothing outside themselves or deeper than themselves. They are neither an index of sensibility nor the expression
of moral impulses: O'Hara is no disciple of Henry James. Nor does
he share in the same tradition as Fitzgerald. Like most 19th-
century novelists of high life, Fitzgerald attributed a spiritual value
to money and social position. "The really rich," he said, "are different from us"—and he meant that they were more beautiful,
more interesting, *better* (though he would have been hard pressed
to define how they were better). Other novelists who have dealt
with the rich have presented them sometimes as better, sometimes
as worse than the rest of us—but always as different, and always
the difference had a meaning. What is curious about O'Hara's preoccupation with the rich is that despite his meticulous care in
describing the way they live and think, he draws no conclusions
from class. Which is to say that he is not a snob. The rich appear
to him most representative of the human condition, because their
lives are frankly, clearly, and fully implicated in the life of society.

O'Hara's concern with sex, and with erratic sexual tastes in
particular, sometimes seems gratuitous, as, for example, when he
devotes several pages to a description of the bedding down of two

peripheral characters. Love-making of all varieties goes on in his books; an O'Hara character is bound to have a very positive sexual personality, especially the women. But mere prurience does not account for these erotic passages—or at least not all of them. In the world of O'Hara, sex is the one area of a man's life in which he can achieve a certain individuality of expression. Everything else belonging to him, defining him, identifying him, comes from environment and returns to it, bit by bit throughout the years. We have no privacy, no inner life, no unique irreducible qualities—no mystery. Except, that is, in the bedroom, the domain of the unpredictable, the individual.

But O'Hara has grown older—he is over fifty now—and he no longer feels satisfied with his original account of life. *Ten North Frederick*, his latest novel, is the most comprehensive picture he has yet given us of Gibbsville. It covers three generations and various social strata of the town, concentrating on the life span of Joe Chapin, Gibbsville's leading citizen, and his wife Edith. The book ends with the following passage:

> There is here, in the biography of Joe Chapin, nothing that could not have been seen or heard by the people whose lives were touched by Joe Chapin's life. . . . Ten years after Joe Chapin's death, the people who remember him slightly or well have to go by what he said and did and looked like, and only rarely by what he did not say or do. Somewhere, finally, after his death, he was placed in the great past, where only what he is known to have said and done can contradict all that he did not say, did not do. And then, when that time was reached when he was placed in the great past, he went out of the lives of all the rest of us, who are awaiting our turn.

The mystery of life has finally caught up with O'Hara in the fact of death, and *Ten North Frederick* is his attempt to reinterpret the universe in the light of that fact. The tone is less jaunty, less smart-alecky than in his previous work; it conveys an impression of a man in quest of answers rather than of a shrewd bird in the know. But it is in the nature of O'Hara's special genius that it should be helpless before questions of meaning, that it should penetrate only so far and no further. The world as he sees it, as he cannot help seeing it, contains no mysteries; at most, it accommodates a paradox or two. His angle of vision is not a matter of choice, but the way he responds to experience, and consequently not to be modified by additions but only by a radical revision.

Ten North Frederick is still written from the same vantage point as *Appointment in Samarra*, except that O'Hara tries to introduce another dimension by acknowledging that a man's life is more than his observable behavior. But on this subject O'Hara has little to say, and the mere presence of the acknowledgment is enough to make the old O'Hara who survives in *Ten North Frederick* less convincing. The drama below the surface in the history of Joe and Edith Chapin is crudely imagined. Joe is animated by the secret ambition to become President of the United States, and when this ambition falls flat his apparently enviable life turns into an insipid affair, ending in alcoholism and moral collapse. Edith is driven by the desire to "own" another human being, and O'Hara gives us to understand that this evil wish poisons her husband's soul. O'Hara never shows the inner struggle between Joe and Edith; it is mentioned many times but remains an unrealized idea. Actually, what comes through as the cause of Joe Chapin's failure is precisely the same error that destroyed Julian English—a tactless move. Joe attempts to further his political career without consulting Mike Slattery, the local boss, and O'Hara is very good when he portrays the disastrous consequences of this offense against the system. For the rest, all the talk about the Joe Chapin-nobody-knew and the "real" Edith Chapin strikes us as a propitiatory gesture toward the gods O'Hara once slighted and whose sovereignty he is now ready to proclaim.

A *Charmed Life* is Mary McCarthy's third novel (or fourth, depending on whether you consider *The Company She Keeps* a novel—I do not). Like *The Oasis* and *The Groves of Academe*, it is a satiric portrait of a community of intellectuals, this time bohemian rather than political or academic. Martha Sinnott, the heroine, returns with her second husband to New Leeds, a town whose "essence was a kind of exaggeration. . . . In wife-beating, child neglect, divorce, automobile accidents, falls, suicides, the town was on a sort of statistical rampage, like the highways on a holiday week-end." She has come back after a long absence to finish a play, though the infectious disorder of New Leeds life frightens her, and in spite of the fact that her first husband, Miles Murphy, from whom she had fled in the night several years earlier to marry John Sinnott, is still in town and still a problem to her. Martha's marriage to Sinnott is a good one, but has lost the aura of excitement that once surrounded it. Under the circumstances, the inevitable happens, and after a drunken party Miles seduces Martha. When she finds that she has become pregnant, the very slight possibility that Miles may have been responsible forces her to seek an abortion. Her desire for a child, reason, arithmetic, and prudence all tell her to have the baby. But intelligence is powerless against Martha's more obscure emotions (". . . the moral part of Martha knew that she would have to have an abortion because all her inclinations were the other way").

On her way to the abortionist, Martha discovers that she is no longer afraid of herself. At that moment her car swerves and crashes, killing her instantly. It is as though, fearless, she were no longer eligible for life.

The story of Martha is standard Mary McCarthy, not as sharply executed as some of the Margaret Sargent stories in *The Company She Keeps*, perhaps, but nevertheless very much worth reading. However, at least half of *A Charmed Life* has to do with other characters and other matters—principally the career of Warren

Coe, a little abstract painter of small mind, silly aesthetic theories, and large heart; and the timid sexual ventures of Dolly Lamb, a fading virgin in her thirties whose goodness is equaled only by her fragility. These sections of the novel are thin and rather flabby. They are Miss McCarthy's experiments in charity, and they seem to register her perception of the helplessness of Good People, but one has the impression that their main purpose is to expand what might have been only a longish story into a full-length novel.

The fact is that good people, helpless or otherwise, are not in Mary McCarthy's line. Neither, for that matter, are bad ones; she seems to me quite indifferent to the ordinary moral categories. Like any good satirist, she creates her own heaven and hell. In the world of Mary McCarthy all activities are equally absurd, all people equally ridiculous. Even Warren Coe, whom she tries very hard to strike off as a figure of dignity, remains pathetic, and so does Dolly Lamb. At first glance, nothing distinguishes the saint from the sinner. There is, however, one traditional virtue which never stimulates Miss McCarthy to suspicion and ridicule —and that is honesty, the will to face the truth about oneself, the desire and ability to be critical of one's own motives. This kind of honesty is, of course, an "intellectual" virtue, presupposing as it does an unusual degree of analytic power. Which is precisely the point: the major distinction Miss McCarthy makes with regard to people, the only distinction that has force and reality to her, is between the intelligent and the stupid. But the intelligent are not those who have read many books or who are always concerned with ideas. They are the people who refuse to harbor illusions about themselves, who are vigilant and severe in flaying the self-deception out of their souls.

Of this virtue Miss McCarthy's heroines are always possessed. A Mary McCarthy heroine examines her soul with the scrupulous, unashamed persistence of a professional model looking herself over in the vanity-table mirror. She knows exactly what she looks like from every angle, and she is not afraid to acknowledge that her nose may be a trifle too long. Indeed, it is of the greatest importance to her that she recognize her own weaknesses, the better to carry them off. But here the comparison ends. For the more a Mary McCarthy heroine knows about herself, the less she is able to control her actions ("The more one knew, the less one could predict, it seemed to Martha Sinnott"). She is driven by impulses that seem to have no relation to what she feels herself to be. To take the most salient example—and the most frequently recurring situation in Miss McCarthy's work—the heroine never goes willingly to bed with a man; she always "finds herself" in bed with someone she dislikes and often hates. What we have in Margaret Sargent (and all the others who follow her, including Martha Sinnott) is a spectator of her own life, yet somehow not a participant, essentially unaffected by her experience and hence not really responsible.

But Miss McCarthy's heroines represent a good deal more than that. In general, it might be said that they dramatize the disjunction—or rather, the hostility—between Reason and Impulse. This is Miss McCarthy's true subject, a theme which underlies her satirical castigations, which calls forth all her famous brilliance, which gives point to her acerbity, and depth to her apparently gratuitous bitterness. She has seen the special relevance of the idea for the contemporary world. The impotence of reason and good intentions against instinct and impulse is, of course, a very old theme of literature. Indeed, it is one of the cornerstones of Christian thought, used by theologians from Augustine to Tillich to prove that man without Grace is helpless against the Devil. It was, too, Freud's great preoccupation; when accused of giving too much license to sex, he retorted that the aim of his new science was to establish for the first time in human history the dominion of reasons over the unconscious. But this ambition was never fulfilled. Freud ultimately claimed that his most enduring achievement was to have dealt the third great blow to human pride, the first two being the Copernican revolution and Darwinism, which proved that man was neither cosmologically nor biologically unique.

A "new philosophy calls all in doubt"—and we have Donne's *Anniversaries* and many Victorian testimonies to give us some sense of the uneasy skepticism caused by the first two revolutions. What Freud called into doubt was our power to control our own characters, much less our own destinies. He taught that no human motive can be "pure," that motivation itself was an incredibly complex phenomenon made up in great part of elements which the actor did not even know were present. He taught that we never quite "outgrow" anything, that the child we once were lives on within us, clamoring to be heard, filing his demands against the adult mind and spirit—and with astonishing success. And here we have the Mary McCarthy heroine: a high-minded adult under the tyranny of a five-year-old brat.

Miss McCarthy, it would seem, has assimilated the lessons of Freud very thoroughly; she has felt them with an intensity no other writer has even approached. Having been raised as a Roman Catholic, and then become an avant-garde intellectual, she was perhaps in an especially good position to understand the implications of Freud's skeptical pessimism, and certainly she responded to it with something like religious fervor. (The analogy between the psychoanalyst's couch and the confessional is always on her mind.) The failure of Reason as a substitute for Grace, and the illusion of free will—she went through, as it were phylogenetically, these adventures of Western culture in her own life:

> She feared that hope might be an illusion, which she had in common with every wreck and derelict who had floated up on the beach. It might be nothing more than the old "free will" of the philosophers, which was a part of the apparatus of consciousness and told nothing one way or the other about reality.

In this scheme of things, hypocrisy—traditionally the main butt of satirists—takes on a new flavor. No one can help being a hypocrite; we are all hypocrites by definition, though some of us are "honest" hypocrites. This, according to Miss McCarthy, is a great joke—on other people:

> The conceit of the "noble" action, he said to himself, chuckling, *l'acte gratuit*, the selfless, improvident, senseless, luxurious, spendthrift action, this had touched the soft spot of the little iron maiden, so resolved to distinguish herself from the others . . . whose ancestors had had to work for a living, by the implacable purity of her motives.

But note how the tone changes when one of her heroines is under scrutiny:

> They still "loved" each other, but this love today was less a promise than a fact of life. If they could have chosen over again, neither would have chosen differently. . . . They could not even imagine an ideal companion they would put in the other's place. From their point of view, for their purposes, they had the best there was. There lay the bleakness; for them, as they were constituted, through all eternity, this had been the optimum—there was no beyond. There was nothing.

The use of "through all eternity" in that passage is, of course, serious, lending grandeur to Martha's difficulties. The relish at having found someone out is transformed into the solemnity befitting the confrontation of a Great Truth. Freud may have deprived Miss McCarthy of her faith in the power of intelligence, he may have convinced her that it is impossible even to be honest, but she will not surrender her feeling of sublimity at the steady contemplation of one's own ruin.

What we respond to in Miss McCarthy, I think, is this show of fearless honesty, this last-ditch stand against cynicism. How courageous, we say, to admit such things, how admirable! But it is, after all, only a show. The "bleakness" inspires no horror. Instead, it seems to generate satisfaction, even complacency. For other people are worse because they are not perceptive or honest enough to admit their own nothingness. Intelligence may be unable to realize itself in action, it may be morally neutral, but how comely a sight all the same!

It is, then, to intellectual vanity—the only form of pride snatched from the flames of three cultural revolutions—that Miss McCarthy's satire appeals. How well she seems to understand our predicament, we who have lost our innocence by knowing too much, the over-conscious, over-critical. How much more attractive she makes us appear than the rest of those people. How well she understands our spiritual fastidiousness, our despair at discovering unworthiness in ourselves. How perfectly she appreciates that the real, the enduring me is the thinking, analyzing me, not the doing, the pragmatic me. How cunningly she salvages my essential purity from the wreck of my life.

In Gibbsville every gesture a man makes is noticed and judged; in New Leeds every movement of his spirit is taken account of and used in evidence against him. In both places the standards are as severely and confidently applied as they are vaguely conceived. A man must always be on guard, for at any moment, and for a reason he may never even understand, someone is likely to take away his membership in the club, or in a bout of despondency he may even tear it up himself. The resident of these places is denied the luxury of taking himself for granted, either socially or morally. No matter what his position, no matter how securely lodged he may seem to be, he must always make a supreme effort, he must continue to justify the space he occupies on the earth. Gibbsville

and New Leeds, different though they look, are nevertheless neighboring communities, and both are in America.
[1956]

II. MISS MCCARTHY AND THE LEOPARD'S SPOTS

A somewhat cynical critic I used to know once remarked that if writers of fiction were forbidden to indulge themselves in elaborate descriptions of dress, furniture, and food—the way freshmen in composition courses are forbidden to use too many adjectives—virtually the whole tribe of contemporary lady novelists would instantly be forced out of business. He had a point, I said, but what about Mary McCarthy? Surely she was different, surely she was better than that. He snorted: an intellectual on the surface, a furniture-describer at heart.

For a long time I thought he was wrong, and yet rarely has any writer allowed the furniture-describing (or the dress-describing or the room-describing or the food-describing) impulse to run as wild as Miss McCarthy permits it to do in her new novel, *The Group*. Here is a fairly typical passage dealing with a young married couple (he works in the theater and she is in Macy's executive training program):

> Once he had brought one of the authors, and Kay had made salmon loaf with cream pickle sauce . . . ("Bake 1 hour," the recipe went, and Kay usually added fifteen minutes to what the cookbook said). . . . Harald did not realize what a rush it was for her, every day now, coming home from work at Mr. Macy's and having to stop at Gristede's for the groceries. . . . He liked the A & P because it was cheaper, and she liked Gristede's because they delivered and had fancy vegetables. . . . Then Harald liked to cook the same old stand-bys (like his spaghetti with dried mushrooms

and tomato paste), and she liked to read the cookbook and the food columns and always be trying something new. . . . She opened a can of beans and dumped them into a baking dish; on top she puts strips of bacon. On the way home on the El she had decided to make Welsh rabbit with beer, to surprise Harald, but now she was afraid to, in case it should curdle and give Harald a chance to lecture her. She pulled apart a head of lettuce and started her salad dressing.

And on the passage drearily drags its flat feet into a discussion of Kay's preference for modern chairs (covered in muslin) over Hepplewhite-style chairs and for Venetian blinds over draperies (to have draperies made, she reflects, would run, even with a Macy's discount, to $100 or $120—"And that was unlined; lined would be even more").

The idea, of course, is that such details enliven a story and provide concreteness; and beyond that, there is the quietly snobbish assumption that they speak worlds about character, at least for those with ears to hear. Being mostly deaf to that kind of thing myself, I only feel safe in giving Kay a demerit for sneering at Hepplewhite-style chairs because I happen to know that liking modern design in furniture is no longer acceptable in Circles that Count. But if my life depended on it, I could not say with any assurance what ghastly moral flaw Harald's fondness for cooking spaghetti with dried mushrooms and tomato paste is supposed to reveal.

There is, however, more to Miss McCarthy's fixation on trivial details here than simple snobbery or feminine gossipiness. One might almost assert, indeed, that the whole point of *The Group* (which is set in the 1930's and deals with the post-collegiate adventures of several upper-class girls just graduated from Vassar) is to proclaim the superior validity of feminine gossipiness as a perspective on reality. Thus, the standard notion that has come down to us about life in America during the Thirties is that it was a hard time but a brave one, a time of terrible misery and passionate belief, of huge foolishness and limitless aspiration. This idea, according to Miss McCarthy, is a piece of sheer romantic nonsense. That is not how it was in the Thirties at all.

What really happened in the Thirties is that Vassar girls began to work, either out of necessity ("Dads" having lost a great deal of money in the crash), or because they felt guilty about their privileges and wanted to do something useful (it being a Depression and all).

What really happened in the Thirties is that Vassar girls began buying objects by Russel Wright like a "cocktail shaker in the shape of a skyscraper and made out of oak ply and aluminum with a tray and twelve little round cups to match—light as a feather and nontarnishable, of course."

What really happened in the Thirties is that young women of breeding began believing that canned goods were not only safe but sensible to use and tasty to eat.

What really happened in the Thirties is that at the same time young women of breeding began feeling "quite out of patience with the unimaginative roasts and chops followed by molds from the caterer that Mother served" and began trying "new combinations and foreign recipes and puffy omelets and soufflés and interesting aspics and just one hot dish in a Pyrex, no soup, and a fresh green salad."

What really happened in the Thirties is that upper-class virgins from Boston began allowing themselves to be deflowered by nasty Greenwich Village types they had only just met, and they also began having themselves fitted with pessaries, without even pretending to the doctor that they were married.

What really happened in the Thirties is that enlightened young mothers began returning to the practice of breast-feeding (even if they were "chestless wonders" like Priss Hartshorn) and observed a strict four-hour schedule.

What really happened in the Thirties is that two-year-olds repaid their mothers for the schedule system by soiling their pants on occasions especially calculated to embarrass any Vassar girl.

What really happened in the Thirties is that normal men and women began to visit psychoanalysts in order to keep from divorcing their wives or husbands, as the case might be.

What really happened in the Thirties is that the English butlers of the rich began acting like English butlers in the movies and became convinced of their superiority to their American masters.

And what really happened in the Thirties is that residents of Oyster Bay, Long Island, began driving over on Mr. Robert Moses's nice new parkways to Mr. Moses's nice new Jones Beach for a swim in the summer, instead of staying in their Oyster Bay country clubs.

Politics? The New Deal is mentioned once or twice (about as many times as the Colony Club); Stalinism is represented by a mild and rather kindly book editor who would like to fight in Spain but goes to an analyst instead; and the Trotskyite movement comes in by way of a quaint German-Jewish refugee who lives in the same rooming house as Polly Andrews and who converts her crazy (but lovable) father to the faith. Not a single person in the book has serious political passions, and it is no accident, comrade (as they used to say in some other Thirties), that one of the few characters Miss McCarthy actually likes is a doctor who never heard of Trotsky.

The Depression? Well, Polly Andrews's father (the crazy lovable one) was ruined and had to work his own farm, but Pokey Prothero's father actually got richer and bought her an airplane so that she could fly in and out of Ithaca where she was studying to be a veterinarian (which is what really happened in the Thirties). The main thing about the Depression, though, was that it forced everyone to watch his pennies. "The Depression, whatever else you could say about it," Priss Hartshorn reflects, "had been a truly wonderful thing for the propertied classes; it had waked a lot of them up to the things that really counted. There wasn't a family Priss knew that wasn't happier and saner for having to scale down its expenditures; sacrifices had drawn the members together."

Miss McCarthy is poking fun here, of course, just as she pokes fun at her characters throughout, but I am very much afraid that the joke is finally on her. For if these girls through whose eyes she portrays the history of the Thirties are so foolish and so peripheral, why is she bothering us with them in the first place? If, on the other hand, they serve to tell us something important about the Thirties, why is she always showing them up as trivial and naive? The answer, I suppose, is that she wants to have it both ways. She wants to be able to say that the Thirties was not a brave and romantic and traumatic period; that the people of those days cared more, far more, about small matters than large; that, indeed, they were deceiving themselves if they thought they even cared about large matters at all. However, she also wants to be sure that we are given no opportunity to accuse *her* of pettiness for taking so petty a view of the world, and hence the ridicule to which she is constantly exposing her characters for *their* pettiness. Which leaves me wondering why it should be a virtue in Miss McCarthy to pay so much attention to the furniture when paying so much attention to the furniture makes Kay a silly girl.

But it would be oversimplifying to leave it at that, for the Thirties are being deflated in *The Group* for a purpose beyond the wicked pleasure it affords Miss McCarthy to cut them down to size. There is a profoundly conservative side to Mary McCarthy, which has been there from the beginning and which has gone largely unnoticed—perhaps because she has always been considered a product of the radical-bohemian milieu that used to center around *Partisan Review*. It is a conservatism that takes many forms (including the unseemly fascination with upper-class life she exhibits here), but it flows ultimately from an ineluctable skepticism about the ability of people to control their own destinies by force of will and idea. Show Mary McCarthy a person with spiritual or moral aspirations—a type she delights to write about—and her eye will immediately and unerringly fly to the discrepancy between these high aspirations and the meanness of his natural impulses. Show Mary McCarthy a person venturing to transcend himself or to overcome the limitations of his background, and she will give you back a contemptible poseur—or a pathetic one, if her mood is benevolent. Show Mary McCarthy an ideal, and she will read you a lecture on Original Sin.

This skepticism of hers goes hand in hand with a sentimental belief in the possibility of saintliness—that is, goodness that comes naturally, as though by Divine Grace. Most Mary McCarthy characters are bad, but, like the little girls in the nursery rhyme, when they are good, they are very very good. So it has been in all her novels and stories, and so it is in *The Group*. The saints (the doctor who marries Polly Andrews, Polly herself, her crazy father, and Dottie Renfrew's mother) are effortlessly saintly. But everyone else is either hopelessly villainous (especially Harald of the spaghetti and tomato paste) or damaged in some way by trying to act in accordance with an idea instead of sticking to the set routines that are presumably natural to the people brought up in them.

Take Kay, for example—a girl of overflowing and abundant vitality who suffers a breakdown and then commits suicide, destroyed by the strain of a life she was never meant to live. Exactly what kind of life she *was* meant to live is hard to tell, but her wedding (Chapter 1) was a sufficiently ominous portent. Neither her parents nor Harald's were present, having done the sensible modern thing and made the young couple a gift of the money it would have cost to travel to New York; there was no honeymoon, for both bride and groom had to return to work immediately (no sentimentality permitted in a time of Depression); and the wedding breakfast, held in a hotel and hosted by the bride herself, featured Eggs Benedict and Baked Alaska (badly prepared, of course). Any Vassar girl of the Class of '33 who could so violate her true nature as to have a wedding like that was bound to jump out of a window sooner or later. The leopard ought to know better than to think he can change his spots.

It is this aspect of the Thirties that Miss McCarthy finally hates the most: the atmosphere of the period demanded of all the leopards that they work as hard as they could at doing something about their spots. Having wilfully blinded herself to the spirit of moral ambition and the dream of self-transcendence that animated this demand, she can see nothing in it but foolishness and insincerity—despite the fact that she herself was produced by that spirit and was beautified once by the dream. The Muses have rewarded her for the *trahison* she is now committing by presenting her with a flatly written and incoherently structured book, a trivial lady writer's novel that bears scarcely a trace of the wit, the sharpness and the vivacity which glowed so often in her earlier work. A well-deserved fiasco, if you ask me.

[1963]

Masses, Classes, & Social Criticism

Paul Goodman, whose latest book is *The Community of Scholars*, and Dwight Macdonald, who has a new collection of essays, *Against the American Grain*, have both been writing for over thirty years, but not until recently has either acquired anything like a large following. Goodman, after making a stir in the avant-garde literary world of the 30's, suffered a long period of neglect, but as he puts it, "the endless drizzle of the Cold War has made my kind of anarchist-pacifism unhappily endlessly relevant to another generation," and he has now become (not altogether comfortably) "a well-known author." His early books—which include fiction, poetry, drama, and literary and social criticism—are gradually coming back into print, and since 1960 new works have been pouring from his extraordinarily prolific pen at the rate of more than one a year. With Goodman, then, the case is one of a writer sticking stubbornly to his guns until the times catch up with him. But the times are never monolithic, and if Goodman is now a success because the radical approach he has always taken answers to a widespread mood of the moment, Macdonald (who also began as a "coterie" writer with a radical point of view) is now a success because his repudiation of radicalism answers to a mood that is perhaps even more widespread within the intellectual community.

"When I came to assemble these essays, written over the last ten years," Macdonald says in the preface to *Against the American Grain*, "I was hardly surprised to find they have a common theme: the influence of mass culture on high culture." The claims to unity that always preface collections of occasional essays are invariably just that—claims—and this one is no exception. I doubt that anyone knowledgeably concerned with the question of the war between mass culture and high culture could learn very much from the two pieces in this book ("Masscult & Midcult" and the review of Raymond Williams's *The Long Revolution*) that actually deal with the subject head-on, let alone from the others (among which are essays on Mark Twain, James Joyce, Ernest Hemingway, James Gould Cozzens, Colin Wilson, the Revised Standard Version of the Bible, the Syntopicon, and the third edition of Webster's Unabridged Dictionary), where the theme is only lightly sounded, if at all.

The truth is that it is not Macdonald's contribution to knowledge or to thought that justifies the reprinting of these pieces, but his consummate artistry as an essayist. To put it mildly, that is justification enough (does anyone expect a poet to introduce his latest volume of lyrics with the statement that he is about to shed light on some large abstract problem?). What makes Macdonald an artist is not merely his easy mastery of the formal requirements of the essay—the skill and grace with which he shapes his material. The more important thing to notice in reading him is that the whole man is talking, such as he is and like him or not: he is *there*, he has not been turned by the discipline of the form into a disembodied brain or a strategist of ideas covering all the exits. This is why people always use words like "lively" or "independent" —qualities of style and personality—in praising Macdonald; they do not often praise his qualities of mind.

He is, of course, intelligent; he knows his way around the relevant issues; he does the necessary homework. For all that, however, there is something incorrigibly unsubtle and unimaginative about his mind: except for their wit (which is an important exception), these essays contain no intellectual surprises; they are a case of "what oft was thought but ne'er so well expressed." Macdonald can document a point superbly, piling up his evidence with the gusto and verve of the born polemicist who knows that winning an argument is as much a matter of getting the audience on your side as of scoring solid hits. But the point being documented is usually a rather obvious one, and the position being attacked is rarely defensible except by dolts or villains. Cozzens's *By Love Possessed*, for example, certainly needed deflating when Macdonald went after it, but it can hardly be said that the job called for, or received, any special critical acumen, or that the poor reviewers who had established the novel's reputation were heavyweight antagonists. In going after the translators of the Revised Standard Version of the Bible, or the compilers of the Syntopicon, or the lexicographers responsible for the third edition of Webster's Unabridged, Macdonald was taking on more formidable opponents, yet even in those three pieces he had the kind of easy time that comes from shelling an overly exposed position. The scholars who have desecrated the King James Version or the lexicographers who are too "democratic" to discriminate authoritatively between good English usage and bad are worth attacking because they have the power to do great damage, but showing up their weaknesses is child's play for a sophisticated critic. Moreover, to the extent that they do present a difficult problem—how to draw the line between legitimate changes in the language and unnecessary or harmful ones—Macdonald is not especially helpful in coping with it theoretically and falls back mainly on taste.

Macdonald's greatest deficiency as a thinker, however, is his inability to move outside the terms in which a given issue is currently being discussed. Here, for example, is how he formulates the much-vexed problem of the relation between high culture and mass culture: "Up to about 1750, art and thought were pretty much the exclusive province of an educated minority. Now that the masses—that is, everybody—are getting into the act and making the scene, the problem of vulgarization has become acute. I see only two logical solutions: (a) an attempt to integrate the masses into high culture; or (b) a contrary attempt to define two cultures, one for the masses and the other for the classes. I am for the latter." (By "classes" Macdonald means an intellectual elite, a kind of Establishment such as exists—to his great envy—in England.)

There are, then, two parties, each with its own "solution," and Macdonald (as he tells us) after having been a member of the one, has now shifted his allegiance to the other. Why has he shifted? For the sake, he says—in a bafflingly cheerful tone, considering how melancholy he shows the situation to be—of culture itself. "The conservatives are right when they say there has never been a broadly democratic culture. . . . So let the masses have their Masscult, let the few who care about good writing, painting, music, architecture, philosophy, etc. have their High Culture, and don't fuzz up the distinction with Midcult." (Midcult is Macdonaldese for middlebrow.)

Thus Macdonald casts his eyes over the scene, notices what practical alternatives (or "solutions") are currently available, pronounces these alternatives to be exhaustive (no utopian he), and makes his choice like a man—never so much as suspecting that the choice he has made is to evade the whole problem. For what can his "solution" solve? Not the problem of culture surely, for there

is no problem except how to "integrate the masses into high culture"—that is, how to bring high culture back into vital relation
with the life from which it springs without destroying standards;
or, to approach it from the other side, how to repair the insult to
humanity that is involved in the peddling of junk by cynical or
ignorant entrepreneurs to people who are *so* hungry for culture
and *so* cut off from their best potentialities that they are willing to
settle for what they can get. If this problem cannot be solved (and
who knows whether it can?), no intransigent effort to preserve
traditional standards—which is all Macdonald is talking about—
can save high culture. Indeed, the Macdonald "solution," by
accepting a situation that (if we wish to speak with historical
sweep) developed only yesterday and that we have no right to
assume is inevitable or ineluctable, condemns high culture to an
eternal isolation and loneliness that would finally end in sterility,
dessication, and mandarinism.

Why does Macdonald fail to see this point? If "the conservatives
are right when they say there has never been a broadly democratic
culture," how does it follow that there never can be, or that the
aim of creating one is any less necessary or any less desirable now
than it was when Macdonald himself supported it? Have the
moral arguments and the philosophical convictions on which this
aim is based ever been refuted in theory or properly tested in
practice? Macdonald obviously thinks they have, which says a
great deal for his readiness to change his mind when the evidence
seems to warrant it, but not very much for his faith in human
possibility.

Just how little faith in human possibility Macdonald has, and
how little this lack of faith can be attributed to a hard-headed
respect for the relevant evidence, becomes immediately apparent
when we compare him to a writer like Paul Goodman. Goodman's
work is informed by the idea that we betray ourselves and "play
along with the forces that are senseless" by settling for anything

less than a society that provides the conditions under which every individual can develop his own grace and fullness of being. The nobility of such an ideal can hardly be disputed; its viability, however, can be and has been endlessly disputed. Goodman, of course, has never doubted its viability for a moment. Since he is convinced that it stems logically from the truth about human nature and from an accurate analysis of the process of human growth, he can simply blame the failure to create the ideal society on the venality of the powerful, the timidity of the wise, and the helplessness of the many. To be sure, there is something exasperating about Goodman's unruffled certainty that he is in possession of the Truth and that only bad will or moral inadequacy prevents everyone else from seeing the truth as well and acting on it. (To make matters worse, he will not even allow villains their villainy or cowards their cowardice: villains and cowards, in Goodman's system, are sick and therefore to be mentioned in patronizing tones of therapeutic compassion.) Yet however unfortunate his tone can occasionally become, it seems to me that Goodman is performing an immense service in showing that the optimistic ideals of the liberal-radical tradition are still capable of holding their own against all comers on the theoretical plane, and that they still supply far and away the most illuminating criteria by which to judge present realities.

The Community of Scholars beautifully exemplifies Goodman's virtues as a social critic, in a less dramatic way, perhaps, than his classic study of juvenile delinquency, *Growing Up Absurd*, but no less impressively: this is a book that deserves comparison with Newman's *The Idea of a University* or Veblen's *The Higher Learning in America*. The theme here is the disruptive effect of administration and the administrative mentality on the proper relation between college students and their teachers in America today, and on the proper relation between the college itself and the surrounding society. As usual with Goodman, the approach is philosophical rather than narrowly political. That is, he does not begin by asking what choices are allowed by the apparently in- eluctable forces of the present (in this instance the growth of an administrative apparatus extraneous and even hostile to the proc- ess of learning); he begins by asking what are the essential prop- erties and purposes of a college, under what arrangements histori- cally have these properties found their fullest expression, and under what conditions can we plausibly imagine that they might be better realized in the future. "Naturally," he remarks, "the schools are tightly involved with the performance, and even more with the style, of the dominant system of society. Any significant reform of them would involve a threat to that dominant system. But that also," he adds casually, "is very well."

The implication is that short of a revolutionary change in our society, not much can be done to improve a situation that has led to "so much waste of effort, and even unnecessary torture, of both students and the teachers." But as we quickly discover, Goodman think that something *can* be done. *The Community of Scholars* is rich in practical proposals (all of them imaginative and some of them very easy to apply, given the will, even within "the dominant system of society"), and the concluding chapter spells out, down to the last item of a projected budget, a daring program for action outside the present collegiate framework. This program, modelled on historical examples, calls for the secession from the system of bands of disaffected professors and the setting up by them, in collaboration with veteran masters of the arts and sciences already outside the academy, of new collegiate communities dedicated solely to the business of teaching and learning. Here, I would say, Goodman falls into much the same error that Macdonald does in advocating the perpetuation of a rigid distinction between mass and high culture, for the problem he so brilliantly analyzes in the body of the book would in effect only be evaded by the secession of the best people now working within the academy. (I think he is on firmer ground when elsewhere in the book he makes a contrary proposal: the periodic return to teaching of veteran practitioners of the arts and sciences, so that the students can acquire a living sense of the practical seriousness of the disciplines they are studying.) Perhaps the system can be reformed significantly from within, perhaps it cannot. But surely the intransigent loyalty to the ideal potentialities of man which has made Goodman so uniquely valuable a social critic also involves a faith in the long-run power of reason and rhetoric to overcome the short-run power of principalities and interests. What I am trying to say is that this splendid book is itself an act, an act that is bound to affect consciousness and through consciousness, conditions. And it is not an act of secession, either.

[1962]

II

Responses

The Young Generation

What makes it especially difficult to characterize the younger generation of intellectuals in this country is that they have not been articulate about themselves. They have found no spokesman to voice their protests or to proclaim their aspirations; nor have they produced a *This Side of Paradise* or a *Farewell to Arms* in which they might imagine themselves defined for all time, in which they could see themselves dramatized, and from which they could derive a sense of their own significance, of their peculiar mission in history. Indeed, so elusive is this generation that one hardly knows where to look for it, one hardly thinks of it as a generation at all. And the fact that its members have not developed a sufficiently strong feeling of identification with one another to emerge as a clearly delineated and self-conscious group only increases the suspicion that perhaps there is no such thing among us as "the younger generation"—perhaps there is only an assortment of discrete individuals with no collective identity: a "non-generation," as it were.

Appropriately enough for a non-generation, the young people who make it up can first of all be distinguished by a negative circumstance: none of them came to maturity during the Depression. That means that they were all born between, say, 1925 and 1935, and that they now range in age from 21 to 31. It also means that the crucial public experience to which they were subjected was the aftermath of World War II and the whole complicated series of events that came to be known as the cold war. If we want to understand this generation, we have to understand how the cold war—and I use the term here not in the narrowly political sense but to describe a moral climate, a condition of culture—affected people who never had any personal involvement with radicalism, who were neither a prey to the illusions nor a beneficiary of the seriousness that together gave the intellectual life of the 30's its special force.

The younger generation grew up in what might be called an atmosphere of intellectual revisionism. The ideological struggle with Communism in this country was in large part conducted not by direct assault on Communism as such—that was too easy—but by an intensive campaign against the pieties of American liberalism which for a variety of reasons had become the last refuge of the illusions of the 30's. But the attack on liberalism was not—could not be—merely political. The social theorists joined in with demonstrations of how simplistic the liberal conception of society was; there were the historians and economists who blasted away at Marxism; there were the sociologists who tore apart cliché after liberal cliché about the nature of American life; there was a rash of articles and books which put American popular culture into a new perspective and argued that the attitude of liberals toward the movies, television, and even the comic strips was a compound of misdirected middlebrow snobbism and vaguely Stalinoid notions about the function of culture; there were, finally, and perhaps most important, the literary critics who implicitly (the New

Critics) and explicitly (Lionel Trilling) brought the liberal picture of human nature into utter disrepute.

Was this a conservative reaction? In a literal sense, yes, but we must be careful to recognize that the main impulse behind it was an effort to redress an imbalance of opinion, not an attempt to replace liberalism with a conservative ideology—though, of course, polemical excess did occasionally give rise to something that looked like a conservative ideology and often even mistook itself for one. In any case, all the disparate forays against liberalism employed the same tactic: they all set out to show that liberalism was guilty of a failure to take a sufficiently complicated view of reality. Complexity became a key word in the discourse of the period, it became one of those words that exercises a thaumaturgic hold on the imagination of the young. The liberal mind was said to conceive of reality, both social and physical, as infinitely manipulable, as wholly subject to human power; revisionism came out for the more subtle, skeptical temper with its inhibiting awareness of human limitations and its "tragic sense of life." With an eye on the liberal emphasis on the rights of man, revisionism pointed to the correlative duties and responsibilities of man.

In general, it might be said that the critique of liberalism added up to a defense of wisdom as opposed to rational speculation, to a defense of the qualities of *maturity* against the values of youth— for at bottom contemporary liberalism was represented as a conglomeration of attitudes suitable only to the naive, the inexperienced, the callow, the rash: in short, the immature. Its view of the world was seen to be an undignified, indeed, dangerous philosophy for the leading nation in the West to entertain; America had grown to a position of great responsibility, and the attitudes of Americans must be made commensurate with the country's new status. But because this defense of maturity had, however indirectly, a political purpose behind it, because it was carried on as a polemic, and because it often involved covert self-castigation, it acquired a passionate urgency rather inappropriate to a literature whose point was to emphasize the virtues of age and pessimism. It was full of excitement and a sense of wonder at the discovery of lost treasures; it was a love-song to the shades of the prison house and a rapturous welcome to the years that bring the philosophic mind; it was probably the happiest, most enthusiastic farewell to innocence in the history of literature.

But it was not only liberalism that was implicated here; the celebration of maturity in the postwar years also constituted an assault on the intellectual life of the 30's itself. At any rate, to the young people educated in the late 40's and early 50's it seemed that a war was being fought in American culture between two styles of asserting one's seriousness as an intellectual: the old style of "alienation," represented by commitment to the ideal of Revolution and an apartment in Greenwich Village on the one hand, and, on the other, the new style of "maturity." The new style was not very clearly defined, but there was no doubt that its shape and color had to express the conviction that a life dedicated to ideas and art was possible *within* "bourgeois" society.

From the point of view of a socialist this is "conformity," but the young people who were attempting to mold their lives according to the new style did not conceive of themselves as conforming to the world around them. Quite the contrary—they were trying to realize its finest and deepest possibilities. For this was a style based on the assumption that the real adventure of existence was to be found not in radical politics or in Bohemia but in the "moral life" of the individual, within the framework of his efforts to do his duty and assume his responsibilities in a world of adults. The mistake of the 30's had been to suppose that society could ever be more than a bad bargain with the absolute: to the young generation, American society seemed on the whole a reasonably decent environment for the intellectual. They had learned from Henry James and Jane Austen that there could be meaning and dignity, even excitement, in the individual's movements through a world with whose basic premises and standards he was, if not quite at peace, then at least not at war. From Hawthorne, Hopkins, Donne, from the Augustinian theologians who became extremely popular during this period, from Hobbes and Burke (who supplanted Locke and Mill as the dominant political philosophers), they discovered that "conformity" did not necessarily mean dullness and unthinking conventionality, that, indeed, there was great beauty, profound significance, in a man's struggle to achieve freedom *through* submission to conditions. D. H. Lawrence taught them that the most important, most exacting, most challenging pursuit of life was the "hard business of human relationship," of friendship and love, while Lawrence the enemy of industrial society could make no impression on them whatever.

The trick, then, was to stop carping at life like a petulant adolescent, to recognize that your own experience as an American in the 20th century was no less valid and interesting than the experience of a 19th-century Englishman, to begin regarding the life around you with respect for its complexity and its drama, and to get down to the business of adult living as quickly as possible. And get down to business the young generation did. A great many of them married early; most of them made firm and decisive commitments to careers of a fairly modest kind, such as teaching; they cultivated an interest in food, clothes, furniture, manners—these being elements of the "richness" of life that the generation of the 30's had deprived itself of. As befitted responsible adults, there was nothing playful or frisky about these young people; their very presence and bearing announced that they were serious men and women with no time for fooling around, burdened with a sense of mortality, reconciled to the sad fact of human limitation. Very much aware of how complicated and difficult all problems were, very much alive to the danger of ideologies and enthusiasms and passions, very much persuaded that *la verité reste dans les nuances,* they struck a perfect attitude of the civilized adult: poised, sober, judicious, prudent.

The young generation has not been unproductive. They have written a great many poems and a fair number of novels. The poems are extremely well-bred, with a surface as impeccable as the poets' taste in clothes and a manner as composed as their behavior at the sober little parties they attend. But the paradox is that despite the early marriages and the devotion to career, the composure has been too easily acquired; it is the kind that comes of being a spectator of life rather than a participant. Everything that happens to these young people seems immediately to be milked of its "meaning" before it has a chance to make an impact; everything must be understood before it gets out of control. The world is seen at a distant remove, commented on quietly and wisely, never struggled with or confronted full in the face.

Nor do the novels written by the young generation bear much trace of direct contact with life. They are full of properly complex ideas about God, Man, Society, Life, Death, Sex; they are beautifully disciplined and shaped, yet one feels that the discipline has been imposed only on very weak impulses. Indeed, the literature that has been produced in our time by people in their twenties is one of the most remarkable phenomena in cultural history. It is a literature written by Olympians who got to the top of the mountain not by inching their way up the slippery faces of the rocks and arriving bruised and torn and bloody, but who were safely deposited there by helicopter and who know nothing about mountains except that the air on the peaks is rarefied. It is a literature of an unearned maturity, a maturity almost wholly divorced from experience, an expression, really, of the fear of experience—a maturity that has become a means of protecting one's neat little existence from the disruptive incursions of experience.

This fear of experience (which readily translates into a fear of taking risks and a concomitant terror of making a fool of oneself) no doubt has some relation to the fact that the prime virtue of a period of cold war and atomic stalemate must necessarily be prudence. It is also related, I think, to the powerful skepticism bred by the cold war itself; one was living in a world of severely limited possibilities, balanced precariously on the edge of an apocalypse. In such a world there was very little one could know, very little one could do.

There is, then, a certain justice in regarding the young generation as a non-generation, a collection of people who, for all their apparent command of themselves, for all the dispatch with which they have taken their places in society, for all their sophistication, for all their "maturity," know nothing, stand for nothing, believe in nothing.

But it would be a mistake to accept the sobriety and composure of the young generation at face value. The truth is that this is a restless generation, and as it grows older it gets more and more restless; it is beginning to feel cheated of its youth (that, I suspect, is the meaning of the recent revival of interest in the 20's). Since this is a generation that willed itself from childhood directly into adulthood, it still has its adolescence to go through—for a man can never skip adolescence, he can only postpone it. And something very wonderful may come about when a whole generation in its late thirties breaks loose and decides to take a swim in the Plaza fountain in the middle of the night.

[1957]

Jewish Culture and the Intellectuals

The publication of *A Treasury of Yiddish Stories* seems to me an event of peculiar significance. This is no mere hodgepodge collection thrown together to provide a suitable gift for Chanukah or Bar Mitzvah, nor is it the usual work of mawkish Jewish apologetics. The book is edited by Irving Howe and Eliezer Greenberg, handsomely published by the Viking Press, and illustrated by Ben Shahn. Among the translators, not only do such familiar figures in Anglo-Jewish journalism as Maurice Samuel, Meyer Levin, and Ludwig Lewisohn appear, but we also find Saul Bellow, Alfred Kazin, Isaac Rosenfeld, and, again, Irving Howe. These latter are all writers who have no professional connection with Judaism and whose work most frequently appears in literary reviews and little magazines. As for the editors, Eliezer Greenberg is himself a Yiddish writer of repute and editor of a Yiddish quarterly, while Mr. Howe, author of books on Sherwood Anderson and Faulkner, is known mainly for his work on American literature and politics.

Ben Shahn, the illustrator, finally, is a distinguished American painter.

Mr. Howe and Mr. Greenberg have collaborated to produce a long, informative, painstaking, and sometimes brilliant introduction, which manages in seventy closely printed pages to supply a sketch of the history of Yiddish literature, a description of this literature in terms of the *shtetl* culture from which it grew, and generally to account for qualities of the literature which might puzzle an unwary American reader. Anyone who is in the least familiar with critical writing in English about Yiddish or Hebrew literature will find this introduction almost as fascinating as the stories themselves, and certainly more unusual. For one thing, the editors have no ax to grind. They simply wish to recommend Yiddish literature to an audience of discriminating readers. They are very—almost overly—careful to make no "extravagant claims" for the work they introduce. While their caution quite rightly does not inhibit them, say, from calling Sholom Aleichem's Tevye one of "the great figures of modern literature," they assure us that Yiddish literature as a whole is of the second rank, and that it contains no Shakespeares, no Tolstoys. When they make the inevitable comparison between 19th-century Yiddish and Elizabethan English, they hasten to add that no comparison is intended between the quality of the works written in the two languages. This temperateness is wholly commendable.

Having made the necessary concessions and qualifications, however, Mr. Howe and Mr. Greenberg feel free to draw on a broad field of general comparisons and references. Certainly Sholom Aleichem, Mendele, and Peretz have never been discussed in such grand, such mostly Gentile company: Kierkegaard, James, Brecht, Kafka, Silone, Turgenev, Jane Austen, Dickens, Dostoyevsky, Tolstoy, Gogol, Chekhov, Gorki, Melville, Rilke, Whitman, T. S. Eliot—these are only a few of the writers mentioned in the introduction. Some of the critics quoted (along with Jewish authorities like Niger, Buber, and Heschel) are Cleanth Brooks, John Crowe Ransom, Robert Penn Warren, Isaac Rosenfeld, and Clement Greenberg.

It should be clear by now that what we have here is Yiddish literature presented under the auspices, so to speak, of the topmost intellectual fraternity. The critics have investigated it and declared it kosher. It is as though the worlds represented by Eliezer Greenberg and Irving Howe, after carrying on a dilatory flirtation for several years, have finally joined hands to acknowledge their kinship. The university and the yeshiva, the big city and the *shtetl*, have come together to explore one another's wisdom, and they find it comfortably possible to speak the same language—English.

I said that the publication of the *Treasury* was a significant event. But this volume is no isolated phenomenon. Within the last few years we have seen Mark Zborowski turning the methods of cultural anthropology on the *shtetl* with striking results. An increasing number of serious writers have dealt with Jews and Jewish experience as one of the *données* of the American scene (Rosenfeld, Malamud, Fiedler, Bellow, Kazin, and Swados, to mention a few). Lionel Trilling has discovered rabbinic overtones in Wordsworth. There is, of course, *Commentary*, which from its inception has sought to fuse an interest in the important intellectual currents of the day with an equally intelligent concern for specifically Jewish issues. Nor is this development confined to Jews alone. *Partisan Review* has printed stories by Isaac Bashevis Singer and others, imparting to these Yiddish works the same air of avant-garde distinction that surrounds the latest literary find from France or Germany. Columbia University instituted a department of Yiddish language and literature several years ago. Edmund Wilson has been learning Hebrew and has recently spoken (in the *New Yorker*) of the contemporary Hebrew novelist, Agnon, as a great writer comparable to Kafka.

Whatever else this phenomenon may indicate, it does seem to betoken a healthier relationship between American Jewish intellectuals and their Jewish experience than prevailed twenty or thirty years ago. But perhaps I may be permitted an autobiographical digression to suggest the qualifications I feel must be introduced into that observation.

While a student at Columbia, I also attended the Seminary College of Jewish Studies, which might be described as the undergraduate liberal arts division of the Jewish Theological Seminary. Naturally, the Seminary took up a good deal of my time. We spent two evenings a week and the whole of Sunday afternoon in classes, and, of course, there were assignments to prepare. I am not sure what drove me to take this additional burden on myself, but whatever my motives may have been, they were unusual. Unlike me, most of my classmates were either preparing for the rabbinate or planning to become Hebrew-school teachers, and almost all of them considered their work at the Seminary more important than their work at college. Many of them were observant Jews, while those who had secular leanings were frequently passionate Zionists training themselves for life in Israel. I was neither religious nor much of a Zionist, so I probably seemed an anomaly at the Seminary, but the fitness of my being there was never questioned. Within my circle of friends at Columbia, however, I was under a continual assault to justify my presence at the Seminary. My friends were grim and earnest young intellectuals, and most of them were Jewish. We considered ourselves the direct heirs and propagators of Western civilization, and we felt chosen to study, teach, and possibly contribute to it. It was a glorious mission, demanding a discipline of mind and spirit as arduous in its way as a monastic calling. But no one felt the glory of this vocation more keenly than we did, and we gave to it a devotion so vigorous and loving that I think we even frightened some of our teachers, who were no mean devotees themselves.

Though our main interest lay in literature, we scorned the scholarly journals like *PMLA*. On the other hand, we read the literary magazines religiously, in particular *Partisan Review* and *Kenyon Review*. Moreover, we thought of ourselves not as Americans or Jews, but as novitiates of the Republic of Letters, a world of whose concrete, physical existence we had less doubt than about the existence of the Midwest. Our Republic included everyone who had ever been instrumental in shaping Western civilization. Herodotus and St. Augustine, D. H. Lawrence and Yeats were all equally distinguished members of the community which we aspired to join. And we conceived of this community in space rather than in time. Despite the fact that we sat at the feet of Lionel Trilling, our sense of history was underdeveloped. Like Mortimer Adler—a Columbia graduate who never grew out of the idea—we saw a "great conversation" going on everlastingly between authors remote from one another in time, space, interest, and intention. We saw them all sitting around a great conference table, discussing the same problems, and always lining up on the same sides. It was the unity of culture, not the differences, that appealed most to our imagination.

But Judaism had virtually no representatives in this parliament of culture. Except for the Old Testament (which was honored both as great poetry and as the "Hebraic" constituent of Western civilization), the Jews did not exist for us. If my friends heard of the Cabbala, it was because Pico della Mirandola had been interested in it, and because it bore some relation to Yeats's occultism. Nothing disgusted my friends so much as the idea that because a man happened to be Jewish it was incumbent upon him to study Jewish culture. This was not "anti-Semitism" (at least not consciously), any more than their conviction that the American novel was inferior to the French, English, or Russian novel could be called anti-Americanism. I think their condescension toward all things Jewish was strikingly similar to their (and my) condescension toward all things American. And it is no accident that the discovery of Jewishness has coincided with the discovery of America for many Jewish intellectuals. The frenetic enthusiasm with which Whitman has been taken up lately may be part of the same process that accounts for the new piety toward Sholom Aleichem. But I should like to say more about that later.

In trying to justify myself against the charges of sentimentality or conformism made by my friends, but feeling in my heart that they were probably right, I used the only arguments that meant anything to them or to me. I said that Jewish culture was worth studying, *as* a culture. I said darkly that their hostility seemed to me suspicious, and that I doubted whether they would attack me for spending three days a week studying Chinese demonology. (I was wrong: they considered me foolish when I enrolled in a new course in Oriental literature—such studies were outside the proper concern of a true fledgling in Western civilization, they were irrelevant and therefore wasteful and therefore sinful.) I tried to recommend Judaism for its special qualities, and my most powerful weapons were two major attitudes which I ascribed to it. The first was that Judaism entertained no dualism of body and soul—an effective argument, because for us dualism was the ubiquitous villain of Western civilization—and the second was that Judaism remained the only culture beside the Greek which believed in learning for its own sake and which honored the sage more than it did the plutocrat. This too was effective, for "bourgeois" standards constituted another of our violent hatreds. My friends were impressed, but they still could not see spending all that time and effort over attitudes which, after all, we had already absorbed from Blake and Lawrence and Flaubert and a dozen other great figures of our pantheon. They would challenge me to produce great writers out of Jewish literature, and my feeble efforts to describe Judah Halevi as a metaphysical poet of the stature of Donne, and Mendele Mocher Seforim as a positively Swiftian satirist, were met with a shrug of the shoulders and a skeptical smile.

I think that the feeling of my friends was a good reflection, given the typical undergraduate intensity, aggressiveness, and exaggeration with which it was held, of the prevalent feeling among American Jewish intellectuals immediately after the Second World War. They were not yet hospitable to the idea that Jewish culture was respectable in their terms, worthy of interest as a thing in itself, apart from whatever relevance it might have to them as Jews. And in any case, they doubted that it was very relevant at all.

But there is another side to this picture. The Seminary is located six short blocks from Columbia College, and for me the walk up Broadway from 116th Street to 122nd Street was like the journey from Paris to the provinces. Undaunted, however, I came rampaging into the Seminary as an apostle, with all the evangelical fervor of a St. Paul bringing the truth that had been revealed to me at Hamilton Hall back to the Jews. The truth I burned to teach was that a fresh stream of thought, disinterested and free of ideology, must be turned on Jewish culture: I was not only St. Paul, I was Matthew Arnold too. It should be pointed out here that the level on which literature was taught and thought about at the Seminary was much lower than the level of Biblical, Talmudic, and historical studies. Some of the courses in Bible and Jewish history were easily a match for analogous courses at Columbia, and some were superior in their kind to anything offered at Columbia. Unfortunately, this was not true of literary studies, a fact which may have reflected the uneasiness Jews have traditionally felt toward literature as a pursuit for its own sake (Mr. Howe and Mr. Greenberg have an excellent section on that tradition in their introduction). It always seemed to me that there was something impurely partisan or insufferably crude in the way both Hebrew and Yiddish literature (which we read in Hebrew translation) were approached. Bialik was apparently honored not as a poet but as a kind of latter-day prophet; Sholom Aleichem was held in higher esteem than Mendele Mocher Seforim (my own favorite) because his picture of Jewish life was more "positive" than Mendele's; and our professors were forever rhapsodizing on how "beautifully" somebody or other wrote Hebrew—so much so that I was unpleasantly reminded of those belle-lettristic Victorian critics against whom the wrath of my beloved quarterly reviews had long been directed. In short, Jewish literature was either a text, an exhortation, a party platform, or it was a milestone in the development of Hebrew as a modern language. My teachers and fellow students seemed to be either Jewish versions of Ralph Fox or of Sir Arthur Quiller-Couch. We had no Eliots, no Leavises, no Trillings, no Ransoms, no Tates, no Brookses. Not, that is, until I arrived on the scene.

My personal crusade to bring the wisdom of Columbia to the Seminary met with no more success than my half-hearted effort to bring the Seminary to Columbia. Of course, I was not very tactful about it, but I doubt if tact really had much to do with the matter. Once, in reporting to a class on a volume of contemporary Hebrew poetry, I nearly caused a riot when I attacked the prosody of a minor Israeli lyric poet by invoking E. E. Cummings as a standard. I was howled down with talk of the blood shed by the six million, I was accused of abysmal ignorance of the Hebrew language, I was told that my comparisons were inept, irrelevant, and even morally reprehensible. (I still think I was right about the poet.) In another class, I was foolish enough to admit that I considered Bialik a second-rate provincial, far inferior to the cosmopolitan Tchernichovsky—and the effort somewhat resembled what might happen if, at a Communist rally, a new party member were to declare Rosa Luxemburg a more profound philosopher than Lenin. My attempts to promote Judah Halevi and Ibn Gabirol as the Hebrew Donne and Marvell were greeted not with skeptical smiles, but with outraged stammerings, coughs, and gnashing of teeth. The only time I provoked no disproportionate opposition was when I said, in one of those everlasting discussions of What Makes a Work of Art Jewish, that Isaac Rosenfeld and Leslie Fiedler were the true American Jewish writers, not Fannie Hurst or Ludwig Lewisohn. But my most notable success came at a Hebrew-speaking summer study camp operated by the Seminary. In teaching a course in Jeremiah, I delighted my fifteen-year-old students by proclaiming that they need not believe God actually spoke to Jeremiah in order to appreciate the greatness of the book. I solemnly expounded Coleridge's theory of the "willing suspension of disbelief" to them, and I hinted that Jeremiah (unlike Isaiah) wanted to be a poet, not a prophet, which is why he was always complaining to God over the slights he had suffered. I presented this agonized religious genius as a sort of Hebraic prototype of the Artist persecuted by a Hebraic prototype of bourgeois society—a Flaubert among the Jewish philistines. (The prophet Amos, incidentally, I was fond of describing as "the first young man from the provinces.") The novelty of this approach was not lost even on fifteen-year-olds.

Meanwhile, something was happening in the world of Columbia that seemed too good to be true. Hasidism, ushered in by Martin Buber and Gershom Scholem like a surprise witness in a sensational murder trial, exploded on the intellectual consciousness of New York. One suddenly found a rash of articles not only on Hasidism, but also on Maimonides, written by people who only yesterday were deep in Eliot, Original Sin, and Kierkegaard. One noticed respectful reviews of Sholom Aleichem, and it began to appear that some of our heroes among the younger critics actually read Yiddish. I remember too with what a sense of personal triumph I first heard that Lionel Trilling was writing an essay on Wordsworth and the Rabbis. About this time also, my friends and I discovered *Commentary*, which was as unsettling to them as it was a delight to me. I was not, after all, alone in the world, there were *others*, and these others were *intelligent*, by which I suppose I meant that they knew all about the New Criticism. I began for the first time to believe my own arguments about the distinction of Judaism as a culture. It did not seem strange to me that the grandsons of Hasidim should travel through Wordsworth in order to get to the *shtetl*. What did astonish me was that the taste for Wordsworth should not have made them despise the *shtetl* and all its works for eternity.

My astonishment was, of course, naive, for the new interest in Jewishness was not quite of the same nature as the interest in Wordsworth. There were many impulses behind it, but the only one that concerns me here was the discovery by many American Jewish intellectuals that they were as much products of Jewish culture as of Western civilization. They became interested in Maimonides and the Baal Shem Tov at least partly because they felt that these men had something to teach them about themselves. However, my impression is that this was a veiled impulse, for publicly and officially, they praised Maimonides and Sholom Aleichem just as I had praised them to my friends—in terms of St. Thomas, Wordsworth, Blake, and Chekhov. In other words, before they would permit themselves the luxury of investigating their own origins, they had to be persuaded that these origins were objects of general interest. They had, as it were, to get the smell of garlic out of the breath of Jewish culture.

I said before that I thought the new interest in Jewishness was part of the same process as the new interest in Americanism, and more specifically, that the way Whitman has been taken up compares with the way Sholom Aleichem has been taken up. But this is not entirely true. For the quality of interest shown in Whitman has reverberations lacking in the quality of attention paid to Jewish writers. For one thing, there is a candid admission on the part of some recent critics of Whitman that they do not, *should* not, read him with the same detachment and by the same standards and for the same reasons that they read Donne or Shakespeare. One feels that the return to Whitman is a family affair, that he is celebrated nowadays not for his great poems on death, but for his teaching on what it means to be an American. And it is quite appropriate that this should be so. Not every litera-ture has produced writers who enjoy a special role as embodiments of the national psyche, because not every culture has found the fact of nationality a problem to be thought about and discussed. Certainly neither the British nor the French, for all their fervent sense of nationality, *worry* about the significance of being French or English. The Russians, on the other hand, the Germans, and we Americans are obsessed with a conscious idea of our own na-tionality. And in this, of course, the Jews occupy a preeminent position. Jewish literature—during the past one hundred fifty years especially—has produced Fichtes, Whitmans, and Gogols, but it has produced nothing else. Which is to say that it differs as radically from other literatures as Jewish history differs from any other history.

And here we have the clue to why my crude attempts to make Jewish culture accessible to myself met with such hostility at the Seminary. I think my teachers rightly resented the arrogant as-sumption that Jewish culture had to be justified in the eyes of the *Kenyon Review* or be set at nought. And yet—raised in what is known as "a good Jewish home," fairly fluent both in Yiddish and Hebrew, highly educated (by American standards) in Jewish culture, and eager to learn "the best that has been thought and known in the world"—I felt that I could approach it by no other road. From their side, my teachers were right in feeling that the terms I wanted to use in interpreting this culture to myself were ultimately an evasion, that they would in the end obfuscate far more than they could clarify. The very characteristic I despised in all of them—their total involvement with their subject, their failure to achieve distance and perspective, their unwillingness even to admit the possibility of detachment—was the only key to a real understanding of Jewishness. For them, there could be no distinction between understanding and a commitment to the destiny of the Jewish people: the very object of understanding was a deepened commitment. All of Jewish culture was a biography of their own souls, and more precious to them even than their own souls. They must have felt that relegating Judah Halevi to the category of a Donne was a way of disposing of him, a way of refusing to meet the challenge he presented—would a man give his life for Donne? For in their view, every Jewish writer presented the same challenge over and over again: what are you going to do about being a Jew? How could I have possibly responded to Bialik when I was not urgently interested in that question? I was right about literature in general: it is both more and less than an invitation to action, and I would have been right in my quarrel with my teachers if any other literature but this one were the issue. For the truth is that neither Hebrew nor Yiddish literature are like any other, to be studied and judged like any other. They refuse to yield their treasures except on their own eccentric terms. They share for good and ill the uniqueness of the people by whom and for whom they were produced.

In their introduction, Mr. Howe and Mr. Greenberg write brilliantly about Yiddish literature. They tell us it has special qualities that we need to become acquainted with—particularly the qualities of love and sweetness. They recommend Yiddish literature as a sort of antithesis to the literature of crisis we all dote on, and they feel it needs no more recommendation than to be seen as an opposing term in the dialectic of modern taste. They even imply—for they are nothing if not honest—that this literature is inevitably, intentionally, and sometimes aggressively parochial, and that it was addressed to readers who were as involved with its lone theme—the meaning of Jewishness—as the writers were. They point out that its emphasis on national destiny is so tyrannical and ruthless that no room is left for an interest in individual character, and they acknowledge that most of us read fiction primarily because we want to see individual character in its eternal struggle with society. This, of course, is tantamount to admitting that these stories cannot claim our attention as readers of fiction, but Mr. Howe and Mr. Greenberg cajole us into believing momentarily that a mature taste, when once it understands the reasons for such a development, will not deny itself the new experience offered. Perhaps.

To be perfectly honest, I cannot say whether I agree with them or not. In reading through this volume—which contains some things I had read before and many that I had not—I was oppressed more powerfully than ever by the feeling that very little of this has anything to do with that part of me which reads English, French, and Russian fiction, and everything to do with that part of me which still broods on the mystery of my own Jewishness. It is not as difficult as it would seem for a Jew to divorce the two parts of himself, and I tried reading the book as Mr. Howe and Mr. Greenberg advise. But I found that the pleasure I derived was quite unlike the pleasure I get from good fiction. It was the pleasure of Old World charm and quaintness, titillating but not challenging, and therefore not to be taken too seriously. What an irony, that this should be the effect of a literature which more than any other demands to be taken with the most apocalyptic seriousness! On the other hand, there were exceptions—a story by Mendele, two by Sholom Aleichem, a few lovely pieces by Abraham Reisen and Lamed Shapiro, the wonderful tale of "Gimpel the Fool" by Isaac Bashevis Singer. Yet the volume as a whole did not, I feel, quite bear out the modest claims of the introduction: I do not think that the book would have convinced my friends in those days at Columbia. I am not saying that most of the writers presented in the volume are not talented enough to deserve a hearing. It is just that a sad, perhaps a tragic, limitation has been imposed upon them, and it is not their fault. But as they themselves would be the first to admit, it's hard to be a Jew.

[1955]

The Article As Art

Anyone who has given much attention to postwar American fiction is likely to have noticed a curious fact. Many of our serious novelists also turn out book reviews, critical pieces, articles about the contemporary world, memoirs, sketches—all of which are produced for magazines and which these writers undoubtedly value far lower than their stories and novels.

Indeed, some novelists (and this applies to many poets too) tend to express their contempt or disdain for discursive prose in the very act of writing it. You can hear a note of condescension toward the medium they happen to be working in at the moment; they seem to be announcing in the very construction of their sentences that they have no great use for the prosy requirements of the essay or the review, that they are only dropping in from Olympus for a brief, impatient visit. But just as often—and this is the curious fact I am referring to—the discursive writing of people who think of themselves primarily as novelists turns out to be more interesting, more lively, more penetrating, more intelligent, more forceful, more original—in short, *better*—than their fiction, which they and everyone else automatically treat with greater respect.

Two examples spring immediately to mind: the late Isaac Rosenfeld and the young Negro author, James Baldwin. Rosenfeld, who died of a heart attack in Chicago two years ago at the age of thirty-seven, was immensely gifted, possibly the most gifted writer to appear in America in the last few decades. Born of immigrant parents and raised in a Yiddish-speaking milieu, he came to own the English language by an act of absolute appropriation. He could make it do anything he wanted—sprout lush flora, like a tropical landscape, or walk in stately simplicity as though it had been designed only to express the basic emotions and the most direct and uncomplicated apprehensions of reality. Beyond that, however, he was intelligent and literate, endowed with wide curiosity and a frisky imagination. He was also prolific: for years his name was ubiquitous in the world of the little magazine, with a story here, a review there, an article yet somewhere else. Though he published only one novel, *A Passage from Home*, and a collection of short stories, *King Solomon's Mines*, he regarded himself and was regarded by others as essentially a novelist.

Yet the truth is that he never produced a piece of fiction which drew on the whole range of his talent and sensibility. You got the impression that in order to write a story, this man had to suppress half of what he knew and saw, that he was possessed of a mind and an eye and an imagination which could not get their full play in a dramatic narrative. Though banality of thought and falsity of feeling hardly ever entered his articles and reviews, his fiction frequently suffered from derivativeness, artificiality, and mere cleverness. You would scarcely have suspected even from his novel that Rosenfeld was more than a bright young man who had read Proust and Joyce and saw himself, like a thousand other bright young men, as a creature set apart by his artistic vocation. You would scarcely have suspected him capable of that marvelous posthumous piece published in *Commentary* called "Life in Chicago," in which the smell and feel of a city and its history are rendered to perfection, in which the meaning of that history is defined through a deliciously fanciful theory of the effect on a city of distance from the sea, in which the combination of love and repulsion that a "rootless" American intellectual invariably feels for his home town is superbly expressed, and in which everything—description, analysis, exhortation, and sheer kidding around—converges in the end on a declaration of faith in the supremacy of the arts and what they represent over the prevalent values of modern life. It is a declaration all the more moving for its directness and candor, and all the more powerful for coming from someone who knows that he is flying in the face of the contemporary spirit—but who also knows that a man at some point in his life has to stop agonizing over his apparent eccentricities and say, simply and without refinement or embellishment, "This is what I stand for."

This essay gives you more of Chicago, more of what it means to be an artist and an intellectual in America, and more of Rosenfeld himself than *A Passage from Home*, which, as it happens, is also about Chicago, the artist in America, and the soul of Isaac Rosenfeld.

The case of James Baldwin is no less striking. Baldwin has so far published three books—a collection of essays, *Notes of a Native Son*, and two novels, *Go Tell It on the Mountain* and *Giovanni's Room*. The essays in *Notes of a Native Son* all appeared originally in magazines; a couple of them are literary criticism, one is a movie review, and the others are memoirs relating to various aspects of a Negro's confrontation with the white world both in America and Europe. Taken together they make up the best book I have ever read about the American Negro, a book that conveys a phenomenally keen sense of the special quality of Negro experience today. What distinguishes these pieces, even apart from the clarity, subtlety, and vividness with which they are written, is Baldwin's complex conception of the Negro as a man who is simultaneously like unto all other men and yet profoundly, perhaps irrevocably, different. The nature of the sameness and the nature of the difference are the subject of the book, and he never allows himself to forget the one term while exploring the other.

But it is precisely the loss of complexity that characterizes his novels. *Go Tell It on the Mountain* is a fairly conventional first novel about a Negro boy in Harlem, and though the hero's milieu (especially the religious background of his life) is well delineated, you nevertheless feel that Baldwin is trying to persuade you that there is no real difference between the situation of John Grimes and that of any other sensitive American boy who is at odds with his environment. But there *is* a difference, and it is not merely one of degree—as any reader of *Notes of a Native Son* can tell you.

Similarly with *Giovanni's Room*, which though it does not deal with Negroes, exhibits the same slurring over of differences in relation to homosexuality. (The white homosexual in America is in the same boat as the oppressed Negro—they are both, as it were, "black" in the eyes of their culture.) Baldwin, in writing about a young American living in Paris who discovers that he is a homosexual, tries very hard to make it appear that a love affair between two men is spiritually and psychologically indistinguishable from a heterosexual romance—which strikes me as at worst an untruth and at best an oversimplification. Here again, then, we have a writer who seems able to produce fiction only at the expense of suppressing half of what he sees and knows, whose discursive prose is richer, more imaginative, and fundamentally more honest than his novels and stories. And with proper qualifications in each case, similar points might be made of James Agee, Mary McCarthy, Elizabeth Hardwick, Randall Jarrell, Leslie Fiedler, and several others.

Now it can, of course, be said that these examples prove nothing —and would still prove nothing even if another twenty were added to them—except that some people are better essayists than novelists. And if I asked why a first-rate essayist should feel obliged to work so hard at turning out second-rate fiction, the answer would be that the novel is to us what drama was to the Elizabethans and lyric poetry to the Romantics, so that an ambitious writer today will naturally make his bid there. In every college in the country, and probably in most of the high schools too, there are kids who want to be novelists when they grow up—who are convinced that a novelist is the most glorious of all things to be, and who are often prepared to make sacrifices in pursuit of this vocation. The aura of sanctity that used to attach to the idea of a poet has now floated over to rest on the head of the novelist—a very congenial switch when we consider that Americans tend to regard poets as sissies and novelists as hard-drinking, hard-loving, hard-fighting men of the world. (Compare the public image of T. S. Eliot and Wallace Stevens to Hemingway's or Faulkner's and you see that the poets and novelists themselves seem driven to play true to type.)

But the prestige of the novel cannot account for the fact that so much good writing about precisely those experiences which are closest to the heart of life in America and which we would suppose to be the proper province of fiction—experiences involving the quest for self-definition in a society where a man's identity is not given and fixed by birth—has been done in our day not in novels but in discursive pieces of one kind or another.

Lionel Trilling made a similar observation in a review of David Riesman's *The Lonely Crowd:*

People of literary inclinations . . . have a natural jealousy of sociology because it seems to be in process of taking over from literature one of literature's most characteristic functions, the in-

vestigation and criticism of morals and manners. Yet it is but fair
to remark that sociology has pre-empted what literature has voluntarily surrendered.

Nor is it academic sociology alone that has "pre-empted what
literature has voluntarily surrendered." The reportage done in
magazines by professional journalists like Dwight Macdonald,
Richard H. Rovere, and a good many others, has carried on a more
exhaustive and more accomplished investigation of our morals and
manners that the bulk of contemporary fiction.

The novel form is honored as never before, yet a feeling of dissatisfaction and impatience, irritation and boredom with contemporary serious fiction is very widespread. The general mood
was well expressed by Leslie Fiedler who opened a fiction chronicle
in *Partisan Review* not long ago with the complaint that the sight
of a group of new novels stimulates in him "a desperate desire to
sneak out to a movie. How respectable the form has become," he
lamented, "how predictable!" Many other critics have tried to explain the low condition of current fiction by declaring that the
novel is "dead," an exhausted genre like the epic and verse drama.
But whether or not the novel is dead (and I myself don't believe
that it is), one thing is certain: that a large class of readers, with
or without benefit of theories about the rise and fall of literary
forms, has found itself responding more enthusiastically to what
is lamely called "non-fiction" (and especially to magazine articles
and even book reviews) than to current fiction.

This is not, of course, a new observation. The popularity of
"criticism"—a word often used as a catch-all term for any writing
about literature or culture in general—has been deplored even
more passionately than the dullness of postwar fiction and poetry,
and has been taken as a sign of the sickness of our present condition. Some years ago, Randall Jarrell, in a famous article, christened
this period, "The Age of Criticism," and complained that nowa-

days young men were taking to their typewriters not to compose poems but to analyze and explicate the poems of others. Personally, I have never been able to understand why Mr. Jarrell was so eager to have everyone writing poetry; we can, after all, take it pretty much for granted that any young man who has it in him to become a poet *will* become a poet, even in an "Age of Criticism." And I should have thought that the danger was not that the popularity of criticism would rob us of poets but that the prestige of the "creative" would rob us of good critics, who have always been rarer, even today, than good poets.

Writing in the heyday of piety toward the "divine faculty of imagination" that succeeded the great flowering of English poetry during the first half of the 19th century, Matthew Arnold provided the best possible retort to Mr. Jarrell:

> Everybody . . . would be willing to admit, as a general proposition, that the critical faculty is lower than the inventive. But is it true that criticism is really, in itself, a baneful and injurious employment; is it true that all time given to writing critiques on the works of others would be much better employed if it were given to original composition of whatever kind this may be? Is it true that Johnson had better have gone on producing more *Irenes* instead of writing his *Lives of the Poets* . . . ?

Arnold's allusion to the distinction between the "critical faculty" and the "inventive" is one that any modern reader would pass over with automatic assent, so accustomed have we all become to thinking in terms of two radically different categories of mind—the imaginative, which is the mind that creates, and the . . . well, there is not even an adequate word for the other kind of mind. "Critical" won't do because it has too restricted a reference; nor will "philosophical" quite serve. The fact is that our attitude reveals itself beautifully in this terminological difficulty:

we call everything that is not fiction or poetry "non-fiction," as though whole ranges of human thought had only a negative existence. We would all admit, if pressed, that books like Freud's *The Interpretation of Dreams* or Tocqueville's *Democracy in America* are as much works of the imagination as *Ulysses* or *The Waste Land*, but we tend in the ordinary course of things to identify "imagination" and "creativity" exclusively with the arts and, where literature is concerned, with poetry, the novel, and the drama. This idea is a legacy of 19th-century aesthetic theory. Throughout the 18th century the word "imagination" (or its synonym, "fancy") was often used pejoratively and sometimes held to be the source of lies and the enemy of reason. Reason was considered the faculty for perceiving truth, and good poetry was regarded as one of its products.

"A poet is not to leave his reason, and blindly abandon himself to follow fancy," declared the critic Thomas Rymer, "for then his fancy might be monstrous, might be singular, and please no body's maggot but his own; but reason is to be his guide, reason is common to all people, and can never carry him from what is natural."

Even before Coleridge formulated his famous theory of the poetic imagination as the highest mode of apprehending reality and credited poetry with a truth superior to the truths of reason and science, early Romantics like William Blake were pushing toward a doctrine that would justify the claims of the poet against those of the "natural philosophers." By the age of Victoria, the Coleridgean view had swept all before it; nothing is more characteristic of the Victorians than the reverence they felt toward poets and poetry (a reverence, as Mr. Jarrell should have remembered, which led to the production of more bad verse than any other period has ever foisted upon the world). The poet was a saint and a sage: the robust-minded Keats became to the Victorians a delicate aesthete languishing away for the sake of beauty and killed by the cruel barbs of the critics, while Shelley—a man up to his neck in politics and causes—was thought of as the wholly spiritual Ariel. The wicked Lord Bryon only added to the charm of these images, and the somber Wordsworth was well suited to the role of Olympian wise man.

One of the consequences of this conception of the poetic faculty was to foster the idea that poetry could be written only in a kind of fit of divine inspiration that had nothing to do with intelligence or consciousness or concern with what was going on in the world. And a plausible relation can be traced between that notion and the decline of poetry in the latter part of the 19th century. It was the novelists of Victorian England, who had not yet quite achieved the status of "creative" and "imaginative" writers and to whom the smell of vulgarity that had once been associated with the novel still clung—Dickens, George Eliot, Thackeray, James— who represent their age most vitally and powerfully. What strikes one today about Victorian fiction is the scope it provided for the exercise of intelligence, the testing of ideas in the medium of experience, the examination of major contemporary problems. The novel flourished partly because it was such a free, amorphous, sprawling form in which almost anything (except, of course, explicit discussion of sex) could go: there was no question of George Eliot's having to suppress half of what *she* knew and saw when she sat down to write fiction. And it flourished because it remained in touch with the world around it, while the poets were busy transcending the mundane and the prosaic.

By now we seem to have reached a point where the novel has taken over from poetry as the sanctified genre, and this has coincided (just as with poetry in the 19th century) with the aftermath of a great flowering. Proust, Joyce, Lawrence, Mann, Kafka, Hemingway, Faulkner are all behind us; in our eyes they have borne out the claims made for the "art of the novel" by Henry James and others, just as Wordsworth, Bryon, Keats, and

Shelley won the case for the superiority of the "poetic faculty" at the bar of Victorian judgment.

In a recent book called *The Living Novel* Granville Hicks, whose benign reviews in the *New Leader* have established him as the most promiscuous admirer of new writing since the days of Carl Van Doren, collected essays by ten well-known novelists aimed at refuting the charge that the novel is dead. Most of the essays are bad—bad thinking and bad writing—but they are interesting for what they reveal of the novelist's view of himself today. The dominant note is one of persecution. Mr. Hicks talks about the "enemies of the novel" and says that the novel has always had enemies. Almost all the contributors throw around words like "vision," "intensity," and, of course, "imagination" to distinguish the novel from other kinds of writing. There is a good deal of bitterness against the critics and a strong implication that they are resentful of "creativity." Saul Bellow (who has fared very well at the hands of the critics) says, for example:

> And so we are told by critics that the novel is dead. These people can't know what the imagination is nor what its powers are. I wish I could believe in their good-natured objectivity. But I can't. I should like to disregard them, but that is a little difficult because they have a great deal of power. . . . And they can be very distracting. But the deadly earnestness with which they lower the boom! On what? after all. On flowers. On mere flowers.

You can't blame Mr. Bellow for being irritated by people who insist that the novel is dead while he is trying to write novels, but it is worth noticing that he does not answer the charge by asserting that good novels are still being produced and then trying to prove it; instead he invokes the name of "imagination" in reverent accents and identifies it with novels (apparently whether they are good or bad), while criticism is a "boom" lowered in metaphorical confusion on the "flowers" around it. Now it would be hard to think of a more infelicitous image for a novel than a flower; novels, if you like, are trees, they are robust and sturdy, not at all delicate. Why should Mr. Bellow have seized on this inept image? Partly to arouse the reader's sense of pathos, I think, but also because the idea of flowers, with its associations of sweetness, fragility, and loveliness, confers an ethereal dignity on the novel.

The idea comes out of the same sort of thinking that was applied to poetry by many Victorians: poetry was delicate, trans-cendant, special, inspired—anything, in short, but the measured discourse of a keen human sensibility operating on a world of men. But a new element has been added to the Victorian view. Not only does "imagination" now sprout "flowers," and not only does it (as in Coleridge) represent the highest faculty of intellection; it has also become the principle of "life" itself, while mind and con-sciousness are now seen as having signed a pact with the Angel of Death. The novel is valuable, we gather from Mr. Bellow and some of his colleagues, because it is the only place left in our world where imagination and its correlatives—sensitivity, responsiveness, passion—still function. (The *reductio* of all this can be found in the "spontaneous bop prosody" of Jack Kerouac.) Mr. Hicks goes so far as to say that "there is no substitute now available for the novel, and those who talk about the death of the novel are talking about the death of the imagination."

I am not one of those who talk about the death of the novel, but I do think that it has fallen on bad days. I also think that the fault lies at least partly with these rarefied and incense-burning doctrines of the imagination, which have had the effect of surren-dering the novel—to apply a remark of F. R. Leavis on Shelley's theory of inspiration—"to a sensibility that has no more dealings with intelligence than it can help." My own criticism of much contemporary fiction would be precisely that it lacks the only species of imagination worth mentioning—the kind that is vital-

ized by contact with a disciplined intelligence and a restless interest in the life of the times. And what the novel has abdicated has
been taken over by discursive writers. Imagination has not died
(how could it?) but it has gone into other channels; these channels are not by any means commensurate with the novel: they are,
in fact, *channels* and not the sea. But there is living water in them
nevertheless.

What I have in mind—and I cheerfully admit that the suggestion sounds preposterous—is *magazine articles*. I won't call them
essays, even though to do so would make the point seem less
disreputable and silly, because the type of thing I am referring to
is not an essay in the old sense. Strictly speaking, the essay requires an audience that has no doubts about where the relevant
subjects of discussion are to be found, and it is therefore written
without any need to persuade the reader that he ought to concern
himself with this particular question. The magazine article, as
they say in the trade, always hangs on a peg; it takes off from an
event in the news, a book recently published, a bill in Congress.
And even then, with its relevance established in the most obvious
way conceivable, it still has to sell itself to a reader who wants to
be told why he should bother pushing his way through it when
there are so many other claims on his attention. This is a tyrannical condition which can, of course, result in the reduction of all
thought to the occasional and the newsworthy. But now and then
a writer whose interests and talent go beyond the merely journalistic can be forced into very exciting pieces of work by the necessity to demonstrate the continuing importance of his special
concerns by throwing them into the buzz and hum around him.

To my mind, the critical pieces of Lionel Trilling offer perhaps
the best example we have of discursive writing that is not only rich
in imagination but animated by an uncanny sensitivity to the life
from which it springs. Trilling has spent most of his time analyzing books—often remote books—but who has told us more than

he about the way we feel and think today? But for the purposes of detailed illustration, I would like to take a less well-known example, an article (published in *Commentary* in 1953) called "The 'Idealism' of Julius and Ethel Rosenberg" by the late Robert Warshow who, like Isaac Rosenfeld, died suddenly at thirty-seven just when his extraordinary powers were developing into full maturity, and who—unlike Rosenfeld—never wrote any fiction.

This article began as a review of the Rosenberg death-house letters which came out around the time the convicted couple went to their execution. Since Warshow was one of those who believed that the world-wide clamor against the death sentence was largely motivated not by compassion for the Rosenbergs or a desire to see justice done, but by political anti-Americanism of one shade or another, one might have expected the review to be a pronouncement on the Communist menace. And certainly the crudity and vulgarity of the Rosenberg letters provided enough opportunity for scoring points against them and the movement to which they gave their lives. But Warshow's imagination would not permit him to turn out a simple polemical tract: what he wanted was an insight into the soul of the Rosenbergs, and it took a powerful act of imagination to find the soul of the Rosenbergs in the mass of depersonalized clichés that make up their correspondence. Considering the patent insincerity of their rhetoric, the temptation was great to deny them any human feelings at all. But again, Warshow's imagination would not allow him to fall into that trap. After quoting several particularly grotesque passages in which they discuss their children, Warshow comments:

> The fact that Julius Rosenberg can speak of a lack of toys as the "materials situation" does not in the least permit us to assume that he did not suffer for his children just as much as anyone else would have suffered. Nor does the impudence of Ethel's appeal to her "sister Americans"—whose lives she had been willing to put in

danger—diminish in any way the reality of the "stab of longing for my boy." On the whole, the Rosenbergs in dealing with their children sound the authentic tone of parental love in the educated and conscientious middle class, facing each "problem" boldly and without displaying undue emotion, though "of course" not denying the existence of emotion either. . . . This is how we all deal with our children, and surely we are right to do so. If it happens that you must "prepare" the children for their parents' death in the electric chair instead of having their tonsils out, then doubtless something better is required. But what, for God's sake? Some unique inspiration, perhaps, and the truth. But we cannot blame the Rosenbergs for their failure to achieve an inspiration, and the commitment for which they died—and by which, we must assume, they somehow fulfilled themselves—was precisely that the truth was not to be spoken. Not spoken, not whispered, not approached in the merest hint.

Warshow goes on to show how the literal truth had ceased to exist for the Rosenbergs as a result of their commitment to Communism, and he connects this brilliantly with "the awkwardness and falsity of the Rosenbergs' relations to culture, to sports, and to themselves" that is evident in their letters:

It is as if these two had no internal sense of their own being but could see themselves only from the outside, in whatever postures their "case" seemed to demand—as if, one might say, they were only the most devoted of their thousands of "sympathizers."
. . . But it is important to observe the dimensions of their failure, how almost nothing really belonged to them, not even their own experience; they filled their lives with the second-hand, never so much as suspecting that anything else was possible. Communism itself—the vehicle of whatever self-realization they achieved—had disappeared for them, becoming only a word to be written in quotation marks as if it represented a hallucination. . . .

In the end, we discover that "they were equally incapable of truth and of falsehood. What they stood for was not Communism as a certain form of social organization, not progress as a belief in the possibility of human improvement, but only their own identity *as* Communists or 'progressives,' and they were perfectly 'sincere' in making use of whatever catchwords seemed at any moment to assert that identity. . . ." It is this, Warshow argues, that makes the Rosenbergs truly representative of the Communism of 1953. But his piece does not really close on a note of analysis or condemnation:

> The Rosenbergs thought and felt whatever their political commitment required them to think and feel. But if they had not had the political commitment could they have thought and felt at all?
> Well, we cannot dispose of them quite so easily. They did suffer, for themselves and for their children, and though they seem never to have questioned the necessity of their "martyrdom" or the absolute rightness of all they had ever done . . . , they wept like anyone else at the approach of death. . . .

I have quoted at length from this short article in order to let the grace and beauty of Warshow's style speak for themselves. It is a beauty that comes not from ornateness or self-conscious finesse, but from a remarkable fusion of feeling and intelligence: to follow this prose is to follow a language in which analysis cannot be distinguished from emotion. When the rhetoric surges ("But what, for God's sake?") it is not for the sake of sweeping the reader away, but in response to a simultaneous movement of the mind and the heart: the heart has discovered something and the mind springs like a panther to formulate its meaning.

A six-page review of a book in a monthly magazine; a discussion of a controversial political question almost completely forgotten only five years later—yet it turns out to be a piece of imaginative and creative writing as good as any we have seen in this gloomy period, a piece that is at once a moving expression of a man's ability to feel for two human beings who sacrificed themselves to a cause he hated and despised, a brilliant analysis of the Communist mentality, and a profound comment on the nature of sincerity. And the rest of Warshow's work—almost all of it as good as and better than the Rosenberg article—remains buried in magazines, mostly in the highly perishable form of movie reviews.*

Why should the magazine article, of all things, have become so important and fertile a genre in our day? Why have so many writers—both "critics" and professional journalists—found it possible to move around more freely and creatively within it than within fiction or poetry? No doubt it has something to do with the spiritual dislocations of the cold war period, but the essence of the answer, I think, lies in an analogy with architecture. It has often been pointed out that functionalism is more an idea than a reality: the products of functional architecture aren't purely functional at all, since they always contain "useless" elements that are there for aesthetic rather than practical reasons. Yet the fact remains that our sense of beauty today is intimately connected with the sense of usefulness: we consider a building beautiful when it seems to exist not for anyone to enjoy the sight of or to be impressed by, but solely and simply to be used. We think of those glass structures like Lever House in New York or the United Nations or the Manufacturers Trust Company building on Fifth Avenue as practical, in the sense that women call walking shoes practical; they have a kind of no-nonsense look about them, they seem to be stripped down to essentials, purged of all superfluous matter.

The same is true of the way we furnish our homes—Scandinavian efficiency is our idea of handsomeness; foam rubber rather

---

* Since this was written, Doubleday has brought out a collection of Warshow's pieces under the title *The Immediate Experience.*

than down our idea of comfort; stainless steel rather than silver our notion of elegant cutlery. I would suggest that we have all, writers and readers alike, come to feel temporarily uncomfortable with the traditional literary forms because they don't *seem* practical, designed for "use," whereas a magazine article by its nature satisfies that initial conditions and so is free to assimilate as many "useless," "non-functional" elements as it pleases. It is free, in other words, to become a work of art.

This is not, of course, an ideal situation for literature to be in, but nothing can be gained from turning one's eyes away in horror. Certainly the rigid distinction between the creative and the critical has contributed to the growth of a feeling that the creative is "useless." Curiously enough, the very concept of imagination as a special faculty—and of novels and poetry as mysteriously unique species of discourse subject to strange laws of their own—itself implies that art is of no use to life in the world. What we need, it seems to me, is a return to the old idea of literature as a category that includes the best writing on any subject in any form. We need a return to this idea and we need it, I should add, most urgently of all for the sake of fiction and poetry.

[1958]

The Know-Nothing Bohemians

Allen Ginsberg's little volume of poems, *Howl*, which got the San Francisco renaissance off to a screaming start, was dedicated to Jack Kerouac ("new Buddha of American prose, who spit forth intelligence into eleven books written in half the number of years . . . creating a spontaneous bop prosody and original classic literature"), William Seward Burroughs ("author of *Naked Lunch*, an endless novel which will drive everybody mad"), and Neal Cassady ("author of *The First Third*, an autobiography . . . which enlightened Buddha"). So far, everybody's sanity has been spared by the inability of *Naked Lunch* to find a publisher,* and we may never get the chance to discover what Buddha learned from Neal Cassady's autobiography, but thanks to the Viking and Grove Presses, two of Kerouac's original classics, *On the Road* and *The Subterraneans*, have now been revealed to the world. When *On the Road* appeared last year, Gilbert Millstein commemorated the event in the New York *Times* by declaring it to be "a historic

---

* It did, of course, find one a few years after this piece was written.

occasion" comparable to the publication of *The Sun Also Rises* in the 1920's. But even before the novel was actually published, the word got around that Kerouac was the spokesman of a new group of rebels and Bohemians who called themselves the Beat Generation, and soon his photogenic countenance (unshaven, of course, and topped by an unruly crop of rich black hair falling over his forehead) was showing up in various mass-circulation magazines, he was being interviewed earnestly on television, and he was being featured in a Greenwich Village nightclub where, in San Francisco fashion, he read specimens of his spontaneous bop prosody against a background of jazz music.

Though the nightclub act reportedly flopped, *On the Road* sold well enough to hit the best-seller lists for several weeks, and it isn't hard to understand why. Americans love nothing so much as representative documents, and what could be more interesting in this Age of Sociology than a novel that speaks for the "young generation"? (The fact that Kerouac is thirty-five or thereabouts was generously not held against him.) Beyond that, however, I think that the unveiling of the Beat Generation was greeted with a certain relief by many people who had been disturbed by the notorious respectability and "maturity" of post-war writing. This was more like it—restless, rebellious, confused youth living it up, instead of thin, balding, buttoned-down instructors of English composing ironic verses with one hand while changing the baby's diapers with the other. Bohemianism is not particularly fashionable nowadays, but the image of Bohemia still exerts a powerful fascination—nowhere more so than in the suburbs, which are filled to overflowing with men and women who uneasily think of themselves as conformists and of Bohemianism as the heroic road. The whole point of *Marjorie Morningstar* was to assure the young marrieds of Mamaroneck that they were better off than the apparently glamorous *luftmenschen* of Greenwich Village, and the fact that Wouk had to work so hard at making this idea seem convincing is a good indication of the strength of prevailing doubt on the matter.

On the surface, at least, the Bohemianism of *On the Road* is very attractive. Here is a group of high-spirited young men running back and forth across the country (mostly hitch-hiking, sometimes in their own second-hand cars), going to "wild" parties in New York and Denver and San Francisco, living on a shoe-string (GI educational benefits, an occasional fifty bucks from a kindly aunt, an odd job as a typist, a fruit-picker, a parking-lot attendant), talking intensely about love and God and salvation, getting high on marijuana (but never heroin or cocaine), listening feverishly to jazz in crowded little joints, and sleeping freely with beautiful girls. Now and again there is a reference to gloom and melancholy, but the characteristic note struck by Kerouac is exuberance:

We stopped along the road for a bite to eat. The cowboy went off to have a spare tire patched, and Eddie and I sat down in a kind of homemade diner. I heard a great laugh, the greatest laugh in the world, and here came this rawhide oldtimes Nebraska farmer with a bunch of other boys into the diner; you could hear his raspy cries clear across the plains, across the whole gray world of them that day. Everybody else laughed with him. He didn't have a care in the world and had the hugest regard for everybody. I said to myself, Wham, listen to that man laugh. That's the West, here I am in the West. He came booming into the diner, calling Maw's name, and she made the sweetest cherry pie in Nebraska, and I had some with a mountainous scoop of ice cream on top. "Maw, rustle me up some grub afore I have to start eatin myself or some damn silly idee like that." And he threw himself on a stool and went hyaw hyaw hyaw hyaw. "And throw some beans in it." It was the spirit of the West sitting right next to me. I wished I knew his whole raw life and what the hell he'd been doing all these years beside laughing and yelling like that. Whooee, I told my soul, and the cowboy came back and off we went to Grand Island.

Kerouac's enthusiasm for the Nebraska farmer is part of his general readiness to find the source of all vitality and virtue in simple rural types and in the dispossessed urban groups (Negroes, bums, whores). His idea of life in New York is "millions and millions hustling forever for a buck among themselves . . . grabbing, taking, giving, sighing, dying, just so they could be buried in those awful cemetery cities beyond Long Island City," whereas the rest of America is populated almost exclusively by the true of heart. There are intimations here of a kind of know-nothing populist sentiment, but in other ways this attitude resembles Nelson Algren's belief that bums and whores and junkies are more interesting than white-collar workers or civil servants. The difference is that Algren hates middle-class respectability for moral and political reasons—the middle class exploits and persecutes—while Kerouac, who is thoroughly unpolitical, seems to feel that respectability is a sign not of moral corruption but of spiritual death. "The only people for me," says Sal Paradise, the narrator of *On the Road*, "are the mad ones, the ones who are mad to live, mad to talk, mad to be saved, desirous of everything at the same time, the ones who never yawn or say a commonplace thing, but burn, burn, burn like fabulous yellow roman candles exploding like spiders across the stars. . . ." This tremendous emphasis on emotional intensity, this notion that to be hopped-up is the most desirable of all human conditions, lies at the heart of the Beat Generation ethos and distinguishes it radically from the Bohemianism of the past.

The Bohemianism of the 1920's represented a repudiation of the provinciality, philistinism, and moral hypocrisy of American life— a life, incidentally, which was still essentially small-town and rural in tone. Bohemia, in other words, was a movement created in the name of civilization: its ideals were intelligence, cultivation, spiritual refinement. The typical literary figure of the 1920's was a midwesterner (Hemingway, Fitzgerald, Sinclair Lewis, Eliot,

Pound) who had fled from his home town to New York or Paris in search of a freer, more expansive, more enlightened way of life than was possible in Ohio or Minnesota or Michigan. The political radicalism that supplied the characteristic coloring of Bohemianism in the 1930's did nothing to alter the urban, cosmopolitan bias of the 1920's. At its best, the radicalism of the 1930's was marked by deep intellectual seriousness and aimed at a state of society in which the fruits of civilization would be more widely available—and ultimately available to all.

The Bohemianism of the 1950's is another kettle of fish altogether. It is hostile to civilization; it worships primitivism, instinct, energy, "blood." To the extent that it has intellectual interests at all, they run to mystical doctrines, irrationalist philosophies, and left-wing Reichianism. The only art the new Bohemians have any use for is jazz, mainly of the cool variety. Their predilection for bop language is a way of demonstrating solidarity with the primitive vitality and spontaneity they find in jazz and of expressing contempt for coherent, rational discourse which, being a product of the mind, is in their view a form of death. To be articulate is to admit that you have no feelings (for how can real feelings be expressed in syntactical language?), that you can't respond to anything (Kerouac responds to everything by saying "Wow!"), and that you are probably impotent.

At the one end of the spectrum, this ethos shades off into violence and criminality, main-line drug addiction and madness. Allen Ginsberg's poetry, with its lurid apocalyptic celebration of "angel-headed hipsters," speaks for the darker side of the new Bohemianism. Kerouac is milder. He shows little taste for violence, and the criminality he admires is the harmless kind. The hero of *On the Road*, Dean Moriarty, has a record: "From the age of eleven to seventeen he was usually in reform school. His specialty was stealing cars, gunning for girls coming out of high school in the afternoon, driving them out to the mountains, making them,

and coming back to sleep in any available hotel bathtub in town."
But Dean's criminality, we are told, "was not something that
sulked and sneered; it was a wild yea-saying overburst of American
joy; it was Western, the west wind, an ode from the Plains, something new, long prophesied, long a-coming (he only stole cars for
joy rides)." And, in fact, the species of Bohemian that Kerouac
writes about is on the whole rather law-abiding. In *The Subterraneans*, a bunch of drunken boys steal a pushcart in the middle
of the night, and when they leave it in front of a friend's apartment building, he denounces them angrily for "screwing up the
security of my pad." When Sal Paradise (in *On the Road*) steals
some groceries from the canteen of an itinerant workers' camp in
which he has taken a temporary job as a barracks guard, he comments, "I suddenly began to realize that everybody in America is
a natural-born thief"—which, of course, is a way of turning his
own stealing into a bit of boyish prankishness. Nevertheless,
Kerouac is attracted to criminality, and that in itself is more significant than the fact that he personally feels constrained to put
the brakes on his own destructive impulses.

Sex has always played a very important role in Bohemianism:
sleeping around was the Bohemian's most dramatic demonstration
of his freedom from conventional moral standards, and a defiant
denial of the idea that sex was permissible only in marriage and
then only for the sake of a family. At the same time, to be
"promiscuous" was to assert the validity of sexual experience in
and for itself. The "meaning" of Bohemian sex, then, was at once
social and personal, a crucial element in the Bohemian's ideal of
civilization. Here again the contrast with Beat Generation Bohemianism is sharp. On the one hand, there is a fair amount of
sexual activity in *On the Road* and *The Subterraneans*. Dean
Moriarity is a "new kind of American saint" at least partly because
of his amazing sexual powers: he can keep three women satisfied
simultaneously and he can make love any time, anywhere (once he

mounts a girl in the back seat of a car while poor Sal Paradise is trying to sleep in front). Sal, too, is always on the make, and though he isn't as successful as the great Dean, he does pretty well: offhand I can remember a girl in Denver, one on a bus, and another in New York, but a little research would certainly unearth a few more. The heroine of *The Subterraneans*, a Negro girl named Mardou Fox, seems to have switched from one to another member of the same gang and back again ("This has been an incestuous group in its time"), and we are given to understand that there is nothing unusual about such an arrangement. But the point of all this hustle and bustle is not freedom from ordinary social restrictions or defiance of convention (except in relation to homosexuality, which is Ginsberg's preserve: among "the best minds" of Ginsberg's generation who were destroyed by America are those "who let themselves be ——————— in the ——— by saintly mortorcyclists, and screamed with joy, / who blew and were blown by those human seraphim, the sailors, caresses of Atlantic and Caribbean love"). The sex in Kerouac's books goes hand in hand with a great deal of talk about forming permanent relationships ("although I have a hot feeling sexually and all that for her," says the poet Adam Moorad in *The Subterraneans*, "I really don't want to get any further into her not only for these reasons but finally, the big one, if I'm going to get involved with a girl now I want to be permanent like permanent and serious and long termed and I can't do that with her"), and a habit of getting married and then duly divorced and re-married when another girl comes along. In fact, there are as many marriages and divorces in *On the Road* as in the Hollywood movie colony (must be that California climate): "All those years I was looking for the woman I wanted to marry," Sal Paradise tells us. "I couldn't meet a girl without saying to myself, What kind of wife would she make?" Even more revealing is Kerouac's refusal to admit that any of his characters ever makes love wantonly or lecherously—no matter how casual the encounter it must always entail sweet feelings toward the girl. Sal, for example, is fixed up with Rita Bettencourt in Denver, whom he has never met before. "I got her in my bedroom after a long talk in the dark of the front room. She was a nice little girl, simple and true [naturally], and tremendously frightened of sex. I told her it was beautiful. I wanted to prove this to her. She let me prove it, but I was too impatient and proved nothing. She sighed in the dark. 'What do you want out of life?' I asked, and I used to ask that all the time of girls." This is rather touching, but only because the narrator is really just as frightened of sex as that nice little girl was. He is frightened of failure and he worries about his performance. For *performance* is the point—performance and "good orgasms," which are the first duty of man and the only duty of woman. What seems to be involved here, in short, is sexual anxiety of enormous proportions—an anxiety that comes out very clearly in *The Subterraneans*, which is about a love affair between the young writer, Leo Percepied, and the Negro girl, Mardou Fox. Despite its protestations, the book is one long agony of fear and trembling over sex:

> I spend long nights and many hours making her, finally I have her, I pray for it to come, I can hear her breathing harder, I hope against hope it's time, a noise in the hall (or whoop of drunkards next door) takes her mind off and she can't make it and laughs—but when she does make it I hear her crying, whimpering, the shuddering electrical female orgasm makes her sound like a little girl crying, moaning in the night, it lasts a good twenty seconds and when it's over she moans, "O why can't it last longer," and "O when will I when you do?"—"Soon now I bet," I say, "you're getting closer and closer"—

Very primitive, very spontaneous, very elemental, very beat.

For the new Bohemians interracial friendships and love affairs apparently play the same role of social defiance that sex used to play in older Bohemian circles. Negroes and whites associate freely on a basis of complete equality and without a trace of racial hostility. But putting it that way understates the case, for not only is there no racial hostility, there is positive adulation for the "happy, true-hearted, ecstatic Negroes of America."

> At lilac evening I walked with every muscle aching among the lights of 27th and Welton in the Denver colored section, wishing I were a Negro, feeling that the best the white world had offered was not enough ecstasy for me, not enough life, joy, kicks, darkness, music, not enough night. . . . I wished I were a Denver Mexican, or even a poor overworked Jap, anything but what I was so drearily, a "white man" disillusioned. All my life I'd had white ambitions. . . . I passed the dark porches of Mexican and Negro homes; soft voices were there, occasionally the dusky knee of some mysterious sensuous gal; and dark faces of the men behind rose arbors. Little children sat like sages in ancient rocking chairs.

It will be news to the Negroes to learn that they are so happy and ecstatic; I doubt if a more idyllic picture of Negro life has been painted since certain Southern ideologues tried to convince the world that things were just as fine as fine could be for the slaves on the old plantation. Be that as it may, Kerouac's love for Negroes and other dark-skinned groups is tied up with his worship of primitivism, not with any radical social attitudes. Ironically enough, in fact, to see the Negro as more elemental than the white man, as Ned Polsky has acutely remarked, is "an inverted form of keeping the nigger in his place." But even if it were true that American Negroes, by virtue of their position in our culture, have been able to retain a degree of primitive spontaneity, the last place you would expect to find evidence of this is among Bohemian Negroes. Bohemianism, after all, is for the Negro a means of entry into the world of the whites, and no Negro Bohemian is going to cooperate in the attempt to identify him with Harlem or Dixieland. The only major Negro character in either of Kerouac's two novels is Mardou Fox, and she is about as primitive as Wilhelm Reich himself.

The plain truth is that the primitivism of the Beat Generation serves first of all as a cover for an anti-intellectualism so bitter that it makes the ordinary American's hatred of eggheads seem positively benign. Kerouac and his friends like to think of themselves as intellectuals ("they are intellectual as hell and know all about Pound without being pretentious or talking too much about it"), but this is only a form of newspeak. Here is an example of what Kerouac consider intelligent discourse—"formal and shining and complete, without the tedious intellectualness":

> We passed a little kid who was throwing stones at the cars in the road. "Think of it," said Dean. "One day he'll put a stone through a man's windshield and the man will crash and die—all on account of that little kid. You see what I mean? God exists without qualms. As we roll along this way I am positive beyond doubt that everything will be taken care of for us—that even you, as you drive, fearful of the wheel . . . the thing will go along of itself and you won't go off the road and I can sleep. Furthermore we know America, we're at home; I can go anywhere in America and get what I want because it's the same in every corner, I know the people, I know what they do. We give and take and go in the incredibly complicated sweetness zigzagging every side."

You see what he means? Formal and shining and complete. No tedious intellectualness. Completely unpretentious. "There was nothing clear about the things he said but what he meant to say was somehow made pure and clear." *Somehow.* Of course. If what he wanted to say had been carefully thought out and precisely articulated, that would have been tedious and pretentious and, no doubt, *somehow* unclear and clearly impure. But so long as he utters these banalities with his tongue tied and with no comprehension of their meaning, so long as he makes noises that come out of his soul (since they couldn't possibly have come out of his mind), he passes the test of true intellectuality.

Which brings us to Kerouac's spontaneous bop prosody. This "prosody" is not to be confused with bop language itself, which has such a limited vocabulary (Basic English is a verbal treasure-house by comparison) that you couldn't write a note to the milk-man in it, much less a novel. Kerouac, however, manages to remain true to the spirit of hipster slang while making forays into enemy territory (i.e., the English language) by his simple inability to express anything in words. The only method he has of describing an object is to summon up the same half-dozen adjectives over and over again: "greatest," "tremendous," "crazy," "mad," "wild," and perhaps one or two others. When it's more than just mad or crazy or wild, it becomes "really mad" or "really crazy" or "really wild." (All quantities in excess of three, incidentally, are subsumed under the rubric "innumerable," a word used innumerable times in *On the Road* but not so innumerably in *The Subterraneans*.) The same poverty of resources is apparent in those passages where Kerouac tries to handle a situation involving even slightly complicated feelings. His usual tactic is to run for cover behind cliché and vague signals to the reader. For instance: "I looked at him; my eyes were watering with embarrassment and tears. Still he stared at me. Now his eyes were blank and looking through me. . . . Something clicked in both of us. In me it was suddenly concern for a man who was years younger than I, five years, and whose fate was wound with mine across the passage of recent years; in him it was a matter that I can ascertain only from what he did afterward." If you can ascertain what this is all about, either beforehand, during, or afterward, you are surely no square.

In keeping with its populistic bias, the style of *On the Road* is folksy and lyrical. The prose of *The Subterraneans*, on the other hand, sounds like an inept parody of Faulkner at his worst, the main difference being that Faulkner usually produces bad writing out of an impulse to inflate the commonplace while Kerouac gets into trouble by pursuing "spontaneity." Strictly speaking, spontaneity is a quality of feeling, not of writing: when we call a piece of writing spontaneous, we are registering our impression that the author hit upon the right words without sweating, that no "art" and no calculation entered into the picture, that his feelings seem to have spoken themselves, seem to have sprouted a tongue at the moment of composition. Kerouac apparently thinks that spontaneity is a matter of saying whatever comes into your head, in any order you happen to feel like saying it. It isn't the *right* words he wants (even if he knows what they might be), but the first words, or at any rate the words that most obviously announce themselves as deriving from emotion rather than cerebration, as coming from "life" rather than "literature," from the guts rather than the brain. (The brain, remember, is the angel of death.) But writing that springs easily and "spontaneously" out of strong feelings is *never* vague; it always has a quality of sharpness and precision because it is in the nature of strong feelings to be aroused by specific objects. The notion that a diffuse, generalized, and unrelenting enthusiasm is the mark of great sensitivity and responsiveness is utterly fantastic, an idea that comes from taking drunkenness or drug-addiction as the state of perfect emotional vigor. The effect of such enthusiasm is actually to wipe out the world altogether, for if a filling station will serve as well as the Rocky Mountains to arouse a sense of awe and wonder, then both the filling station and the mountains are robbed of their reality. Kerouac's conception of feeling is one that only a solipsist could believe in—and a solipsist, be it noted, is a man who does not relate easily to anything outside himself.

Solipsism is precisely what characterizes Kerouac's fiction. *On the Road* and *The Subterraneans* are so patently autobiographical in content that they become almost impossible to discuss as novels; if spontaneity were indeed a matter of destroying the distinction between life and literature, these books would unquestionably be It. "As we were going out to the car Babe slipped and fell flat on her face. Poor girl was overwrought. Her brother Tim and I helped her up. We got in the car; Major and Betty joined us. The sad ride back to Denver began." Babe is a girl who is mentioned a few times in the course of *On the Road;* we don't know why she is overwrought on this occasion, and even if we did it wouldn't matter, since there is no reason for her presence in the book at all. But Kerouac tells us that she fell flat on her face while walking toward a car. It is impossible to believe that Kerouac made this detail up, that his imagination was creating a world real enough to include wholly gratuitous elements; if that were the case, Babe would have come alive as a human being. But she is only a name; Kerouac never even describes her. She is in the book because the sister of one of Kerouac's friends was there when he took a trip to Central City, Colorado, and she slips in *On the Road* because she slipped that day on the way to the car. What is true of Babe who fell flat on her face is true of virtually every incident in *On the Road* and *The Subterraneans*. Nothing that happens has any dramatic reason for happening. Sal Paradise meets such-and-such people on the road whom he likes or (rarely) dislikes; they exchange a few words, they have a few beers together, they part. It is all very unremarkable and commonplace, but for Kerouac it is always the greatest, the wildest, the most. What you get in these two books is a man proclaiming that he is *alive* and offering every trivial experience he has ever had in evidence. Once I did this, once I did that (he is saying) and by God, it *meant* something! Because I *responded!* But if it meant something, and you responded so powerfully, why can't you explain what it meant, and why do you have to insist so?

I think it is legitimate to say, then, that the Beat Generation's worship of primitivism and spontaneity is more than a cover for hostility to intelligence; it arises from a pathetic poverty of feeling as well. The hipsters and hipster-lovers of the Beat Generation are rebels, all right, but not against anything so sociological and historical as the middle class or capitalism or even respectability. This is the revolt of the spiritually underprivileged and the crippled of soul—young men who can't think straight and so hate anyone who can; young men who can't get outside the morass of self and so construct definitions of feeling that exclude all human beings who manage to live, even miserably, in a world of objects; young men who are burdened unto death with the specially poignant sexual anxiety that America—in its eternal promise of erotic glory and its spiteful withholding of actual erotic possibility—seems bent on breeding, and who therefore dream of the unattainable perfect orgasm, which excuses all sexual failures in the real world. Not long ago, Norman Mailer suggested that the rise of the hipster may represent "the first wind of a second revolution in this century, moving not forward toward action and more rational equitable distribution, but backward toward being and the secrets of human energy." To tell the truth, whenever I hear anyone talking about instinct and being and the secrets of human energy, I get nervous; next thing you know he'll be saying that violence is just fine, and then I begin wondering whether he really thinks that kicking someone in the teeth or sticking a knife between his ribs are deeds to be admired. History, after all—and especially the history of modern times—teaches that there is a close connection between ideologies of primitivistic vitalism and a willingness to look upon cruelty and blood-letting with complacency, if not downright enthusiasm. The reason I bring this up is that the spirit of hipsterism and the Beat Generation strikes me as the same spirit which animates the young savages in leather jackets who have been running amok in the last few years with their switch-blades and zip guns. What does Mailer think of those wretched kids, I wonder? What does he think of the gang that stoned a nine-year-old boy to death in Central Park in broad daylight a few months ago, or the one that set fire to an old man drowsing on a bench near the Brooklyn waterfront one summer's day, or the one that pounced on a crippled child and orgiastically stabbed him over and over and over again even after he was good and dead? Is that what he means by the liberation of instinct and the mys-teries of being? Maybe so. At least he says somewhere in his article that two eighteen-year-old hoodlums who bash in the brains of a candy-store keeper are murdering an institution, committing an act that "violates private property"—which is one of the most morally gruesome ideas I have ever come across, and which indi-cates where the ideology of hipsterism can lead. I happen to believe that there is a direct connection between the flabbiness of American middle-class life and the spread of juvenile crime in the 1950's, but I also believe that juvenile crime can be explained partly in terms of the same resentment against normal feeling and the attempt to cope with the world through intelligence that lies behind Kerouac and Ginsberg. Even the relatively mild ethos of Kerouac's books can spill over easily into brutality, for there is a suppressed cry in those books: Kill the intellectuals who can talk coherently, kill the people who can sit still for five minutes at a time, kill those incomprehensible characters who are capable of getting seriously involved with a woman, a job, a cause. How can anyone in his right mind pretend that this has anything to do with private property or the middle class? No. Being against what the Beat Generation stands for has to do with denying that inco-herence is superior to precision; that ignorance is superior to knowledge; that the exercise of mind and discrimination is a form of death. It has to do with fighting the notion that sordid acts of violence are justifiable so long as they are committed in the name of "instinct." It even has to do with fighting the poisonous glorification of the adolescent in American popular culture. It has to do, in other words, with one's attitude toward intelligence itself.

[1958]

The New Nihilism and the Novel

If you take a random sampling of novels published over the past few months, what strikes you most forcibly is the remarkable degree to which writers, both here and in various European countries, have again become preoccupied—though in a different key and a new perspective—with the theme of the loss of values. In America, at least, the deep concern with this theme that informed almost every poem and novel of the modernist movement became for a time either incomprehensible or boring (which, when we are talking about attitudes as expressed in works of art, amounts to much the same thing)—and with good cause. First of all, the modernist movement had exhausted itself by the mid 1940's: the avant-garde in literature was dead, and the few experimental writers who remained were able to bring no fresh life to the attitudes of the movement. It is this, and not a mere deficiency of technical ingenuity, that explains why such writers daringly continued to repeat experiments so revolutionary that they were already on the reading lists of freshman survey courses in English literature. Concern over the loss of values became a received idea, a cliché, and the best anyone could do with it was to trot out mechanical symbolic allusions; only a scholar with the statistical thoroughness of Miss Caroline Spurgeon would have the stamina to tabulate the number of deserts, rats, ruined mansions and the like that have cropped up in the last ten or fifteen years of American writing. Beyond this, however, the whole question of the loss of values was soon removed from the hands of the literary men who had raised it in the first place and given over to the tender embraces of the theologians, thus turning what had been a "non-sectarian" diagnosis of the spiritual condition of modern man into a point of doctrinal contention between "humanists" and "religionists." Not that the literary men offered any great resistance to this usurpation, for the terms in which some of them had posed the problem led inevitably (or so it appears today) to a religious solution. If God is dead—as Nietzsche had proclaimed—and his death (with all that the metaphor implies) has rendered life intolerable—as Kafka and Lawrence and Eliot went on to say—why, then, He must be speedily resurrected. Eliot, in his best disingenuous manner, once complained that when *For Launcelot Andrewes* appeared, a reviewer "made it the occasion for what I can only describe as a flattering obituary notice . . . he pointed out that I had suddenly arrested my progress—whither he had supposed me to be moving I do not know—and that to his distress I was unmistakably making off in the wrong direction." We all know whither Eliot's early admirers had *not* supposed him to be moving, but at any rate the direction he himself took was representative of the direction taken by the attitudes toward modernity that animated the great literary flowering in which he played so prominent a role. When the theologians stepped in—and they stepped in gleefully, announcing that the poets had borne eloquent confessional witness to the disasters of the flight from religion—the voice of the spiritual engineer was bound to drown out the voices crying from the wilderness. And so it did. The prophet had said: "Things fall apart; the centre cannot hold; / Mere anarchy is loosed upon the world, / .... / The best lack all conviction, while the worst / Are full of passionate intensity." And the priest (in the words of Professor Stanley Romaine Hopper) answered: ". . . there are many otherwise creditable (and even distinguished) literary people whose knowledge of what is taking place in theology today is almost sublimely unenlightened. Their creative works are therefore legitimate but uninformed fumbling after solutions to problems of the spirit, works which could have been more efficiently ordered and more accurately construed had the author or the artist been working within the framework of a well articulated world-view."

Once this emphasis was established, the theme of the loss of values suffered debasement into a strictly polemical device for attacking the secularizing forces at work in Western civilization—science, industrialism, and liberal democracy. And having shrunk from being the vital expression of the consciousness of an age to the status of a plank in the platform of the Church party, the theme could no longer serve the uses of a living literature. Moreover, this hitching of the responsibility for all our woes on science, industrialism, and liberal democracy was badly timed, coming as it did to a head precisely at a moment when everyone (soldiers to a man in the cold war) was busily engaged in rediscovering the values latent in the "American way of life." True, there was, and is, a great deal of blabbering about the religious foundations of Western civilization on the one hand and "godless Communism" on the other, as though the conflict between the democratic West and the totalitarian East were at bottom a struggle between faith and atheism. But the most energetic intellectual impulse of the period was pushing toward the idea that the main enemy, both in culture and politics, was the "true believer," the fanatic of whatever complexion, the prisoner of ideology. This being so, the loss of values could be seen as a positive virtue, a symptom of our progressive liberation from rigid systems of belief. What we in the West stood for was the skeptical empiricist temperament, the very temperament that makes for a healthy political system (since it discourages fanaticism), a prosperous economic life (since it is the basis of technological efficiency), and a flourishing culture (since concreteness is the soul of art). Something of the elation you find in the early defenders of natural philosophy like Bacon and Sprat was in the American air for a few years at the discovery that the whole liberal-humanist complex contained within itself an answer to those who were attacking it for being incompatible with good life. And Lionel Trilling was there to tell us that the progressives in our midst had betrayed the liberal tradition by perverting it into an ideology. The old battle between the rationalist and the empiricist philosophers was lustily being fought again, and thinkers as diverse as Hannah Arendt, Hans J. Morgenthau, Michael Polanyi, and George Kennan were providing (in some instances inadvertently) arguments from every corner for a crusade against the rationalists of today (i.e. the ideologists). The upshot, so far as American youth was concerned, was not that we had lost our values, but only our taste for ideology, and good riddance to it. Our values were implicit in the complexities of our behavior from day to day; they were not the kind that could easily be systematized and translated into slogans to compete with the slogans of the Communists for the "uncommitted minds" of the world: here lay the source of our weakness in the cold war, but also of the moral superiority of our position. It was because the sociologists, led by David Riesman, were doing more than anyone else to confirm this proposition, to uncover a coherent pattern in our daily behavior, that sociology became so prominent a field of study in those years.

Only one major literary effort was generated by the ethos I have been trying to describe—*The Adventures of Augie March*—and if we want to understand why the hot-blooded love affair between the intellectuals and America cooled off before it ever got to the altar, we can do no better than go to Mr. Bellow's celebrated novel. Both in its attempt to create a new idiom that could express the intellectual's joyous sense of connection with the common grain of American life and in its assertion that individual fulfillment is still possible in this fluid and rootless society of ours ("I may well be a flop at this line of endeavor. Columbus too thought he was a flop, probably, when they sent him back in chains, which didn't prove there was no America"), *Augie* speaks for that period, roughly between 1948 and 1955, that some have called the age of conformity and neo-Conservatism and others the era of "intellectual revisionism." But in its failures as a novel—the willed spontaneity of the writing, the abstractness of the hero—we can also detect the uncertainty and emotional strain that lurked on the underside of the new optimism. The elation in the discovery of America was indisputably sincere, but it was a temporary mood, as deceptive an indication of the feelings within as the surface texture of Mr. Bellow's prose. Not nearly enough conviction stood behind this mood to sustain it against the slow inexorable grinding of the years of atomic stalemate, the grinding and the anxiety which would not be denied. Mr. Bellow himself went on to the agonies of *Seize the Day* (in my opinion the best thing he has so far written), and the rest of us dispersed on our separate ways, a few crying for a return to radicalism, a few once again hawking the wares of the church. Surely the reception accorded Jack Kerouac and Allen Ginsberg, whose work combines an appearance of radicalism with a show of intense spirituality, testifies to the hunger that has grown up on all sides for something extreme, fervent, affirmative, and sweeping; five, or even three, years ago the Beat Generation would simply not have been noticed. On another level altogether, there is the magazine *Dissent*. When you consider that it speaks largely in the tired accents of an old-fashioned Central European socialism, you can only conclude that its growing influence indicates a nostalgia for the grand passions and the selfless dedication that democratic socialism once had no trouble breeding in its adherents. I imagine that many American readers of *Dissent* regard it with a kind of envy and perhaps even with humble reverence, much as a sin-stricken man in quest of religious faith might look upon the inhabitants of a monastery. And finally, there is Richard Chase's exciting book *The Democratic Vista*, the first truly relevant, if not altogether convincing, effort to redefine the need for a cultural radicalism and to argue that avant-garde attitudes are still worth passionate support. Chase is the first writer who has tried to bring the 1930's up to date, but as things are going, he will almost certainly not be the last.

A renewed sense, then, of the loss of values is beginning to impose itself, only this time it seems to be taking the form of a recognition that in losing our taste for ideology we have also lost our capacity for passion. But though one can decide which values to defend, and though one can try on ideologies like suits of clothes, one cannot choose to be passionate. It is impossible to will oneself into powerful convictions; something from the outside has to take over the mind and spirit, has to "startle this dull pain, and make it move and live." The dilemma today is that nothing seems to be left in our world to set an honest man's feelings on fire.

Three recent novels by young American writers bear discussion in this connection as different responses to the new mood which has been developing in the past year or two. The most recalcitrant of the three, and the least interesting, is Frederick Buechner's *The Return of Ansel Gibbs*, a terribly solemn little book about a patrician statesman who runs into trouble with a know-nothing midwestern senator when his appointment to a cabinet post comes up for confirmation. The contrast between Gibbs and the senator is much too crude to yield anything significant, and to make matters worse, Buechner drags in a contrived and wholly unconvincing bit of complicated business involving the hero's daughter and the son of a man for whose suicide many years earlier Gibbs still feels responsible. None of this is any good at all, but in the portrait of Ansel Gibbs himself, Buechner gets hold of something real; he handles it ineptly, but it is something real nevertheless. Gibbs is a rather stuffy and pompous man (one wonders whether Buechner is aware of the extent to which he has endowed his hero with these unattractive qualities), but he has breeding, cultivation, and intelligence (or anyway a reasonable facsimile of intelligence—the breeding and cultivation seem authentic enough). His political enemies accuse him of having once responded to the question, implausibly put to him by an irate soldier when he was in Washington during the war without a uniform, "Well, my friend, and what are you doing to save civilization?" with the calm reply, "I am civilization." Civilization, we quickly discover, means for Buechner a consciousness of the "tragic ambivalence" of life, and being civilized exacts a severe toll: Gibbs suffers from a certain deficiency of feeling, a certain remoteness from the natural processes and the elemental emotions. He is almost incapable of passion (sobriety, judiciousness, detachment, moderation, tolerance being the civilized virtues), and he can no more satisfy his old teacher's demand that he become a prophet than he can prate sentimentally like the senator about Mom's apple pie. The novel raises the question of whether such a man can be relied upon to guide the fortunes of others, and after making all the necessary concessions (and a few gratuitous ones as well) to the opposing camp, it answers in the affirmative. Not, mind you, a strong affirmative; only a "civilized" one, full of "tragic ambivalence."

Buechner is saying that the inability to commit oneself passionately can still be regarded as a positive value: he is on the side of those who belive in the intrinsic superiority of what I have shorthandedly called the skeptical empiricist temper. But notice how weak and defensive his tone is by comparison with the elation that accompanied this position a few years ago. "Civilization" in

Buechner's sense has clearly lost the power to generate even a surface enthusiasm by now. It seems to be all played out.

George P. Elliott's first novel, *Parktilden Village*, is a much better book than *The Return of Ansel Gibbs*; indeed, Elliott seems to me one of the most promising new figures to have appeared on the literary scene in a long time. He writes with that air of cool judicious detachment that is now universally recognized as one of the signatures of serious fiction in this period, but after reading a few pages of *Parktilden Village*, you become pleasantly aware of the absence of portentous solemnity in the tone, and you begin to see that for once the cool judiciousness is doing something more than calling your attention to the author's subtlety and good taste: it is working to define a critical attitude toward the main character. This bland and pleasant young sociologist is ultimately to be shown as capable of the most vicious irresponsibility and the most heedless cruelty. But we soon understand that Elliott's intention is not to indict the individual Hazen; he is attacking the whole culture personified by Hazen for breeding emotional sterility and moral emptiness—in short, for having no values. For the purposes of a polemic against the "scientific" or "positivistic" view of life, Hazen is well conceived. He is tall, handsome, and affable in manner, a kind of human counterpart to the shiny, comfortable, and efficient uniformity of the apartments in the California housing development where he lives; except for those habits in himself which are susceptible or being affected by an act of conscious determination (he is a great maker of resolutions), he dismisses all self-confrontation as wasteful and meaningless; and he refers everything in his experience to neat categories, refusing to be bothered with nice discriminations. For all this, however, Hazen is blood brother to some of the less amiable elements in American life, his sociological research projects being mainly a pretext for reading comic strips (and then creating a successful one himself) and hot-rodding with the leather-jacket gang on the drag-strip. Here, I think, the novel is at its best: Hazen comes through vividly as not very different in spirit from the wild kids he is "studying," and Elliott's point—that the rise of positivism and the malignant spread of adolescent recklessness are both expressions of the same spiritual vacuum in our society, a vacuum which is itself most clearly exemplified by mass culture—gets established without too much prompting from the wings.

Judging from a coy hint at the end, Elliott's answer is God. But the hint is so coy and so timidly brought forward that we are left with some doubt as to whether and to what degree he really means it. Under the assumption that he does, and assuming further that Elliott can be taken as a representative spokesman, *Parktilden Village* becomes an extremely revealing document of the current feelings in the "Church party" about the loss of values. Except for the last section of the book, where there is a sudden and unexpected shift in attitude toward Hazen, Elliott's tone throughout is critical but hardly heated. He pokes fun at Hazen and he attributes most of our troubles to the usual trio of science, industrialism, and the liberal ethic, but despite this, you get no sense of a refusal to accept the reality of Hazen. Elliott is neither horrified nor repelled: when he describes Hazen's simultaneous involvement in affairs with the middle-aged wife of one of his former teachers and her teen-age daughter, he writes of the incident not (as Graham Greene, say, might) as a sinister matter with diabolic overtones, but as the kind of occurrence that no longer seems so outrageous. It is only when he comes to the end and spells out the pain Hazen's behavior has caused others that he feels impelled to express shock and to bring in an allusion to the need for prayer and faith in God. Even here, however, there is ambivalence, for the character who is the vehicle of this message is too silly and superficial a person to take seriously herself. In other words, *Parktilden Village* would appear to indicate that sheer habituation to the nihilism of American life—for a nihilist, a believer in nothing, is precisely what Hazen is—has infected even the proponents of a religious solution, who now find it hard to assert anything more powerful against it than a mild irony, a fairly stale argument, and a willed outrage.

Nihilism is given its full head in what from my point of view is the best of the three novels in this group, J. P. Donleavy's *The Ginger Man*. The book is undramatic, badly paced, and very uneven indeed, with more weak passages than it can comfortably assimilate, but it is also an extremely funny novel, and its vitality is more than merely rhetorical. In a furiously exuberant prose style that suggests wild horses let loose, Donleavy lashes about with abandon at everything in sight, only to find that he has been flailing the empty air, so utterly has the once solid structure of middle-class respectability disintegrated from lack of any conviction to prop it up. His hero, Sebastian Dangerfield, is a young expatriate American studying in Dublin on the G.I. Bill, where he has forced his English wife and their baby to live in squalor and poverty. The studying is a farce; he has no intention of becoming a lawyer or anything else. All he is doing is marking time until his prosperous father dies, and he intends to go on marking time for the rest of his days when he comes into his inheritance. He is a drunkard, a philanderer, a cheat, a liar, and even a petty thief. At first, we respond to him as we do to any character in fiction who allows us to participate in the fantasy of complete release, especially when the release largely takes the form of constant drinking and jumping from bed to bed. And so it comes as a momentous shock when we begin to realize that Dangerfield is not an endearing "Rabelaisian" rascal. Not only does he treat his wife with appalling cruelty, but we learn that because he has been stealing their baby's milk money, the infant has developed a case of rickets. This is no joke, and it jolts us right out of the realm of pleasant fantasy into the most sordid of realities—which, of course, is exactly what Donleavy wants it to do. Why, then, do we continue to feel the attraction of Dangerfield? What claim does he exert on our sympathies? The decisive factor, I think, is his honesty. Unlike almost everyone else in the book (and incidentally unlike Kerouac's heroes, with whom he has been foolishly compared), he never simulates feelings that he does not in fact feel, he refuses to make excuses, and he will not hide behind empty pieties. He is not a bum and a scoundrel out of ill will or malice or insensitivity. On the contrary, he strikes us as a man who has looked into himself and found nothing, and then looked about the world and found no set of values (neither "traditional" nor "liberal") in sufficiently robust condition to exert any pull over his soul. Dangerfield, in short, is not exacting a fantasy of release, he is living by the truth of his times. Nor is he a rebel, for there is nothing to rebel against, everything gives way before him. He is—to use the terminology adopted by Alfred Kazin in a brilliant article in the current issue of *Psychoanalysis and the Psychoanalytic Review*—an example of the "stranger" as hero, an example of what becomes of the impulse toward rebellion at a moment in history when the only conventions in existence are anachronistic survivals of a moribund ethos, shadows without substance. Donleavy takes no joy in this situation —his joy is in the honest exposure of it. Nor is he able to offer any answers. The only positives in the novel—an earthgoddess type of girl who falls in love with Dangerfield, and the warm friendship that exists among the few people who, like Dangerfield, are in on the ghastly secret of our times and act upon it— are literary clichés derived from Joyce and Hemingway. *The Ginger Man* is fundamentally a book without hope (Dangerfield is even cut out of his father's will at the end) and it reflects, more directly than Elliott or Buechner, I think, the true spiritual contours of this period. It is a response not to the death of traditional values, not to the dislocations caused by industrialism and technology—there are no memories of an older, more settled way of life here—but precisely to the final collapse of the bourgeois era, a book that comes out of a moment in history when the old world has died and the new one about to be born may never struggle its way out of the womb.

It was, of course, Camus who first spotted the significance of this new style of nihilism and identified it, in *The Stranger*, with the pathological apathy of the narrator Meursault—the French were far in advance of the Americans in seeing that the "rebel" was giving way in our day to the "stranger." In his latest book, a collection of stories called *Exile and the Kingdom*, Camus continues to deal with the predicament of men and women moving dully through an indifferent universe (he is very much a man in quest of solutions, and not at all content with mere diagnosis), but my impression is that he has lost the firm grasp he had on the problem in his earlier work. The decline set in with his last novel, *The Fall*, a book that seems to me only a mechanical repetition of what he had already accomplished before, and even at their best these new stories have nothing of the clear brilliance and beauty of *The Stranger* or the thickness of texture that distinguished *The Plague*. Nevertheless, Camus is in a different class from the three American writers I have just been discussing, not only because he brings a much wider historical and philosophical perspective to bear on the common theme, but because for him the Meursaults exist as a sinister possibility, they are a projection of what he himself might so easily become, rather than an image of what he already is. The source of his power is not in my opinion his superior artistry (indeed, as a craftsman of the novel he is rather poorly endowed by comparison with a dozen lesser writers), but in the very delicate balance he manages to strike between identification with the nihilists he writes about and detachment from them. Reading Camus is like watching a man plunge over a precipice and then grab the edge of the cliff with his nails and hold on by God knows what miraculous instinct to survive. It hardly matters that this instinct is inarticulate, that Camus's solutions (submitting to the knowledge of the predicament, sharing the burdens of the oppressed) are no solutions—or at least nothing more than individual solutions. What matters is that he has looked upon the face of death and lived, that he has visited chaos and returned with the message that all we can do is try to *think* our way back into a world of meaning, to create a new world of meaning that makes no concession to the bankrupt philosophies of church or state.

What Sartre calls the "anti-novels" of Nathalie Sarraute seem, so far as I can make out from the only one as yet published in this country, *Portrait of a Man Unknown,* to present a total submission to meaninglessness of existence. Mme. Sarraute has plunged over the cliff, landed on her feet, and then begun to stroll calmly through the void as we watch dimly and incredulously from above. There is something rather horrible in this coolly presented picture of nothingness, this absolute taking for granted that life is a Chinese box and that as you painfully pry open each successive lid you are rewarded with yet another vacuum. What appears at first to be the insanity of the narrator, who speaks paranoically of "They" and who for no reason whatever becomes obsessed with a shadowy couple, an elderly man and his spinster daughter living together in hatred and mutual contempt, turns out to be intended as a picture of the actual state of affairs in our world. There are no characters in the book, for individuality is an illusion that can no longer be maintained; no communication between persons, for there is nothing left to communicate except, as Sartre points out in his introduction, the most generalized of commonplaces. No other writer, not even Beckett or Ionesco, has gone quite as far as Mme. Sarraute, and further than this it would be impossible to go, since her extraordinary novel is written at the point where literally everything, including the six senses themselves, are just about to dissolve into thin air.

Thomas Hinde's interesting novel, *Happy as Larry*, provides a good illustration of how the new nihilism is being treated in England. Here again we have a hero who is shiftless, irresponsible, and unable—with justification, given what we see of the possibilities for engagement in the novel itself—to get interested in anything. Larry Vincent is also capable of horrendous behavior: he runs off pretending not to have noticed when he sees his wife (whom he loves) hit by a car, and he spends the rest of the novel trying to do penance by tracking down a compromising photograph which can damage the career of a close friend—an act that he has decided will help him get a fresh start in life. The book is imbued with the same sense of the purposelessness of the common routines that you come upon in John Wain's *Hurry on Down*, and a strong feeling that everyone in the modern world, ordinary people no less than self-conscious questioners, is at heart a nihilist:

> Suffering was hidden away—in hospitals and asylums. As a result they had no attitude to it—except resentment that it should be brought to their notice. The suffering they didn't know about, which wasn't illness or hunger, but just empty unhappiness—that was hidden too, behind their prosperous faces, behind the hire-purchased walnut suite, the four-seater saloon with mother in the back. . . .

As for the hero himself, his terrible confusions are seen as a product of the absence of any values in the society he inhabits which he can accept happily or rebel against (either course would give his life meaning):

> "Can you imagine not knowing the difference between right and wrong?" [he asks a girl.]
> "No."
> "I can. One person says do this, another do that. I like them both. I understand exactly why they say what they say and think the other absurd. I can think the way either of them think. What should I do?"

"You must feel."

"I sometimes genuinely don't—or rather I feel both. Then what am I to do? Start arguing? I haven't the intelligence. Anyway it's a life work."

The only exceptions to this rule are a few Bohemians whose protest against the emptiness of modern life is to "refuse to do what doesn't interest them."

The paralyzing gloom of *Happy as Larry* stands in the sharpest possible contrast to the destructive exhilaration of *The Ginger Man:* Hinde can hardly bear the pain of looking at what his own book reveals. Yet beneath this gloom, one senses the presence of a notion that the problem is fundamentally social, and therefore solvable by political action. Unlike his American literary contemporaries, Hinde, I would guess, believes that the process of disintegration he finds in the world around him is reversible—an understandable sentiment in a country where technology and mass culture are so much less taken for granted than here (what American writer would use the fact that people communicate by telephone as an occasion for reflecting that machines were robbing us of the "common feeling . . . before nature, to God"?) and where the inevitable social changes that have been gathering steam in the last few years can so easily seem, to those suffering from the attendant dislocations, a matter of free choice, like voting for or against commercial television. (C. P. Snow has said that most English literary people still haven't come to terms with the industrial revolution.)

Hinde is usually associated with the rather heterogeneous group of writers now irrevocably known as the Angry Young Men. These writers are often described as lower-class rebels against the Establishment who are bitter about the decline of British prestige in the world and/or—so the usual cliché goes—the drabness of life in the Welfare State. There is a slight touch of truth in this description, but apart from the fact that it oversimplifies and ignores the element of genuine rejoicing on the English Left (where all but one or two of the AYM can be found) at Britain's retirement from the colonial scene and her increasing egalitarianism, its main weakness is that it misses the jauntiness and the underlying *optimism* of Amis, Wain, and even Osborne—an optimism that derives from their excitement at the prospect of a new society coming into being which has the opportunity to create a healthy "organic" culture for the first time since the industrial revolution. To my ears, it is a jauntiness remarkably reminiscent of the tone of much American writing of the 1930's (writing, by the way, which is greatly admired in England today—the early plays of Lillian Hellman and Clifford Odets have been recommended by the influential young drama critic Kenneth Tynan as a model for the British theater to follow). But many other things besides tone in the British cultural atmosphere today also recall the spirit of the American 1930's. To take a vivid, though possibly trivial example: during the few days when DeGaulle's access to power was still in doubt, a number of English writers hired a hall in London to protest against the impending murder of freedom in France and formed a Committee to Save the Fourth Republic. (It was later reported that the Committee's message of solidarity to certain French anti-Gaullistes caused bewilderment even in Paris, where this fervent gesture seemed, as the English themselves would put it, "a bit thick," given the temper of the times.) If I remember rightly, the protest meeting was organized by the *Universities and Left Review,* a new socialist magazine which has a fresh, naive bounciness that stands out in bold relief against the tired, almost worldly sophistication of its American counterpart *Dissent* (for once, the tables of European "maturity" and American "innocence" have been turned), and a hopeful belief in the possibility of social solutions to problems of culture that reminds one of *Partisan Review* in its youthful phase. The H-bomb, one might say, is to the English Left today what the Depression was to the American Left of the 1930's—a disaster that stimulates enthusiastic intellectual activity.

The conclusion to be drawn from this admittedly sketchy analysis is that England, as usual, represents a special case. English writers—at least on the Left—are as deeply preoccupied with the new nihilism as the Americans or the French, but they tend to identify it with the specific domestic conditions of their own country, and in particular with the refusal of moribund Establishment values to lie down and die. (John Osborne, who is the most extreme exponent of this point of view, has declared that the British masses are "not conditioned to seriousness but to totem worship" by the monarchy, by the church, by "people sodden in the culture-mores of Oxford and Cambridge," and by "implicit ruling-class ideals like 'restraint,' 'good taste,' 'healthy caution,' and so on," and he voices the hope that "there will be singing one day" . . . under socialism.)

But confidence in the possibility of a social answer to the new nihilism seems confined to England. Ignazio Silone's latest novel, *The Secret of Luca*, projects as an ideal the heroic individual who triumphs by following his own deepest convictions against the demands of society. Since these convictions include a belief that the law has no business prying into his private affairs, Luca refuses to defend himself against a false murder charge, and he spends forty years in prison until he is exonerated by the actual criminal's deathbed confession. If this were all, we could accept Silone's contention (in a recent interview) that his book is a defense of the right of privacy, though the weaknesses in his argument would still be very damaging. What sense does it make for a man to claim the right of privacy when he has been accused of a crime? Is any sane principle being served when such a man goes to jail rather than reveal his whereabouts on the night of the crime? On the evidence of the novel itself, however, it is not Luca's defense of a principle more sacred than the law that draws Silone's admiration. It is, quite simply, his astonishing ability to hold out against all pressure for what he believes is right. But we cannot be moved by Luca's heroism without respecting the conventions of chivalry and honor to which he has sacrificed himself, and they are of a kind that can only seem silly today (to have accounted for his movements when the murder was committed would, in his eyes, have besmirched the reputation of a married woman with whom he was in love, despite the fact that nothing had ever happened between them). Even a very great novelist would have been hard put to give meaning and dignity to this heroism. All Silone—a very good and very intelligent writer—can do is impress us with the pathos of Luca, and it is a tribute to his humane artistry that only once, when Luca weeps with unabated passion while reading the diary of the lady he had loved at a distance for forty years, do we feel unequivocally that this is man too ridiculous to bother with. It turns out, then, that even Silone, who is second only to Malraux as a distinguished writer with an honorable career of *engagement*, is now having difficulty in proclaiming the possibility of absolute dedication to a moral code. Surely it is significant that in order to assert the supreme value of passionate inner conviction he should have had to wander off into a wholly foreign area of feeling and assumptions, and that he should precisely have hit upon a code that can no longer command any respect—quite as though he were inadvertently confessing that the "secret" of Luca is of precious little relevance today.

Only, I think, against some such background as the one I have been trying to sketch can the wonder that has greeted Bernard Malamud's last two books, his novel *The Assistant* and his collection of stories *The Magic Barrel*, be fully understood. Many reviewers have made a stab at describing the unique flavor of his work, but what they have said in specific matters less than their agreement that a highly special—and highly elusive—quality exists that very nearly beggars definition. Since he writes so well about Jews, and poor ones at that, and since he has succeeded in catching the very life of Yiddish speech better than any of the countless American writers who have tried before him, the natural thing to do has been to look for a handle in "Jewishness" or Sholom Aleichem or even the Bible. None of this seems to me of much help; in fact, I would argue that Malamud's conception of Jewishness and his idea of what Jews are really like come out of his own head and cannot be supported, except in a vague general way, by precedent in Yiddish or Hebrew literature. To Malamud, the Jew is humanity seen under the twin aspects of suffering and moral aspiration. Therefore any man who suffers greatly and who also longs to be better than he is can be called a Jew. (Frankie Alpine's formal conversion to Judaism at the end of *The Assistant* is almost gratuitous, since he became a Jew, in the only sense that Malamud understands the word, many chapters before.) It is not so much that this idea is wrong—whatever that would mean—as that Malamud holds to it with an unqualified intensity and directness that actual observation of the East European immigrant Jews he is portraying would not appear to warrant. And here lies the source of that strangeness we are puzzled to account for in his Jewish characters—they are so beautifully drawn in their physical being (their speech, their gestures, their ordinary social attitudes, their milieux) that we never think to question their authenticity as East European immigrant Jews, when all the while their spiritual lineaments have been quietly copied not from any models on earth but from an idea in the mind of Bernard Malamud.

The point is that Malamud's unique and marvellous ability to write without embarrassment or falsity of the simplest and most basic emotions, his power to say "And there were days when he was sick to death of everything," or "They pressed mouths together and parted forever" (the last line of "The Loan," one of the three stories in this collection that deserve to live forever, the

other two being "The Bill" and, of course, "The Magic Barrel")
depends on a certain blindness to the full realities of the world
around him. The trick he has turned is not unlike what Yeats did
with magic: in the absence of a culture that could supply him with
a secure basis for the things he needs to believe, he has created a
folk, partly out of what actually exists and partly out of what his
spirit demands. You would not go to Bernard Malamud for a
balanced and reliable picture of the East European immigrant
Jew, but you would go to him for profounder truths about human
beings than mere observation can yield.

Malamud has elicited wonder and astonishment from the most
heterogeneous body of readers because he has managed to escape
both the corrosions of modern life and the deepenings of insight
that have accompanied these corrosions. He is a genuine "sport"
who has travelled his own idiosyncratic road, almost as untouched
by literary influences as by the historical currents in which the rest
of us are being swept away. And his work, when it is good—which
sufficiently often it is—seems a kind of miracle, an act of spiritual
autonomy perfect enough to persuade us that the possibility of
freedom from the determinings of history and sociology still exists.
That wacky, wonderful voice we hear in a Malamud story is one
of the few sounds remaining in our world that cannot be accounted for in terms of anything but itself. For it is a voice that
speaks of people who belong to no period in particular, and in a
language that belongs not to history but to nature.
[1958]

Norman Mailer: The Embattled Vision

Norman Mailer is one of the few postwar American writers in whom it is possible to detect the presence of qualities that powerfully suggest a major novelist in the making. Anyone trying to describe these qualities would be likely to dwell on Mailer's extraordinary technical skill, or on the boldness and energy of his mind, or on his readiness to try something new whenever he puts pen to paper. What seems even more remarkable, however, is that his work has responded to the largest problems of this period with a directness and an assurance that we rarely find in the novels of his contemporaries. Mailer is very much an American, but he appears to be endowed with the capacity for seeing himself as a battleground of history—a capacity that is usually associated with the French and that American writers are thought never to have. He is a man given to ideologies, a holder of extreme positions, and in this too he differs from the general run of his literary contemporaries, so many of whom have fled ideology to pursue an ideal of sensible moderation both in style and philosophy. To follow

Mailer's career, therefore, is to witness a special drama of development, a drama in which the deepest consciousness of the postwar period has struggled to define itself in relation to the past, and to know itself in terms of the inescapable, ineluctable present.

Now for many people the only Mailer worth considering is Mailer the realist, and for these *The Naked and the Dead* is the only one of his three novels that matters at all. It is true, I think, that Mailer's phenomenal talent for recording the precise look and feel of things is his most impressive single gift, and there is some ground for arguing that in deserting realism he has made insufficient use of this power. But it was not by arbitrary choice that Mailer abandoned realism, any more than it was by arbitrary choice that he wrote as a realist in the first place. Far from merely being a technique selected for its suitability to the author's talents, the realism of *The Naked and the Dead* is in itself an expression of his response to a certain structure of experience. The world of *The Naked and the Dead* is one in which a varied group of clearly defined individuals are pitted in a very direct and simple way against two allied enemies—the army and nature. Nature brings violent storms and intolerable heat, it provides jungles to be crossed and mountains to be climbed, and it also sets limits to the physical strength of the men exposed to its rigors. The army, on the other hand, is a society, tightly organized, efficiently ruled, and almost as confident of its power as nature itself. From the point of view of the individual, driven by a hunger for absolute freedom, hardly any distinction can be drawn between them. Just as nature threatens him with pain and fear and death, so the army threatens him with moral destruction, aiming finally to destroy his will altogether and reduce him to a mere servant of its own ends. To keep himself alive physically, he must be strong, resourceful, and determined; to keep himself alive spiritually, he must have enormous reserves of inner resistance.

This was an ideal situation for a writer with Mailer's natural

gift of observation. Something palpable was there to describe and
he described it brilliantly, down to the last quiver of a particular
muscle in a man's thigh as he was climbing the face of a rock,
down to the last twitch of temptation as he was saying no to an
offer of promotion. The availability of a great literary tradition—
a tradition which had itself developed out of just such situations
in an age when society seemed as solid and substantial and un-
shakable as the army is in *The Naked and the Dead*—certainly
helps to explain how it came about that a first novel by a young
man of twenty-five should have exhibited mastery of so high an
order. But there is more to the success of the best passages in
The Naked and the Dead than a happy confrontation of talent,
circumstance, and tradition. The rainstorm that descends on
Anopopei shortly after the division has landed; the episode in
which the platoon drags four huge guns through the muddy jungle
in the black of night; the climb up Mt. Anaka—all these are so
good and so moving because they are written by someone who in
the deepest reaches of his being believes that the world is made
up exclusively of stone walls and that life consists in a perpetual
crashing of the head against them. It is as though the war provided Mailer with a never-ending succession of examples that confirmed everything he had ever felt or thought about human existence, and one can almost detect the relish with which he piled
up the evidence in scene after astonishing scene.

The *Naked and the Dead*, however, cannot simply be read as
an expression of Mailer's feelings about life in general; it also attempts to make certain specific statements about World War II,
the American army, and the character of American society. In 1948
Mailer—who was shortly to become a leading figure in Henry
Wallace's campaign for the Presidency—subscribed to the notion
that our postwar difficulties with Russia were the sole responsibility
of American capitalism. We had gone to war against Hitler not
because the American ruling class was anti-fascist, but because

Hitler had shown himself unwilling to play the capitalist game according to the rules, and the next step was to dispose of Russia, the only remaining obstacle on the road to total power. World War II, then, was the first phase of a more ambitious operation, while the army had been used as a laboratory of fascism, a preview of the kind of society that the American ruling class was preparing for the future. These ideas are brought into *The Naked and the Dead* in various ways. Some of them emerge from the long discussions between General Cummings (the commander of the division that has invaded the island of Anopopei) and his young aide Lt. Hearn (a rich midwesterner whose political sympathies are with the Left and whom Cummings is trying to convert to his own special brand of fascism). Another channel is supplied by the "Time Machine" flashbacks, which are there partly in order to demonstrate Mailer's contention that American society is essentially a disguised and inchoate form of the army. But it is in the main line of the plot that the politics of the novel are most heavily emphasized. The scheme of *The Naked and the Dead* is to follow a single campaign from the preparations for invasion to the mopping-up operation, and the technique is to shift back and forth between command headquarters and one small platoon in the division. This enables Mailer to observe the campaign both through the eyes of the man who is running it and in terms of the day-to-day fortunes of those who are affected in the most immediate way by his every move. The experience of the enlisted men serves throughout as an ironic commentary on the general's behavior, but the irony becomes most pronounced in the last third of the novel when Cummings decides to send a patrol to the rear of the Japanese positions for the purpose of determining the feasibility of a daring new plan that he has just conceived. This decision, prompted not by the interests of victory but by vanity and opportunism, results in the death of three men and in immeasurable misery for several others—all of it wasted. Even after the Japanese have surrendered, the patrol (which has not yet heard the news) is still being dragged up Mt. Anaka, again ostensibly in the interests of victory but really in order to further the mad ambitions of the platoon sergeant, Croft.

The army, then, is evil and the individual caught in its grip has only two basic choices: he can either submit without resistance (and eventually be led into identifying himself with his persecutors) or he can try to maintain at least a minimum of spiritual independence. To be sure, there are many degrees of submission, from Stanley's abject brown-nosing to Wilson's easy-going indifference, but only one character among the enlisted men in the book is still completely unbroken by the time we come upon them: the ex-hobo Red Valsen. As for the officers, they are all (with the exception of Hearn) willing instruments of the evil power embodied in Cummings. Like Cummings and Croft, Hearn and Valsen represent the same principle on different levels of articulation and self-consciousness: they are rebels who do what they have to do but who will not permit their minds or their feelings to be drawn into collaboration with the system. The army proves too strong even for them, however, and ultimately both men are beaten down in much the same fashion.

Mailer's intentions are thus perfectly clear. Cummings and Croft exemplify the army's ruthlessness and cruelty, its fierce purposefulness and its irresistible will to power, while Hearn and Valsen together make up a picture of the rebellious individual who, for all *his* determination and courage, is finally defeated in an unequal contest. But no sooner do we become aware of this intention than we notice that there are forces at work in the novel whose effect is to subvert the general scheme. The most insidious of these, perhaps, is Mailer's tone: *The Naked and the Dead* simply does not *sound* like a book drawing up an angry indictment, though the things it says explicitly provide plenty of ground for indignation. The tone, indeed, is rather more disinterested than

partisan; it is the tone of a man whose capacity for political indignation is inhibited by a keen sense of the world as a very complicated place, not easily to be understood by grand formulas. And
the strength of this sense manifests itself unmistakably in Mailer's
treatment of Valsen and Hearn, who turn out to be less sympathetic than their role in the general scheme would seem to require, just as Cummings and Croft somehow develop into more
admirable figures than they were ever meant to be.

Hearn, the rich Harvard graduate, and Valsen, the penniless
hobo, have a great deal in common. They are both incapable of
attaching themselves to anything or anyone, and they share the
nihilistic belief that "everything is crapped up, everything is
phony, everything curdles when you touch it." Their rebellion
against the system is sterile and ineffective, for it involves nothing
more than a determination to preserve their "inviolate freedom,"
as Hearn puts it, "from . . . the wants and sores that caught up
everybody [else]." What Mailer tells us in a key passage about
Hearn is also true of Valsen: "The only thing to do is to get by on
style. He had said that once, lived by it in the absence of anything
else. . . . The only thing that had been important was to let no
one in any ultimate issue ever violate your integrity." Style without
content, a vague ideal of personal integrity, a fear of attachment, and a surly nihilistic view of the world are not enough to
save a man in the long run from the likes of Cummings and
Croft, and certainly not enough to endow him with heroic stature
—and Mailer knows it. His desperate effort to redeem Hearn
toward the end comes too late and in any case lacks conviction:
perhaps the weakest passage in the whole novel is the one dealing
with Hearn's decision on the night before he is killed to resign his
commission and take a principled stand against everything that
Cummings represents.

The same desperation shows through Mailer's effort to deflate
Cummings and Croft. Like Valsen and Hearn, the platoon

sergeant and the general have so much in common that they seem
to be the same person in two different incarnations. They are
both immensely competent; they are both very brave; they are
both contemptuous of weakness; they both suffer from a sexually
determined hunger to dominate. Most important of all, what they
are both pursuing is the dream of absolute freedom, the dream of
exercising will without obstruction or limit. Man, Cummings tells
Hearn, is a being "in transit between brute and God," and his
deepest urge is to "achieve God." It is this urge that drives Croft
to drag the platoon up Mt. Anaka, just as it provokes Cummings
to feats of military brilliance. But it is also what establishes the
two men as the *natural* heroes of *The Naked and the Dead*. If life
is truly what *The Naked and the Dead* shows it to be—a fierce
battle between the individual will and all the many things that
resist it—then heroism must consist in a combination of strength,
courage, drive, and stamina such as Cummings and Croft exhibit and
that Hearn and Valsen conspicuously lack. Moreover, Cummings
and Croft are the only characters who point to anything like an
adequate response to life as we see it in the novel. They are, of
course, reactionaries, but they demonstrate (as reactionaries often
do) the workings of the radical spirit—which is to say that the
principle of their behavior is a refusal to accept the limitations
inherent in any given situation as final, a refusal stemming from
the conviction that the situation itself need not be regarded as
final in advance. The trouble with Hearn and Valsen is their inability to transcend the terms of the given; they know perfectly
well that these terms are intolerable, yet they cannot envisage any
conditions other than the ones before their eyes, and therefore
they are reduced to apathy, cynicism, and despair. Croft and
Cummings also know that the terms are intolerable, but the
knowledge acts as a stimulus to their energies and a goad to their
imagination. Though the laws of nature seem to prohibit a man
from climbing to the top of Mt. Anaka, Croft, who cannot bear

to remain imprisoned within the boundaries of what has already been accomplished, dares to attempt the climb, while Hearn and Valsen shrug helplessly at the sight of the peaks: like liberalism itself, they lack the vision and the drive to push toward the top of the mountain. All this being the case, Mailer either had to give up his liberalism or forcibly prevent Croft and Cummings from running away with *The Naked and the Dead* altogether. Because he was not yet ready to write liberalism off and because it seemed impossible to find virtue in Cummings and Croft without also finding virtue in fascism, he had no alternative but to violate the emotional logic of his novel by destroying them as best he could. The destruction of Croft is spread thin throughout the novel, but the disposal of Cummings is only effected at the end, when Mailer contrives by a shocking twist of plot to rob him of credit for winning the campaign.

The Naked and the Dead, then, shows an exceptionally gifted young writer in the years immediately after the war discovering what he did not know he knew—that American liberalism is bankrupt because it cannot provide an answer to the challenge with which history has presented it. Not only does liberalism confine itself to the terms of the given at a time when there can be no hope of working within these terms, but it is animated by a vision of the world that neither calls forth heroic activity nor values the qualities of courage, daring, and will that make for the expansion of the human spirit. In the "absence of anything else," however, and out of his awareness that it was impossible to "get by on style" as so many intellectuals of his generation were trying to do, Mailer held on stubbornly to his liberal views, even as he was beginning to recognize that his real values tended in an anti-liberal direction. So little, indeed, did liberalism affect his deepest judgments that the most compassionate writing in *The Naked and the Dead* is devoted to the tribulations of the pathological anti-Semite Gallagher when he receives the news of his wife's death in childbirth. Fascist or no fascist, Gallagher is a violent, passionate man, and this was enough to turn the balance in his favor, just as the timidity and mediocrity of Roth, Wyman, and Brown are the decisive factors in the adverse judgment Mailer passes on them. Ultimately what Mailer was looking for—and has continued to look for—is not so much a more equitable world as a more exciting one, a world that produces men of size and a life of huge possibility, and this was nowhere to be found in the kind of liberalism to which he committed himself in the earliest phase of his literary career.

It is characteristic of Mailer—and, I believe, of the essence of his strength as a novelist—that he never pays much attention to intellectual fashion. In 1948, when everyone of any sophistication understood that Henry Wallace had been duped by the Communists, Mailer was campaigning vigorously for the Progressive party, and if this amounted to a confession of political naivety, it also exhibited a healthy reluctance on his part to be guided by the experience of others. He must always work everything out for himself and by himself, as though it were up to him to create the world anew over and over again in his own experience. He abandoned what was then being called "unreconstructed" liberalism only when he could see at first hand why it was wrong to support it, and even then he did so in his own good time and for his own special reasons. Certainly he must be the sole American example of a liberal who responded to the cold war by rushing to embrace revolutionary socialism. There was nothing "nostalgic" about Mailer's new radicalism; only a man who had been affected by Marx and Trotsky down to the core would have been capable of writing *Barbary Shore,* and it is because he was so profoundly affected that he could blithely ignore all the good arguments against Marx and Trotsky that were in currency at the time. It would be impossible to guess from a reading of this novel that the case it constructs with such loving care had ever been challenged or refuted or in the least damaged. Nor would it be easy to guess that objective conditions played their own imperturbable part in the break-up of revolutionary socialism as an active political movement. Everything in *Barbary Shore* seems to hang on the will of the people involved, and in this sense Mailer is right to describe the book as "existentialist" in spirit.

In Marx and Trotsky, Mailer found a system that brought the courage, vision, and uncompromising determination of Cummings and Croft into the service of freedom and equality rather than class and privilege, and consequently there is no conflict between idea and feeling in *Barbary Shore* of the kind we have seen operating in *The Naked and the Dead*. But if *Barbary Shore* exhibits an almost perfect internal coherence, it also suffers from a certain straining for effect, a certain shrillness and melodramatic solemnity of tone often verging on the pretentious that contrast very sharply with the flawless pitch of *The Naked and the Dead*. The source of this trouble seems to be Mailer's unwillingness to make any use whatever of the techniques he learned to handle so well in *The Naked and the Dead* and his attempt to write in a completely new style. Here again we see him beginning from scratch, repudiating the help of his own past as vigorously as he repudiates the help of everyone else's. But there is more to Mailer's desertion of realism than that. To write realistic fiction a novelist must believe that society is what it seems to be and that it reveals the truth about itself in the personalities it throws up, the buildings it builds, the habits and manners it fosters; all the writer need do is describe these faithfully, selecting whatever details seem to him most sharply revealing and significant, and the truth will be served. But Mailer's point in *Barbary Shore* is precisely that our society is *not* what it seems to be. It seems to be prosperous, vigorous, sure of itself, and purposeful, whereas in fact it is apathetic, confused, inept, empty, and in the grip of invisible forces that it neither recognizes nor controls. To write about this society as though the truth of it lay embedded in its surface appearances would be to endow it with a solidity and substantiality that it simply does not possess. The only hope of making any sense of such a society is with reference to the invisible forces that work in and through it and that cannot be described but that can be talked about abstractly and pictured allegorically. In delineating the world of the cold war, then, what Mailer tries to do is convey a sense of the strangeness of the way things are and to evoke a feeling for the overpowering reality of the invisible forces that supply a key to this strangeness.

Since an extremely bad press and a climate unfavorable to political radicalism resulted in a tiny readership for *Barbary Shore*, let me summarize its plot briefly before making any further observations. Most of the action takes place in a rooming house in Brooklyn Heights which turns out to be the refuge of a man calling himself McLeod, who—we eventually learn—had once been notorious throughout the world as the "Hangman of the Left Opposition." After breaking with the Communist party on the signing of the Nazi-Soviet pact, McLeod had come to the United States to work for the State Department and had subsequently run off again, this time to devote himself to a Marxist analysis of why the revolution went wrong. An FBI agent, Hollingsworth, is also living in the rooming house under an assumed identity, and the plot centers around his efforts to recover a mysterious "little object" which had disappeared from the State Department along with McLeod. Neither Hollingsworth nor anyone else knows what the "little object" is, but he assumes that it must be worth a fortune and is planning to steal it himself once he gets it away from McLeod. The landlady, Guinevere, a former burlesque queen secretly married to McLeod, is in league with Hollingsworth, and he also has the help of a girl named Lannie Madison who had literally been driven out of her mind by the assassination of

Trotsky and who hates McLeod because he is the "undertaker of the revolution." The story is told by another tenant, Michael Lovett, a would-be novelist who is a victim of total amnesia and so can remember nothing whatever of his past but who, it develops, had been almost as deeply involved in the Trotskyite movement as Lannie. In the end, Lovett decides to devote his life once again to the hopes that had been shattered for him by the wartime collapse of revolutionary socialism, and this decision makes it possible for McLeod to pass the "little object" on to him instead of surrendering it to Hollingsworth, as he had finally agreed to do. In a rather hasty climax, McLeod commits suicide, Hollingsworth runs off with Guinevere before the police arrive, and Lannie is taken into custody. Lovett is left alone with McLeod's will and the "little object," charged with the responsibility of keeping the flame of "socialist culture" alive while he waits for the apocalyptic war that is inevitably to come, hoping against hope that out of the conflagration a new opportunity may arise for realizing the goals that were betrayed in the first great revolution of this century.

Barbary Shore is obviously an allegory, but of what? Most of the reviewers in 1951 took it to be an extravagant view of McCarthyism, but McCarthyism as such is actually a negligible element in the book. Mailer's real subject is the effect on modern life of the failure of the Russian revolution, and if there is an extravagant assumption at work in *Barbary Shore*, it is that *all* our difficulties (political, spiritual, psychological, and sexual) are directly traceable to this failure. "The growth of human consciousness in this century demanded—for its expanding vitality—that a revolution be made," Mailer wrote some years later, and in this sentence, I think, we have the key to *Barbary Shore*. The Russian revolution figures here not as one important historical event among many but (in the words of Lovett) as "the greatest event in man's history," the culmination of an evolutionary process dictated by the inner necessities of the human spirit. The race, in Mailer's view, must either grow into greater possibilities or retreat into less; there can be no stagnation. But the retreat into less is not merely a matter of shrinking or cowering; it involves a disruption of the whole organism, a radical dislocation—it is a disease that infects the life of individuals no less than the behavior of nations. *Barbary Shore* is an investigation of this disease, a pathology of the modern spirit.

The two characters in the book who have been most directly affected by the failure of the revolution are Lovett and Lannie. After his first political discussion with McLeod, Lovett begins to recall his days as a member of a Trotskyite study group, and he describes them in a remarkably evocative passage:

> I was young then, and no dedication could match mine. The revolution was tomorrow, and the inevitable crises of capitalism ticked away in my mind with the certainty of a time bomb, and even then could never begin to match the ticking of my pulse. . . . For a winter and a spring I lived more intensely in the past than I could ever in the present, until the sight of a policeman on his mount became the Petrograd proletariat crawling to fame between the legs of a Cossack's horse. . . . There was never a revolution to equal it, and never a city more glorious than Petrograd.

Lovett's amnesia is the consequence of the death of this passion, and its effect has been to cut him off from everything, including his own experience. He represents the modern consciousness, and the weird unfamiliar world that we see through his eyes is in fact intended as a picture of the world we all inhabit. In Lannie, we get an image of the modern consciousness in its most violently pathological aspect. The loss of hope in her case has taken the form of guilt for having presumed to think "that there was a world we could make," and her insanity consists in a total surrender to the given—submitting herself with grim enthusiasm to the brutal handling of Hollingsworth and to the bewildered narcissism of Guinevere. This surrender constitutes insanity because the given (as Lannie herself says in an extraordinary outburst to Lovett) is a world whose nature has been most sharply revealed in the Nazi death camps. What follows from the surrender, moreover, is a frantic attempt to reinterpret the moral meaning of things: "There is neither guilt nor innocence," she tells Lovett, "but there is vigor in what we do or the lack of it," and it is in Hollingsworth and Guinevere that she imagines she sees vigor. Hollingsworth she believes to be strong and purposeful, for to her he is the embodiment of those who now rule the earth, while to the raucous, grotesque, and vulgar Guinevere she makes her sick love, calling what Guinevere symbolizes good and beautiful and begging it to discover its goodness and beauty in her eyes, just as she wants only for the powerful to discover their strength in exercising it upon her.

If Lannie and Lovett together make up a picture of the modern consciousness, Guinevere and Hollingsworth must be regarded as different aspects of the disease engendered by the failure of the revolution. Nothing could be more fantastic than the way everyone takes Guinevere to be the fulfillment of his own special desires. Her vitality, however, is only superficial, the air of abundance about her is a lie, and she lacks the wherewithal to deliver on her vast promise. Given all this, I would suggest that she figures in the allegorical scheme as an image of the life outside politics, the attempt to live by and for self, the purely private life, and that she is Mailer's comment on the sorry possibilities of such a life in America today.

Hollingsworth's role is easier to formulate, since it is described explicitly by McLeod in an analysis of the forces that make the Third World War inevitable. Today, he says, "the aim of society is no longer to keep its members alive, but quite the contrary, the question is how to dispose of them." This is "the first stage of cannibalism" in a process leading inexorably to the destruction of the world, and it expresses itself initially in the rise of a class of bureaucrats who come to power "at the very moment they are in the act of destroying themselves." Far from being strong and purposeful, then, Hollingsworth is the creature of conditions he neither controls nor comprehends and the victim of inner compulsions he neither respects nor recognizes. Sick with greed and with homosexual longings, he can only find relief in outbursts of petty sadism and in the symbolic seduction of McLeod (whose crimes, Lannie declares at one point, were responsible for his very existence). Mailer, however, gives him a moment of genuine self-consciousness in which, like a character in poetic drama, he is suddenly permitted to enunciate the principle of his own being with force and conviction:

> More modesty. We ain't equipped to deal with big things. If this fellow came to me and asked my advice, I would take him aside and let him know that if he gives up the pursuits of vanity, and acts like everybody else, he'd get along better. Cause we never know what's deep down inside us . . . and it plays tricks. I don't give two cents for all your papers. A good-time Charley, that's myself, and that's why I'm smarter than the lot of you.

This is the doctrine by which the disease being investigated through Guinevere and Hollingsworth calls itself health and by which the blindness to reality that is one of its major symptoms claims the right to be known as "realism."

At the center of *Barbary Shore* stands McLeod, the incarnation of the revolutionary spirit itself. His biography amounts to a moral history of that spirit—its early achievements, its subsequent crimes, its temporary abdication, and then its agonized attempt to find new strength by a humble return to "theory." The "little object" that McLeod has stolen from the State Department is never identified, but we can be fairly confident in thinking of it as Hope or Dedication or Vision or a "coagulation" of all three—the loss of it is what accounts for the gradual and subtle derangement of the system and the possession of it by this lone individual entails the most fearful of responsibilities. Vision and hope and dedication, at any rate, are the qualities that separate McLeod from all the other characters and that finally enable him to jolt Lovett out of his stupor and to win the support of Lannie. By the rigorous terms set up in *Barbary Shore* he points to the only possible course left to the modern consciousness—which is to hold on with all its might to the "little object" while crying a plague on both your houses to the two contending powers in the cold war who are irrevocably committed to the cause of death. The heritage Mc-Leod passes on is a feeble thing, but it means feeling for Lovett where there was apathy before and relatedness where there was absolute isolation.

What it meant for Mailer, however, was another matter entirely, since the grand heroic life he was looking for could no more be found in revolutionary socialism than in liberalism. If the one is bankrupt in drive, vision, and imagination, the other is dead in practice, frozen in outworn categories, and cut off from the living realities of the present. Several years after the appearance of *Barbary Shore* Mailer declared (in replying to Jean Malaquais' attack on his *Dissent* article "The White Negro") that Marxism had failed in application because it was "an expression of the scientific narcissism we inherited from the nineteenth century" and motivated by "the rational mania that consciousness could stifle instinct." One might almost take this as a criticism of the cold, tense, claustrophobic brilliance of *Barbary Shore* itself; and indeed, Mailer's abandonment of revolutionary socialism in favor of the point of view he calls "Hip" was as much a repudiation of ideological thinking in general as of Marx and Trotsky in particular. Here again we have an example of the curious relation to intellectual fashion that appears to mark the movements of Mailer's mind. Just as he remained untouched by all the sophisticated arguments against "unreconstructed" liberalism that were circulating so energetically through the intellectual atmosphere of 1948 until he had discovered their truth for himself and in his own good time, so he had to go through a period of revolutionary fervor and ideological rigidity before beginning to yearn (as so many former radicals had done before him) for a breath of fresh air and a supple, open-ended point of view. Unlike the great majority of his literary contemporaries, who knew all about the deleterious effects of ideological commitment without ever having tasted the accompanying passion, Mailer was able to experience both the passion and the rigidity on his own pulses, and when he finally turned against ideology it was with the roar of a man betrayed, not with the complacency of the wise at one remove. And again—as in the case of his shift from liberalism to revolutionary socialism—he followed a wholly unexpected path in making his escape from the constrictions of ideological commitment.

In the Hipster (whom he calls the American existentialist) Mailer believes he has found an effective mode of rebellion against the terms of the given neatly combined with the flexibility and openness to life that were lacking in revolutionary socialism. In contrast to Lovett—who had nothing to do once he accepted the "little object" from McLeod but drift from one back alley to another while waiting for the apocalypse to come—the Hipster has developed a strategy for living fully and intensively in the present. He too refuses to have any truck with the world around him and he too recognizes that collective death is the goal toward which our society is moving, but he differs from Lovett in the further refusal to pin his hopes on the future. Having no future, he cares nothing for the past and therefore he is totally consigned to the fluctuating dimensions of the "enormous present." In effect, the

Hipster as Mailer describes him in "The White Negro" is a man who follows out the logic of the situation in which we are all presumably caught: a man who, faced with the threat of imminent extinction and unwilling to be a party to the forces pushing toward collective death, has the courage to make a life for himself in the only way that conditions permit—by pursuing the immediate gratification of his strongest desires at every moment and by any means.

The full consequences of this new position for Mailer's work are yet to emerge, but several results have already become visible in *The Deer Park*—which, though written before "The White Negro," belongs to Mailer's Hip phase—and in the completed sections of the ambitious novel on which he is currently engaged. The most important consequence, perhaps, is that Hip, with its "burning consciousness of the present" and the "terribly charged" quality of experience it involves, has allowed Mailer to make a more intensive use of his great powers of observation than he has done since *The Naked and the Dead*. Whereas *Barbary Shore* seems to have been produced by a mind shut in upon itself and glowing with the febrile intensity of a lonely intellectual passion (it is a book such as might have been written by one of those brooding, distracted students who haunt the pages of Russian literature), *The Deer Park* exhibits a newly liberated capacity for sheer relish in the look and feel and sound of things. Mailer is now back in the world that he deserted in *Barbary Shore*, though it is by no means the same world that he evoked in *The Naked and the Dead*. What he sees in Hollywood is the image of a society that has reached the end of its historical term, a society caught between the values of an age not quite dead and those of a new era that may never crawl its way out of the womb. The defining characteristic of such a society is a blatant discrepancy between the realities of experience and the categories by which experience is still being interpreted—a discrepancy that can make simultaneously for comedy and horror. The reality is that the scruples, inhibitions, and conventions which were once effective in restraining the natural egoism of the individual no longer work very well because the values from which they drew their strength no longer command much respect. No one, however, is willing to admit this, and they all go on talking and sometimes acting as though what they "really" wanted were the things that people used to want when their basic psychological drives were still roughly in harmony with their professed values—when, that is, these values were powerful enough to create internal needs that became almost as pressing as the primary needs themselves. This situation reveals itself in every department of life, but it is in sex that its contours are most clearly defined, and therefore it is on the sexual affairs of his characters that Mr. Mailer concentrates in *The Deer Park*. What he gives us is a remarkable picture of people saddled with all the rhetoric of the monogamous while acting like some primitive tribe that has never heard of monogamy and is utterly bewildered by the moral structure on which this strange institution rests. It is a world of people who talk incessantly about being in love and craving "decent, mature relationships" but who are in fact tightly imprisoned in their own egos and who have no true interest in anything but self. For them sex has become a testing ground of the self: they rate one another on their abilities in bed, and the reward of making love is not so much erotic satisfaction or spiritual intimacy as a sense of triumph at being considered "good." Mailer's attitude toward all this—I mean the attitude built into his tone and his emphases—is very tricky. There is an unmistakable note of shocked disapproval at many of the things he is describing, yet he insists on treating them with the respect due a major fact of experience. What follows from that respect is a highly disciplined refusal to dismiss the "decadent" narcissistic sexuality of his characters either as immoral or (what comes to the same thing) immature, either as sinful or unhealthy.

It would be difficult to exaggerate the originality of this approach, for it is almost impossible to think of another serious American novelist who has even so much as attempted to study contemporary sexual life on its own terms, let alone one who has brought to the subject anything resembling Mailer's readiness to find the organizing principle, the principle of meaning, that may be implicit in these terms.

The Deer Park takes place largely in Desert d'Or, the favorite resort of the Hollywood movie colony, and it centers mainly on Charles Francis Eitel, a famous and very talented director who has been blacklisted for refusing to cooperate with a Congressional investigating committee and who, after holding out for a whole year against all the pressure to capitulate, finally collapses and gives in. This, of course, is the standard Mailer situation—the rebellious individual crushed by the powers that be—but we do not have to read very far into the novel before we realize that Mailer's view of the nature of the conflict has changed considerably since *The Naked and the Dead*. Hearn and Valsen were defeated in a contest against a hopelessly strong adversary; it is not, however, the strength of his adversaries that defeats Eitel. The two producers Teppis and Munshin are formidable enough in their own way but they are also—what Cummings and Croft could never be—figures of comedy and objects of ridicule. For the first time in Mailer, then, victory over the system has become possible to those who can see through it and who are sufficiently brave to act on what they see. Eitel, a sensitive and intelligent man, understands the secret of the system quite as well as the two characters in the novel who succeed in overcoming it—the narrator Sergius and the diabolical young pimp Marion Faye—but he fails because he lacks the courage to disregard "all the power of good manners, good morals, the fear of germs, and the sense of sin," and to turn himself into a complete and ruthless egoist.

Sergius and Marion are thus the natural heroes of the world

of *The Deer Park*, as Cummings and Croft were the natural heroes of *The Naked and the Dead*, and since Mailer is aware of this, there is no need for him to wrench our sympathies in a direction that the novel itself refuses to support. He does, however, make several positive assertions about Sergius and Marion that are as unwarranted aesthetically as the negative assertions made in *The Naked and the Dead* about Cummings and Croft. It is impossible, for example, to believe that the Sergius we see moving around in *The Deer Park* could ever have developed into the author of this novel.* Not only is he simple-minded, unimaginative, affected, and basically sentimental, but (what is perhaps more to the point) utterly dismissing in his view of other people. When Eitel, who has been his good friend, finally capitulates to Teppis and Munshin and the Committee, Sergius cuts him off brutally—he has failed and is therefore entitled to no further consideration. There is no question that this is the final judgment Mailer himself passes on Eitel, but it is only a final judgment and it is qualified and complicated by the rich, full picture we get of the process that brought Eitel to the painfully sorry pass in which we see him in the last chapter of the novel. Now it is hard to credit that the man who could respond so insensitively to his friend's failure would ever have been able to summon up the subtlety and the insight to understand how a failure of this sort comes about. Nor could such a man conceivably have produced the account of Eitel's affair with Elena, where every nuance in the progress of a vastly complicated relationship is registered with a delicacy and a precision that recall Proust himself. He would also have been incapable of the brilliant comic portraits of Munshin and Teppis,

---

* To forestall the obvious objection, I ought to explain that Sergius's role as narrator is comparable not to Nick Carraway's in *The Great Gatsby* but to Marcel's in Proust. Moreover, he is an active character in the story, one of whose purposes is to explain why he rather than Eitel must be considered the true artist.

which are so good precisely because they are *not* dismissing—
Mailer devastates the two producers while allowing them their full
due. Nothing we see of Sergius in the novel could explain how he
might have come to compose the marvellous letter of self-justifica-
tion that the drunken Elena sends to Eitel after she has gone to
live with Marion—that letter in which a girl who has been universally snubbed and patronized because of her social crudity suddenly bursts forth with astonishing power as a woman of feeling
and perception.

But if Sergius could not conceivably be the author of *The Deer
Park*, Eitel very easily could; what Mailer has done here is to
endow Sergius with Eitel's sensibility, just as he tries to endow
Marion's nihilism with grandiose theological significance. The
reason, I think, can be found in "The White Negro," where
Mailer tells us that the nihilism of the Hipster is really a creative
force. In Hip "incompatibles have come to bed, the inner life
and the violent life, the orgy and the dream of love, the desire to
murder and the desire to create." Yet the curious thing is that the
Hipster who "lives out, acts out, follows the close call of his instinct as far as he dares," who is the herald of a revolution moving
"backward toward being and the secrets of human energy," and
whose subversiveness takes the form of a constant pursuit of immediate gratification—the curious thing is that this "adventurer"
of the night is deeply suspicious of feeling and mortally afraid of
passion. The nihilism of Marion Faye, for example, amounts to a
rebellion *against* feeling, a kind of Nietzschean repudiation of his
"civilized" or Christian self. Everything he does is done precisely
because it is repugnant to him, and he believes that "there is no
pleasure greater than that obtained from a conquered repugnance."
He is not naturally cruel and therefore he forces himself to be
hideously cruel; he is not naturally vicious and therefore he cultivates the vices with the grimness of a hermit scouring himself in
the desert. Similarly with Sergius, who bends all his efforts toward

the perfection of a style based on the suppression of spontaneous feeling: above all he wants to be *cool*.

The irony is that with Sergius and Marion we are back again to Hearn—and he is still trying to get by on style and an ideal of personal integrity. It is much the same style and derives from much the same source (the unavailability of radical political solutions), but in the rank atmosphere of cold-war stalemate it has grown and matured and begun to mistake itself for a portentously weighty philosophy. At the time of the Korean War, when the apocalypse seemed about to descend at any moment, Hearn (who had been killed off in *The Naked and the Dead* before his newly formed resolve to throw off his surly nihilism could be tested) reappeared in *Barbary Shore* split into the amnesiac Lovett and the madwoman Lannie. The loss of the political faith that would have sustained him in the 30's was now seen by Mailer as worse than simply a sign of spiritual inadequacy—it was a sickness of the mind and a disease of the soul. But his brave attempt to recapture that faith proved to be only a dramatic gesture in the face of a dramatic situation; when the situation lost its drama and settled into the dull round of aimless anxiety that has marked the Eisenhower years, the gesture lost its air of glory, as all apocalyptic gestures inevitably do when the apocalpyse itself takes too long in coming. Under these circumstances, Mailer turned back to the old Hearn and began to cast about for hidden resources of creativity where before he had seen only the emptiness of mere style, and for stature where before he had perceived only a well-intentioned mediocrity. In identifying himself finally with Hearn, he has in effect acknowledged his kinship to the intellectuals of his own generation—that generation of whose failings he has always been the most intransigent critic and whose qualities he has always tried so hard to extirpate from his own character. His espousal of Hip indicates that he is still trying—for what else is Hip as he defines it but a means of turning away in

despair (as most of his contemporaries have done) from the problems of the world and focusing all one's attention on the problems of the self without admitting that this must automatically entail a shrinking of horizons, a contraction of the sense of possibility, a loss of imaginative freedom?

One can only sympathize with Mailer's latest effort to maintain
a sense of huge possibility, even if one is totally out of sympathy
with some of the doctrines he has recently been preaching. In my
opinion, his great mistake is to attribute direction and purpose to
the Hipster (and I think that the weakness of Sergius and Marion
as imaginative creations indicates that the novelist in Mailer is
once again resisting the commands of the theoretician). Hipsterism, it seems to me, is a symptom and not a significant protest,
a spasmodic rather than an organized response. The Hipster is the
product of a culture (exemplified beautifully in the Hollywood
of *The Deer Park*) whose official values no longer carry any moral
authority, and he reacts to the hypocrisy, the lying, and the self-
deception that have contaminated the American air during the
cold-war period by withdrawing into a private world of his own
where everything, including language, is stripped down to what
he considers the reliable essentials. To this extent, his response to
the America of Eisenhower bears a certain resemblance to Hemingway's response to the America of Woodrow Wilson. As many
critics have pointed out, Hemingway's prose was generated by the
wish to liberate language from the fine lying rhetoric in which
Wilsonian idealism had cloaked the horrid realities of the First
World War; like the personal style Hemingway elaborated in his
stories—the code of courage and craft in the face of a constantly
threatening universe—the prose style itself was the expression of an
effort to establish a truth of human experience that would be proof
against the distorting encrustations of "culture" and "civilization,"
a truth (as it were) of the state of nature, a truth at rock bottom.
But the difference between Hemingway and the Hipster is the

difference between mastering a bad situation and being victimized by it, between exercising intelligence, sensibility, and discipline in order to overcome the rot of history and seizing upon the rot of history as an excuse for resigning from the painful responsibility to exercise the mind at all.

If it is true that Mailer has been reading things into Hip that are simply not there—and just those things that Hip would need to satisfy his demand for size and importance and a sense of huge possibility—then we can be fairly certain that sooner or later his restless imagination will light out for some other territory. Indeed, he has already shown signs of an impulse to drop his original emphasis on the political significance of Hip in favor of what he takes to be its theological implications. The idea, apparently, is that God is "no longer" omnipotent and therefore needs the help of man to fulfill the "enormous destiny" with which He has been charged (by whom Mailer does not say). Here is how he put it spontaneously to an interviewer:

> . . . I think that the particular God we can conceive of is a god whose relationship to the universe we cannot divine; that is, how enormous He is in the scheme of the universe we can't begin to say. But almost certainly, He is not all-powerful; He exists as a warring element in a divided universe, and we are a part of—perhaps the most important part—of His great expression, His enormous destiny; perhaps He is trying to impose upon the universe His conception of being against other conceptions of being very much opposed to His. Maybe we are in a sense the seed, the seed-carriers, the voyagers, the explorers, the embodiment of that embattled vision; maybe we are engaged in a heroic activity, and not a mean one. . . .

The attraction of this fantastic collection of ancient Christian heresies for Mailer comes out explicitly a little later in the interview:

This involves new moral complexities which I feel are far more interesting than anything the novel has gotten into yet. It opens the possibility that the novel, along with many other art forms, may be growing into something larger rather than something smaller, and the sickness of our times for me has been just this damn thing that everything has been getting smaller and smaller and less and less important, that the romantic spirit has dried up. . . . We're all getting so mean and small and petty and ridiculous, and we all live under the threat of extermination. . . .

We get some notion of what Mailer means by these "new moral complexities" from the prologue to his novel-in-progress which was published in the Fall 1958 issue of *Partisan Review* under the title "Advertisements for Myself on the Way Out." The reader, he announces, must be prepared "for a dissection of the extreme, the obscene and the unsayable" in this "tale of heroes and villains, murderers and suicide, orgy-masters, perverts, and passionate lovers," and it is abundantly clear that the exploration of these "mysteries" is to be made without the help of any traditional moral assumptions. Murder is not necessarily to be regarded as evil, perversion is not necessarily to be considered perverse, suicide is not necessarily to be looked upon as an act of simple self-destruction, and so on. We can now only wait to see what comes of all this, and Mailer being so unpredictable a writer, the one safe guess we can make is that it will turn out to be very different from what many readers of "Advertisements" have assumed—very different and very much more exciting than most of the fiction that is being produced by most of the other novelists of his sorely beleaguered generation.

[1959]

The Adventures of Saul Bellow

Most serious critics today—at least those who have concerned themselves at all with current writing—would probably single out Saul Bellow as the leading American novelist of the postwar period. There are many reasons for this. First of all, Bellow is an intellectual, by which I do not only mean that he is intelligent, but also that his work exhibits a closer involvement with ideas than the work of most other writers in this period. Alfred Kazin, one of his warmest admirers, for example, calls attention to the fact that Bellow's characters "are all burdened by a speculative quest, a need to understand their particular destiny within the general problem of human destiny," and he compares Bellow to " 'metaphysical' American novelists like Melville, for he identifies man's quest with the range of the mind itself." Nor is it simply that Bellow is concerned with ideas; the concern itself operates on a high level of sophistication and complexity—higher, even, than Norman Mailer's, if not more audacious. He is an educated, exquisitely self-conscious writer, at the opposite pole from someone like James Jones, and yet not in the least academic or Alexandrian. His books, whatever else we may say of them, *mean* something: they are charged with the urgency and the passion of a man to whom the issues he writes about are matters of life and death. And finally, Bellow is a stylist of the first order, perhaps the greatest virtuoso of language the novel has seen since Joyce.

But these qualities alone do not account for the special, almost personal, interest that serious critics have always taken in Bellow. For an adequate explanation, we also have to look, I believe, at the changing historical context out of which his novels have come and in terms of which their impact has been registered. Bellow began writing fiction at a time when the literary avant-garde in this country had reached a point of sheer exhaustion, and when the moral and social attitudes associated with it no longer seemed relevant either to life or to literature—and he was the first gifted American novelist to search for another mode of operation and a more viable orientation to the world of the postwar period. Since a large and influential body of intellectuals was engaged on a similar quest, Bellow naturally assumed a position as spokesman and leader. There is, indeed, a sense in which it may even be said that the validity of a whole new phase of American culture has been felt to hang on whether or not Saul Bellow would turn out to be a great novelist.

The direction in which Bellow would find himself going in search of this new orientation was evident as far back as his first novel, *Dangling Man*, a short bitter book about a Chicago intellectual who is told to hold himself in readiness for the army and then waits around in lonely idleness for nearly a year before the draft board finally acts. If we think of *Dangling Man* as a war novel, we can see how far Bellow's starting-point was from Mailer's, to whom the experience of war offered an opportunity for establishing continuity with the past—with, that is, the conventions of naturalism and the progressive ideas that were its traditional ally. The war for Bellow did not mean an exposure to the great realities of hardship, violence, and death; nor did it mean a confrontation between the virtuous individual and the vicious instrument of a vicious society. On the contrary: it meant the disruption of continuity with the past, the explosion of a neat system of attitudes that had for a time made life relatively easy to manage. These attitudes can be summed up in the word "aliena-tion," provided we understand that the term refers not merely to the doctrines of a small group of radicals bred on Marx, but to the hostile posture toward middle-class society adopted by nearly all the important writers of the modern period, whatever their particular political persuasion. T. S. Eliot and Ezra Pound on the right, or the largely non-political Hemingway, Fitzgerald, and Faulkner, were no less "alienated" from the America of the 20's and 30's than John Dos Passos and James T. Farrell on the left. What distinguished the 30's in this regard is simply that a temporary alliance was struck between the avant-garde in literature and radicalism in politics, so that a phenomenon like *Partisan Review* could develop, and a critic like Edmund Wilson could conclude his book on symbolism with the assertion that Marxism had provided a "practical" answer to the questions posed by the modernist movement. Those writers and intellectuals who decided around the time of the Moscow trials that Stalin had betrayed the revolution might altogether have lost their faith in the possibility of a practical solution to the spiritual problems of the age if not for the fact that a third alternative presented itself in the form of a new proletarian revolution led by Trotsky. With America's entry into the war, however, the few shreds of revolutionary hope that had managed to survive the end of the decade disintegrated completely. Yet the collapse of revolutionary hopes only killed the belief in a *practical* or political solution to the spiritual problems of the age; it did not kill the problems themselves, nor did it destroy the sharpness with which writers and intellectuals experienced those problems. (That was left to the 50's to accomplish.)

From this perspective, we can see why *Dangling Man* ought to be called a prescient book. Published in 1944, it was one of the first expressions of the dislocation that set into American intellectual life during the 40's, when a great many gifted and sensitive people were quite literally dangling, like the Joseph of Bellow's novel, between two worlds of assumption and were forced back upon themselves to struggle with all the basic questions that had for so long been comfortably settled. At 27 Joseph has not only repudiated the radicalism of his immediate past, but has come to believe that there can be no political answers to problems of the spirit. There is, he admits, something about modern society that creates special and unprecedented difficulties for the individual who aspires to the best that mankind has been able to accomplish—to wholeness of being, grace of style, and poise of spirit. But he also feels that we abuse the present too much: surely it must still be possible to do again what so many others have done before. Though he continues to "suffer from a feeling of strangeness, of not quite belonging to the world," he refuses to accept alienation as a strategy for getting by. Alienation, he says, "is a fool's plea. . . . You can't banish the world by decree if it's in you. . . . What if you declare you are alienated, you *say* you reject the Hollywood dream, the soap opera, the cheap thriller? The very denial implicates you," and if you decide that you want to forget these things, "The world comes after you. . . . Whatever you do, you cannot dismiss it." It may even be that it is a "weakness of imagination" that prevents people from seeing "where those capacities have gone to which we once owed our greatness." Nevertheless, a man must protect himself from the world, and if he has no recourse either to alienation as a style of life or to political activism, how is he to live? Perhaps, Joseph thinks, "by a plan, a program . . . an ideal construction, an obsessive device." But it would be better to get along without such an "exclusive focus, passionate and engulfing," partly because there is always "a gap between the ideal construction and the real world, the truth," and partly because "the obsession exhausts the man," often becoming his enemy.

What Bellow is attempting to do here, then, is challenge the standard idea of the heroic that dominates 20th-century literature in general and the fiction of the 30's in particular: the idea that under modern conditions rebellion is the only possible form of heroism. He is saying, in effect, that all the traditional modes of rebellion (including—and perhaps especially—the simple act of conscious dissociation from society) have been robbed of their relevance by the movement of history. Heroism as Bellow envisages it in *Dangling Man* would consist in accepting the full burden of time and place, refusing to hold oneself aloof, and yet managing not to be overwhelmed or annihilated. The image he has in mind, in other words, is neither Prometheus nor Ahab, but Beethoven, Shakespeare, Spinoza—men who have achieved (to use the phrase that was soon to become so fashionable) the tragic sense of life. It goes without saying that Joseph is very far from this goal; but he has the ambition, and the main thing that happens to him in the course of the novel is that he is pushed by suffering into recognizing that the sober, balanced, Olympian attitudes of his earlier self were an evasion rather than a stage in his progress. In a word, he discovers evil—the reality that must be contended with before the tragic sense of life can develop. He also discovers how far he still has to go and how pitifully ill-equipped he is for making the journey—which means that he has experienced a necessary humiliation. At the end, he hurls himself with a kind of joyous bitterness into the army and the war, hoping to learn through "regimentation of spirit" what he had been unable to learn as an isolated "free" man.

Yet it is hard to believe that Joseph will do very much better in the army than he managed to do in his lonely room. He is too self-consciously eager for further humiliation, too ready to extract the wisdom from suffering before it even comes to a boil, too little endowed with the robust toughness that would be needed to make him seem a plausible candidate for the destiny to which he aspires. Thus, what Bellow has actually succeeded in creating in Joseph is not a character whose job it will be to find a way of realizing the highest human possibilities under modern conditions, but an extraordinarily intelligent portrait of a type that was to come into great prominence in the years following World War II. Joseph is still the alienated modern man who has been a leading figure in the literature and social thought of the 20th century, but he differs from his immediate ancestors in lacking a plan or program or obsessive device to justify, support, and enrich his estranged condition. Like Mailer's Lovett in *Barbary Shore*, he is doomed to alternate bursts of aimless hysteria and pathological apathy; and again like Lovett, he is forced to drag himself through the world without the help of the past and without a sense of wide future possibilities. ("I, in this room, separate, alienated, distrustful, find in my purpose not an open world, but a closed, hopeless jail. My perspectives end in the walls. Nothing of the future comes to me.") As he himself observes, "the greatest cruelty is to curtail expectations without taking away life completely," and it is to this cruelty that he is exposed, the more so because he can find nothing in the life he leads to "hold and draw and stir" him. Whereas the answer to this predicament was once art (but he is not an artist) or revolution (but revolution is impossible), Joseph's answer is to accept the society of which he is inescapably a part and to work toward transcending it. The fact that this answer exists within the novel only as an abstractly stated proposition rather than a concrete presence, is, of course, a major failing, just as it is the main reason for the book's imaginative thinness. Written in the form of a journal, *Dangling Man* hardly ventures beyond the consciousness of the central character and is so highly self-involved that even when Bellow does move outside Joseph's mind and into the world around him, the novel remains cheerless and claustral, giving the impression of a universe barren of people and things, a kind of desert beaten by the wind and sleet of a foul Chicago winter.

Cheerlessness also characterizes the world of Bellow's second novel, *The Victim* (1947). Here the Chicago winter gives way to a New York summer, and instead of emptiness we get a sense of crowds milling, seething, and sweating. "On some nights New York is as hot as Bangkok" is the opening sentence, and this association of the city with an exotic primitive place is unobtrusively reinforced throughout the narrative, until we begin to understand that what we have in *The Victim* is a vision of the city as a tiny village surrounded on all sides by a jungle that threatens at any moment to spill over and engulf the precarious little human oasis at its center. This is New York seen through the eyes of a writer overwhelmed by the sheer animality of the human species, and nagged by the suspicion that "civilization" may be a gigantic and desperate illusion—and an illusion that is becoming more and more difficult to sustain.

Discussing the conviction he once had of the mildness of his own character and trying to rationalize his horror of violence, Joseph tells us in *Dangling Man* that the famous passage from Hobbes which describes life in the State of Nature as "nasty, brutish, and short" was always present to his mind, and one imagines that the same passage was always present to Bellow's mind as he was writing *The Victim*. The central figure, Leventhal, is a man of even greater spiritual timidity than Joseph, though not being an intellectual, he has no theories to bolster his timidity. He goes through life with the feeling of having "got away" with something, by which he means that he might very easily have fallen among "that part of humanity of which he was frequently mindful—the lost, the outcast, the overcome, the effaced, the ruined."

But it gradually becomes clear in the course of the novel that what Leventhal really fears is crossing over a certain boundary of the spirit, beyond which lies not merely failure, but violence and the darker passions: he is afraid of being "drowned at too great a depth of life." In order to keep from drifting out of the shallow water, he has always resorted to various psychological tricks ("principally indifference and neglect"), and *The Victim* is about a crisis that crashes through his wall of defenses and jolts him into reconsidering his life and his character. The crisis takes the form of his pursuit by the down-and-out anti-Semite of patrician origin, Kirby Allbee, who accuses Leventhal of having maliciously caused his ruin, and (less importantly) Leventhal's simultaneous involvement in the illness and death of his brother's child. With great subtlety and brilliance Bellow traces the process by which Leventhal is drawn into acknowledging responsibility for Allbee, not because Allbee's accusations against him are justified (they are not), but because he learns to recognize a kinship with Allbee himself, who embodies everything he most fears in the world and in his own soul.

From a purely literary point of view, *The Victim* represents a great step forward for Bellow. Whereas in *Dangling Man* we get the feeling that the few dramatic incidents included are brought in only to create the spurious impression that Joseph's theoretical speculations are anchored in the events of his life, in *The Victim* the abstract metaphysical questions that are so important to Bellow arise naturally and spontaneously (and ingeniously) out of the story. The book, moreover, is beautifully constructed and paced, so that Leventhal's growing sympathy for the repulsive Allbee sneaks up on the reader as insidiously and surprisingly as it sneaks up on him. The sub-plot is managed with less dexterity; there is something perfunctory and perhaps a little schematic about it, as though Bellow thought it necessary to provide Leventhal with an experience of death in case his crisis should seem lacking in dimension and profundity.

From the point of view of Bellow's quest for a new orientation to the world around him, however, *The Victim* is not so much an advance over *Dangling Man* as a companion piece to it. If *Dangling Man* challenges the strategy of alienation under the altered conditions of the postwar period, *The Victim* launches an assault on the prudence, caution, and spiritual timidity that Bellow believes to lie behind alienation in a post-radical world. "You people take care of yourselves before everything," Allbee says to Leventhal. "You keep your spirit under lock and key. . . . You make it your business assistant, and it's safe and tame and never leads you toward anything risky. Nothing dangerous and nothing glorious. Nothing ever tempts you to dissolve yourself." There is, of course, a certain justice in the charge, as Leventhal goes on to discover, but there is also something to be said in his favor. He lives by a sensible idea of responsibility as against Allbee's insistence that no one can be held responsible for the terrible things that happen to him, and he knows far better than Allbee that a price has to be paid for avoiding the awful dangers of "cannibalism." At the same time, however, Leventhal has been denying the darker sides of his nature, and it is these that he learns to respect and acknowledge in the course of his relations with Allbee. He comes to see that if Allbee is an animal and a monster, so too is he an animal and a monster, capable of savagery and malice and gratuitous cruelty, and he also comes to recognize that his timidity has robbed him of warmth and sympathy and the capacity to reach into the being of another.

Yet it is important to notice that these profound lessons carry no startling practical consequences. In an epilogue to the novel, we come upon Leventhal some years later, and the only change that has taken place is that "Something recalcitrant seemed to have left him; he was not exactly affable, but his obstinately unrevealing expression had softened. . . . And, as time went on, he lost the feeling that he had, as he used to say, 'got away with it.' " In other words, he is now more at peace with himself than before. He has not ventured into the "depths" that he once feared would drown him; he has merely (like a successfully analyzed patient) learned something about himself that has helped him come to terms with the world and make a settlement. During his difficulties with Allbee, he had reflected that "Everybody wanted to be what he was to the limit. . . . Therefore hideous things were done, cannibalistic things. Good things as well, of course. But even there, nothing really good was safe. . . . There was something in people against sleep and dullness, together with the caution that led to sleep and dullness." *The Victim* is concerned with criticizing "the caution that led to sleep and dullness," but Bellow wishes to do so in a complicated way, never blinking at the "cannibalistic things" that can erupt once this caution is overthrown. In the end, he does not advocate that it be overthrown; all he does is recommend that the anti-cautious impulses be acknowledged and accepted, and it is perhaps his feeling that nothing more ambitious can be offered that accounts for the oppressively pessimistic tone of the novel. I call it oppressive because it is a pessimism over the human condition even darker than Freud's in *Civilization and Its Discontents*. In *The Victim*, the making of a settlement (that is, the stifling of the instincts) is seen as bringing no positive rewards or compensations of any significance—no increase of energy through sublimation, no powerful Faustian drive; it merely has the negative virtue of preventing the outbreak of "cannibalism." Nor is Bellow's pessimism here of a piece with the grim view of life that led Hobbes to insist on the necessity of a strong social authority. Bellow wants no strong authority to enforce repression, and he knows that such authorities as do exist are—deservedly—in a seriously weakened condition. *The Victim* is thus highly characteristic of the postwar ethos, restricting itself to a consciousness of how difficult and complicated things are and seeing little hope of remedial action of any kind whatever. Taking itself as a tragic view of life, this attitude is in reality a form of the very cautiousness and constricted sense of possibility that Bellow attacks both in *Dangling Man* and *The Victim*.

By the early 50's, however, while Bellow was working on *The Adventures of Augie March*, the ethos of which his first two novels had been among the early premonitions was also in process of consolidating itself, and as its outlines grew clearer, it gained steadily in confidence and militancy. The first stage (reflected, it may be, in the pessimism of *The Victim*) was an almost reluctant admission that America had become the only protection against the infinitely greater menace of Soviet totalitarianism. But what began as a grim reconciliation to the lesser of two evils soon turned into something rather more positive, ranging from the jingoism of a few ex-radicals who travelled as far to the right as they could go, to the upsurge of an exhilarating new impulse to celebrate the virtues of the American system and of American life in general. So powerful was this new impulse that it even found its way into the pages of *Partisan Review*, which had always been the very symbol of the attitudes now under attack.

The spiritual atmosphere of this phase of American cultural history was fully captured and expressed for the first time in a novel by *The Adventures of Augie March*, which perhaps explains why the book was greeted with such universal enthusiasm and delight when it appeared in 1953. The attitudes of what its enemies called "the age of conformity" and its friends "the age of intellectual revisionism" were all there; the prevailing tone of the age was there; and a new Bellow, reborn into exuberance and affirmation, was there too. "I am an American, Chicago-born," ran the opening words of the novel, and anyone who knew Bellow's earlier work immediately understood him to be asserting that he had managed to cut through all the insoluble problems over the proper relation of the self to society with which he had been wrestling for ten years—cut through them to this wonderfully simple declaration of his identity. The man who had been dangling had finally come to rest in a new maturity of style and vision; the victim of a cruel universe offering only the consolations of an uneasy settlement was now rushing headlong into a world of possibility: he was discovering the richness and glory of the life around him, and everywhere he looked there were treasures to reap. Instead of a bleak Chicago or a threatening New York, we are swept in *Augie* through whole continents, each more vividly colored than the other. Instead of puny characters forever taking their own pulses and dragging themselves onerously from one day to the next, we are introduced in *Augie* to huge figures like the crippled Einhorn whom Bellow belligerently compares to Caesar, Machiavelli, Ulysses, and Croesus ("I'm not kidding when I enter Einhorn in this eminent list"); like Grandma Lausch, who is portrayed as a giant among formidable old women; and like Thea Fenchel, who is reviving the art of falconry and captures poisonous snakes with her bare hands. Most important of all, perhaps, we get a new prose style, the first attempt in many years to experiment with the language in fiction. In contrast to earlier experiments, however, this one expresses not an attempt to wall off the philistines, but precisely a sense of joyous connection with the common grain of American life. And finally, there was the form of the novel itself. Bellow had done his duty by the well-made novel, writing in the shadow of the accredited greats who were sanctioned both by the academy and the literary quarterlies—Flaubert, Kafka, Gide, Henry James—and again he anticipated a widespread feeling in his implicit declaration that this tradition had become a burden rather than a help. For *Augie* he looked back to another tradition —the picaresque, with its looseness of structure, its saltiness of language, its thickness of incident, its robust extroversion. And the fact that one of the greatest of all American novels (whose title is echoed by his own) itself derived from this tradition made it all the more obvious that he had hit upon the right mode for a novel that was setting out to discover America and the American dream anew.

In certain respects, Augie March is a familiar figure, an image of modern man living in a hopelessly fluid society, forced to choose an identity because he has inherited none, unable to find a place for himself. He is rootless, cut off, even (if you like) alienated. But far from responding to this situation with the usual anxiety, he is "larky and boisterous," and his rootless condition makes life endlessly adventurous and endlessly surprising. His uncertainty about his own identity, moreover, is represented as a positive advantage, leading not to the narcissistic self-involvement of a Joseph or a Leventhal, but rather to a readiness to explore the world, a generous openness to experience. Nor is his optimism superficial or blind. He understands that there are powerful arguments against his position, and he knows that optimism is a faith which, like any other, must be maintained in the teeth of the opposing evidence. "What I guess about you," one of his friends tells him, "is that you have a nobility syndrome. You can't adjust to the reality situation. . . . You want to accept. But how do you know what you're accepting? You have to be nuts to take it come one come all. . . . You should accept the data of experience." Augie's reply is significant: "It can never be right to offer to die, and if that's what the data of experience tell you, then you must get along without them."

Here, then, was the hero Bellow had been looking for since the start of his literary career; here, it seemed, was a way out of the impasse at which the mode of alienation had arrived—a way that offered the possibility of participating fully in the life of the time without loss of individuality, a way that pointed toward a fusion of mind and experience, sophistication and vitality, intelligence and power. Since this was also the way that so many of Bellow's contemporaries had marked out for themselves, it is not surprising that they should have approached *The Adventures of Augie March* with a ready disposition to take the novel's pretensions wholly at face value. Yet the truth is that like the ethos of which it was the most remarkable reflection, *Augie* was largely the product not of a state of being already achieved, but rather of an effort on Bellow's part to act as though he had already achieved it. As a test case of the buoyant attitudes of the period, in other words, *Augie* fails— and it fails mainly because its buoyancy is embodied in a character who is curiously untouched by his experience, who never changes or develops, who goes through everything yet undergoes nothing.

The strain it cost Bellow to maintain this willed buoyancy becomes most strikingly evident in the prose style he invented for *Augie*. It is a free-flowing style that makes use of three apparently incongruous rhetorical elements—cultivated, colloquial, and American-Jewish—each deriving from a different side of Augie's character and announcing, in the very fact of their having been brought together, the new wholeness of being to which Bellow had always aspired. When it works, as it does at many isolated moments in the novel, this style is capable of extraordinary effects:

> [Mama] occupied a place, I suppose, among women conquered by a superior force of love, like those women whom Zeus got the better of in animal form and who next had to take cover from his furious wife. Not that I can see my big, gentle, dilapidated, scrubbing, and lugging mother as a fugitive of immense beauty from such classy wrath . . .

But the rightness, the poise, and easy mastery of this passage are not typical of *Augie* as a whole. More often Bellow seems to be twisting and torturing the language in an almost hysterical effort to get all the juices out of it:

> The rest of us had to go to the dispensary—which was like the dream of a multitude of dentists' chairs, hundreds of them in a space as enormous as an armory, and green bowls with designs of glass grapes, drills lifted zigzag as insects' legs, and gas flames on the porcelain swivel trays—a thundery gloom in Harrison Street of limestone county buildings and cumbersome red streetcars with metal grillwork on their windows and monarchical iron whiskers of cowcatchers front and rear. They lumbered and clanged, and their brake tanks panted in the slushy brown of a winter afternoon or the bare stone brown of a summer's, salted with ash, smoke, and prairie dust, with long stops at the clinics to let off clumpers, cripples, hunchbacks, brace-legs, crutch-wielders, tooth and eye sufferers, and all the rest.

The frantic and feverish pitch betrays the basic uncertainty that I have been pointing to in the Bellow of *Augie March*: it tells us that there was simply not enough real conviction behind the attitudes out of which the novel was written. And it tells us to expect the radical shift of mood that did indeed come over Bellow in his next book, *Seize the Day*.

Probably it would be foolish to relate this change too closely to the parallel shift in mood that occurred among American intellectuals in general during the same period. Nevertheless, the parallel is worth noticing, for it suggests that the optimism of the intellectuals about America was as strained and willed as the prose of *Augie March* itself. The irrepressible doubts that lurked on the underside of the new optimism were bound to emerge once more as the dreary Eisenhower years wore on, but when they did emerge, it was in a form very different from the ones they had taken in the decades before World War II. To be sure, the old idea that the modern world was suffering from a "loss of values" came back again, but even that idea soon began to seem inadequate to account for the dimensions of the spiritual vacuum that many intellectuals saw lying beneath the surface prosperity and apparent confidence of the Eisenhower Age. The more and more frequent outbreaks of juvenile violence; the sharp rise in the consumption of narcotics (including legal drugs like tranquillizers and sleeping pills); the fantastic divorce rate; the suicides; the breakdowns—all this showed how great a gap had developed between the realities of experience in America and the moral vocabulary of the age.

It is against this background, I think, that the upsurge during the late 50's of various forms of anti-rationalism must be understood. The sudden popularity of Zen, Reichianism, and existentialism reflected the growth of a conviction that the source of our trouble lay deep in the foundations of Western civilization— deeper than politics could reach, deeper than a mere opposition to capitalist society or middle-class values could cure. We were a people so far removed from nature, so lost in abstraction, so cut off from the instinctual that only—as Norman Mailer put it—a "revolution backward toward being" could save us. Bellow, of course, has never gone as far in this direction as Mailer—he has too skeptical a mind to go far in any theoretical direction—but his last two novels, *Seize the Day* and *Henderson the Rain King*, seem to indicate an equally strong awareness on his part of the depth to which the contemporary crisis has cut. The world of *Seize the Day*, indeed, might fairly be compared with the world of the *The Deer Park*, for each in its own way is an image of a society at the end of its historical term, a civilization whose particular compromise with nature has all but broken down.

Like *The Victim*, *Seize the Day* is set in New York, but if Bellow once saw the city as a tiny village holding out desperately against the surrounding jungle, here he sees it as "the end of the world, with its complexity and machinery, bricks and tubes, wires and stones, holes and heights." So far has the divorce of man from nature proceeded that "the fathers are no fathers, and the sons no sons," and money—that most refined of all abstractions—rules in place of the natural affections. Communication is no longer possible under these circumstances ("Every other man spoke a language entirely his own, which he had figured out by private thinking"), and there is no telling "the crazy from the sane, the wise from the fools, the young the old or the sick from the well." Love has disappeared along with communication, and what remains is a world full of lonely men, "a kind of hell [or] at least a kind of purgatory. You walk on the bodies. They are all around. I can hear them cry *de profundis* and wring their hands . . . poor human beasts."

This, then, is a civilization on the edge of collapse:

> Seven per cent of this country is committing suicide by alcohol. Another three, maybe, narcotics. Another sixty just fading away into dust by boredom. Twenty more who have sold their souls to the Devil. Then there's the small percentage of those who want to live. That's the only significant thing in the whole world of today. Those are the only two classes of people there are. Some want to live, but the great majority don't. . . . They don't, or else why these wars? I'll tell you more . . . The love of the dying amounts to one thing; they want you to die with them.

The central figure of the story, Tommy Wilhelm, is one of those who want to live, though it is part of Bellow's complex purpose to reveal this fact only gradually both to the reader and to Wilhelm. He is presented at first as a weak, blundering, self-destructive man riddled with self-pity and totally lacking in the resources of character that would enable him to redeem the mess

he has made of his life. Only when we reach the closing scene do
we realize that his desperate appeals to his father for help and his
wild gamble on the commodities exchange were unconsciously
motivated (like all the crucial decisions he has ever made) by a
saving impulse to liberate himself from the false values that have
always dominated his soul. These values are money and success,
the pursuit of which has perverted a whole civilization, turning
millions of people into slaves of the social system, enemies of
themselves, monsters with murder in their hearts who go resentfully and hideously to their graves never knowing why life has
been so bitter. Indeed, there is probably no more frightening picture of old age in literature than the one Bellow draws in *Seize the
Day*—the men like Wilhelm's father meanly and coldly and
selfishly clutching at his withered life, or like the retired chicken-
farmer Rappaport ("I'm older even than Churchill") who sits day
after day at the commodities exchange greedily waiting for a rise
in rye or barley or lard. This is what the pursuit of success and
money finally amounts to in the world of *Seize the Day*, and it is
what Wilhelm—as he dimly comes to recognize in the closing
pages—has always resisted by blundering over and over again
into failure.

Because of its masterful concentration, its vividness of detail, its
brilliance of characterization, and its grandeur of theme, *Seize the
Day* probably deserves its reputation as the best thing Bellow has
so far done. It is so good, in fact, that one wonders what prevents
it from being great. My guess would be that Bellow was putting
the brakes on himself in writing the story, that he allowed a certain timidity in the face of his own most powerful response to life
—and I mean to life, not to the historical circumstances of the
moment—to soften the impact of his material. This response, to
judge by all those things in his work that carry the most conviction, is one of angry resentment and bitterness—precisely the kind
of bitterness that is expressed in the terrible line in *King Lear*:

"As flies are we to the wanton gods; they kill us for their sport." Even the comic side of his talent participates in this bitterness, for comedy in Bellow's fiction is almost always directed against the utopian theorizers (like Robey, Thea Fenchel, and Bateshaw in *Augie March*), who simply cannot understand how little help there is for being human. For some reason, however, Bellow has never been willing to give his bitterness free rein; he is always trying to stifle it or qualify it, and it is this refusal of anger, I believe, that robs *Seize the Day* of the great power it might have had.

The answer to Wilhelm's predicament, we are given to understand, is love, and we gather from the description of a momentary revelation he had once experienced that by love Bellow means something like the Christians *agapé*. And with a good many Christian writers, he seems to believe that a man's capacity to "seize the day"—that is, to live fully in the present—depends on his capacity to know himself as kin to all other men. The nature to which Bellow wishes to return in *Seize the Day* is not the instinctual nature that Norman Mailer talks about, but nature as the theologians have conceived of it: a harmonious universe ruled over by God, a universe in which man has reassumed his proper place in the cosmic hierarchy. "We are bleeding at the roots, because we are cut off from the earth and sun and stars, and love is a grinning mockery, because, poor blossom, we plucked it from its stem on the tree of Life, and expected it to keep on blooming in our civilized vase on the table." This is not, of course, Bellow; it is D. H. Lawrence. Yet the passage fairly characterizes the doctrinal core of *Seize the Day*, and another remark of Lawrence's points toward the "positive" values implied in the novel: "Augustine said that God created the universe new every day; and to the living, emotional soul this is true. Every day dawns upon an entirely new universe, every Easter lights up an entirely new glory of a new world opening in utterly new flower. And the soul of man and the soul of woman is new in the same way, with the infinite delight of life and the ever-newness of life."

But this is a theory, and Bellow, we know, is skeptical of theories, which is perhaps one reason why he puts these sentiments, cruelly vulgarized, into the mouth of Dr. Tamkin, a charlatan, a fake, and a liar. Making Tamkin the spokesman of his own views, however, is perhaps also his way of saying that today even those who know the truth are caught up in the false values of our civilization—the churches, as it were, are corrupt, the prophets are fools and probably a little crazy. Nevertheless, the fact that he is skeptical of the theory does not prevent Bellow from allowing it to inhibit the response which his story, in its primary emotional impact, demands. "You see," Tamkin tells Wilhelm, "I understand what it is when the lonely person begins to feel like an animal. When the night comes and he feels like howling from his window like a wolf." And Wilhelm agrees. "One hundred falsehoods," he says to himself of Tamkin's remarks, "but at last one truth. Howling like a wolf from the city window. No one can bear it any more. Everyone is so full of it that at last everyone must proclaim it. It! It!" What the reader waits for in *Seize the Day* is exactly this howl, some expression of wrath, some violent uproar which would release the "great knot" in Wilhelm's chest that has been strangling him by inches, and which would express the full extent of Bellow's outrage at life. It never comes. All Bellow gives us at the end is a fit of weeping that, he says, carries Wilhelm "toward the consummation of his heart's ultimate need." We have already been told what this need is—it is love. If, however, Bellow had been ruthless in following out the emotional logic of *Seize the Day*, it would almost certainly have been murder—and *Seize the Day* would almost certainly have become a great book.

In *Henderson the Rain King*, Bellow's latest novel, the ideology of love does not so much inhibit him as obscure his central intention. Returning to the loose picaresque mode of *Augie March*, Bellow tells the story of a middle-aged millionaire, the ne'er-do-well scion of an old patrician family, who runs off to Africa in a state of crisis and is transformed by a series of fantastic adventures he encounters there. The Africa of the novel bears very little relation to the real Africa; it is an imaginary place, and Bellow might have avoided a certain amount of misunderstanding if he had given it an imaginary name. Similarly, if he had presented Henderson in frankly allegorical terms instead of confusing the issue by making him a Hudson Valley aristocrat, he would not have left himself open to the charge of having failed to create a believable hero, or of having failed at the end to put Henderson's regeneration to the test back in the "real" world. In my opinion, while Henderson is obviously not believable as a Hudson Valley aristocrat, he is completely convincing as an allegorical personification of the vague malaise, the sense of aimless drift and unused energy, that seems to afflict a prosperous and spiritually stagnant society like our own. And while Henderson's regeneration cannot be accepted as a total transformation of character, it seems to me wholly credible as an *experience*, the kind of experience that religious converts speak of when they say they have been re-born.

The important question is: to what, precisely, is Henderson re-born? Here and there, and especially in the concluding pages, Bellow makes several pious gestures in the direction of Love, but this only confuses the issue even further, for if anything Henderson is saved by being re-born into more rather than less self-involvement. The transforming revelation he experiences with the help of King Dahfu is that the world from which he has fled is not to be confused with reality: reality is in the self and not in the circumstances or conditions that surround the self. "The world of facts is real, all right, and not to be altered. The physical is all there, and it belongs to science. But then there is the noumenal department, and there we create and create and create." A voice inside him had been crying "*I want! I want! I want!*" He had never known what it wanted, but now he knows:

It wanted reality. How much unreality could it stand? . . . We're supposed to think that nobility is unreal. But that's just it. The illusion is on the other foot. They make us think we crave more and more illusions. Why, I don't crave illusions at all. They say, Think Big. Well, that's baloney of course, another business slogan. But greatness! That's another thing altogether. . . . I don't mean pride, or throwing your weight around. But the universe itself being put into us, it calls out for scope. The eternal is bonded onto us. It calls out for its share. This is why guys can't bear to be so cheap.

With *Henderson*, then, Bellow seems to have come very close to surrendering the idea that the world of postwar America is a rich and inviting world and that the strategy of alienation is—as he called it in *Dangling Man*—a fool's plea. He is still resolutely non-political, for when he talks in *Henderson* about the "world of facts" that cannot be altered, he makes no effort to exempt the world of social facts from the category of the unalterable. So, too, he is still fixed on the notion that it is only spiritual timidity or —to take another phrase from *Dangling Man*—"a weakness of imagination" that robs us of the capacity to achieve true wholeness of being, true grace of style, true poise of spirit. For all that, however, *Henderson*, properly understood, represents a further stage in Bellow's development away from the forced affirmations of *Augie March*—here, at least, as in *Seize the Day*, he writes with a sharp awareness of the extent to which the problems of contemporary life are more than merely a matter of individual pathology. What one awaits is a novel by Bellow that would unambiguously locate the source of the malaise that afflicts Joseph, Leventhal, Wilhelm, and Henderson in the institutions under which they are forced to live—in that particular "world of facts" which belongs not to science but to politics, not to nature but to history, not to the realm of the physical but to "the noumenal department" where we "create and create and create." Bellow could find no better target than this for the rage that is contained within him and that has perhaps always been stifled only for lack of its proper object.

[1959]

The Best Catch There Is

Not long ago, in an article in *Commentary*, Philip Roth complained that the world we live in "is a kind of embarrassment to one's own meager imagination" as a novelist. "The actuality," Roth went on to say, "is continually outdoing our talents, and the culture tosses up figures almost daily that are the envy of any novelist. Who, for example, could have invented Charles Van Doren? Roy Cohn and David Schine? Sherman Adams and Bernard Goldfine? Dwight David Eisenhower?" Anyone who follows the daily newspapers or watches television with some regularity will understand what Roth is getting at. We do often seem to be inhabiting a gigantic insane asylum, a world that, as Roth puts it, alternately stupefies, sickens, and infuriates. No wonder the American writer has so much difficulty "in trying to understand, and then describe, and then make *credible* much of the American reality."

I think Roth's observation goes far toward explaining why Joseph Heller's *Catch-22* has provoked more enthusiasm than any first novel in years. Though ostensibly about an air force squadron in the Second World War, *Catch–22* is actually one of the bravest and most nearly successful attempts we have yet had to describe and make credible the incredible reality of American life in the middle of the 20th century. To describe and make credible; not, however, to *understand:* the secret of Mr. Heller's success lies precisely in his discovery that any effort to understand the incredible is bound to frustrate the attempt to describe it for what it really is. The way to portray insanity, in other words, is to show what insanity looks like, not to explain how it came about.

To be sure, Mr. Heller is a very good writer, with an exceptionally rich talent for comedy (both high and low) and a vitality of spirit that is nothing short of libidinal in its force. But I doubt whether even those virtues would have been enough to produce *Catch–22*; what was needed was the heroic power to resist all the temptations to understanding (or, if you like, sympathy) that must have arisen during the eight years it took to write this novel. I use the word "heroic" here without irony, for I can imagine that Mr. Heller was continually plagued by the fear that if he did not bow more deeply in the direction of simple plausibility, no one would find his story credible, and his characters and the fantastic situations he was putting them through would be understood as comic exaggerations rather than as descriptions of what the world actually does look like to a rational man. Who could have invented Charles Van Doren or Dwight David Eisenhower? Not, surely, a conventional painter of portraits, perhaps not even a great conventional painter of portraits. But Dickens could have invented them—only in this case he would not have been caricaturing (if in fact he was ever caricaturing); he would have been performing an act of photography. So too with Mr. Heller, whose gift for caricature has made it possible for him to achieve a very credible description indeed of the incredible reality around us.

The hero of *Catch–22* is a bombardier named Yossarian who is convinced that everyone is trying to kill him. This idea makes various people angry, especially his friend Clevinger. Clevinger is a man who believes passionately in many principles and who is also a great patriot.

"No one's trying to kill you," Clevinger cried.

"Then why are they shooting at me?" Yossarian asked.

"They're shooting at *everyone*," Clevinger answered. "They're trying to kill everyone."

"And what difference does that make?"

Clevinger is certain that Yossarian is crazy. Yossarian, for his part, has not the slightest doubt that Clevinger is crazy. In fact, everyone is crazy who thinks that any sense can be made out of getting killed. When Yossarian is told that people are dying for their country, he retorts that as far as he can see the only reason he has to fly more combat missions is that his commanding officer, Colonel Cathcart, wants to become a general. Colonel Cathcart is therefore his enemy. So is the German gunner shooting at him while he drops his bombs. So is the Nurse in the hospital who doesn't like him, and so are countless others (including bus drivers all over the world) who want to do him in. He is in constant peril of his life. All men are, but no one seems to realize it as keenly as Yossarian and some of his friends—Dunbar, for example, who cultivates boredom because boredom makes time go slowly and therefore lengthens his life. Everywhere, Yossarian reflects in contemplating the war, "men went mad and were rewarded with flying medals. Boys on every side of the bomb line were laying down their lives for what they had been told was their country, and no one seemed to mind, least of all the boys who were laying down their young lives." But Yossarian minds. He minds so powerfully that he can think of nothing else. After gorging himself on a marvelous meal one day, he wonders awhile if it isn't perhaps "all worth it." But not for long. The very next sentence reads: "But then he burped and remembered that they were trying to kill him, and he sprinted out of the mess hall wildly and ran looking for Doc Daneeka to have himself taken off combat duty and sent home."

Yossarian may mind about getting killed to the point of madness himself, but there is no question that we are meant to take his paranoia not as a disease but as a sensible response to real dangers. Colonel Cathcart, who keeps upping the number of combat missions the men in his command are required to fly before being sent home, is—just as Yossarian says—an idiot who cares only about becoming a general. General Dreedle and General Peckem and Colonel Cargill and Colonel Korn are all idiotic too, always engaged in ridiculous jurisdictional disputes and petty personal rivalries which are usually settled by the mail clerk at headquarters, ex-P.F.C. Wintergreen, through the simple expedient of forwarding one general's communications through channels and dropping the other's (whose prose Wintergreen considers too prolix) into the waste basket. There is also Milo Minderbinder, the mess officer, running a huge syndicate called M & M Enterprises in which the Germans too have a share (Milo even accepts a contract from the Germans to bomb his own outfit). Meanwhile, Yossarian has to go on bombing people he doesn't know, and men on the ground go on firing flak at Yossarian, whom *they* don't know. It is all very strange and bewildering.

The whole system is governed by Catch-22, which permits the authorities to do anything they please while pretending to a respect for the rights of the individual. Catch-22 contains many clauses. The most impressive we learn about early in the book, when the flight surgeon Doc Daneeka explains to Yossarian why he cannot ground a crazy man, despite the fact that the rules require him to ground anyone who is crazy. The catch is that the crazy man must ask to be grounded, but as soon as he asks he can no longer be considered crazy, since "a concern for one's own safety in the face of dangers that are real and immediate is the process of a rational mind." Yossarian is "moved very deeply by the absolute simplicity of this clause of Catch–22." So is Doc Daneeka, whose terror of death (and of being shipped to the Pacific where so many dread diseases can be contracted) is almost as great as Yossarian's and whose attitude toward the world is correspondingly similar: "Oh I'm not complaining. I know there's a war on. I know a lot of people are going to suffer for us to have to win. But why must I be one of them?"

What is the war in *Catch–22* all about? The only explanation anyone ever seems able to offer is that men are dying for their country and that it is a noble thing to give your life for your country. This idea Mr. Heller takes considerable pleasure in ridiculing. What does Colonel Cathcart's desire to become a general have to do with anyone's country? And what is a country anyway? "A country is a piece of land surrounded on all sides by boundaries, usually unnatural," an ancient Italian who has learned the arts of survival tells the nineteen-year-old Lieutenant Nately. "There are now fifty or sixty countries fighting in this war. Surely so many countries can't *all* be worth dying for." Nately is shocked by such cynicism and tries to argue, but the old man shakes his head wearily. "They are going to kill you if you don't watch out, and I can see now that you are not going to watch out." (This prophecy later comes true.) And in answer to Nately's declaration that "it's better to die on one's feet than to live on one's knees," the old man tells him that the saying makes more sense if it is turned around to read, "It is better to *live* on one's feet than die on one's knees."

The interesting thing is that there is scarcely a mention until the end of the novel of Nazism or fascism as an explanation of why the war may be worth fighting; if there were, Mr. Heller's point of view would have had a far greater degree of resistance to contend with than he actually allows it to encounter throughout most of the book. That he is aware of this problem is obvious from a dialogue between Yossarian and Major Danby (a "gentle, moral, middle-aged idealist") that takes place in the closing pages. Danby reminds Yossarian that the Cathcarts and the Peckems are not the whole story. "This is not World War One. You must never forget that we're at war with aggressors who would not let either one of us live if they won." Yossarian is provoked by this unanswerable argument into taking back everything he has previously stood for:

I know that . . . Christ, Danby . . . I've flown seventy goddam combat missions. Don't talk to me about fighting to save my country. I've been fighting all along to save my country. Now I'm going to fight a little to save myself. The country's not in danger anymore, but I am. . . . The Germans will be beaten in a few months. And Japan will be beaten a few months after that. If I were to give up my life now, it wouldn't be for my country. It would be for Cathcart and Korn. . . . From now on I'm thinking only of me.

This statement comes as a surprise: one had supposed that Yossarian had been thinking only of himself all throughout the novel. If we take what this new Yossarian says seriously, then the whole novel is trivialized, for what we had all along thought to be a remorselessly uncompromising picture of the world written from the point of view of the idea that survival is the overriding value and that all else is pretense, lying, cant, and hypocrisy, now becomes nothing more than the story of a mismanaged outfit and an attack on the people who (as Yossarian puts it with a rhetoric not his own) always cash in "on every decent impulse and every human tragedy." No, the truth is that Mr. Heller is simply not prepared to go all the way with the idea that lies at the basis of his novel and that is the main tool he has used in making an incredible reality seem credible. He is simply not prepared to say that World War II was a fraud, having nothing whatever to do with ideals or values. I don't blame him for not being prepared to say that; it would not be a true thing to say. Yet for the purposes of this novel, it would have been better if he *were* prepared to say it, for in shrinking from the final ruthless implication of the premise on which *Catch*-22 is built—the idea that nothing on earth is worth dying for—he weakens the shock of the whole book.

Are we then to conclude that Mr. Heller doesn't really mean what *Catch*-22 so unmistakably seems to be communicating for most of its first four hundred pages? I think we must, for if he really meant it, it would not have been possible for him to end the book as he does, with Yossarian heroically refusing to seek his own advantage through cooperating with the Cathcarts and the Korns. (The ancient Italian who lectures Nately and who really does believe that survival is the only thing that counts would most certainly have accepted the opportunity that Yossarian turns down.) Nor, for that matter, would Mr. Heller have been capable of the gusto and exuberance which is *Catch*-22's most attractive quality: the morality of survival is more likely to breed a quiet and weary irony than the kind of joyful energy that explodes all over the pages of this book.

Perhaps without quite knowing it, Mr. Heller has given us in Yossarian another brilliant example of a figure who first appeared in J. P. Donleavy's *The Ginger Man* a few years ago: the youthful idealist living in a world so insane that he can find nothing to which his idealism might genuinely attach itself, and who therefore devotes all his energies to exposing the pretenses of everything that claims to be worthy of his aspirations and his loyalty. He hungers desperately for something that might be worth laying down his life for, but since nothing is available and since he is above all an honest man, he tells himself that he has in effect chosen to live only for his own survival and that he had better not kid himself about it. But of course he *is* kidding himself—he is not capable of the ruthlessness and opportunistic cunning it takes to live such a life. Now that he has learned that preserving his honor means more to him than saving his skin, the only way out is to run off somewhere, to extricate himself from the insane and murderous world that has somehow grown up around him. And so Yossarian bolts and will try to make it to Sweden. Only—I find myself wanting to ask Mr. Heller—what will Yossarian come upon there, in that peacefully neutral place, that is worth dying for? After all, a life devoted to preserving the "self" is not so very different from a life devoted merely to staying alive, and you have just told us that Yossarian needs something bigger to attach his spirit to. So you see, there are more clauses in Catch–22 than even you knew about.

[1962]

The Gloom of Philip Roth

Philip Roth's first full-length novel, *Letting Go*, is an extremely depressing book, and not only because it has so many sad stories to tell. More fundamentally, it is depressing in the way of all bad novels which are also serious: it arouses great expectations in the reader without ever managing to satisfy them.

A busy, diffuse, ambitious book running to some 600 closely printed pages, *Letting Go* is more or less organized around a five-year period in the lives of two young men, Gabe Wallach and Paul Herz, both of whom teach English at the University of Chicago. Though Gabe has written a dissertation on Henry James and Paul is working on a novel, neither of them seems especially passionate about literature, and teaching they regard as a drag and a chore. What Gabe (who serves as the narrator except when it suits Roth's convenience to switch into the third person) tells us about himself is also true of Paul: "I knew it was not from my students or my colleagues or my publications, but from my private life, my secret life, that I would extract whatever joy—or whatever misery—was going to be mine." As we shall soon see, however, very little joy turns up in Gabe's private life, and even less—to put it mildly—in Paul's.

When we first come upon Gabe, he is brooding over the death of his mother and is also deeply involved in a moral and psychological struggle with his father, whose lonely demands for love he is unable to satisfy. His next important adventure is an affair with Martha Reganhart, a young divorcée who loses custody of her two small children because of her illicit relations with him. Later, when one of the children (in full view of the reader) accidentally kills the other while they are away with their father, Martha breaks off the affair and reconciles herself to marrying a man she does not love. Heartbroken, guilty and wounded, Gabe then embarks on a mad escapade connected with the baby that he has helped Paul Herz and his wife adopt. This leads to what appears to be a temporary nervous collapse, and when we finally take our leave of him, Gabe is wandering around Europe in search of his new identity.

But the miseries that Gabe experiences and witnesses are as nothing beside the tribulations that dog every step taken by poor Paul Herz in this novel. In contrast to Gabe (there are many such contrasts between the two young men), Paul is married—to an intense, hysterical girl always on the verge of a breakdown that for some mysterious reason never comes. This marriage, like every relation of any kind that we see acted out in *Letting Go*, is unrelievedly grim and cannibalistic. Nor is the grimness mitigated in the least by the fact that Paul and Libby are really in love. On the contrary, it only seems to deepen their misery by adding to the guilt they feel at having to fail each other over and over, again and again.

Failure, indeed, is the keynote of the Herzes' existence. When they decide to get married while still in college, his parents object because she is Catholic, and her parents object because he is Jewish. When they go ahead and get married anyway, both families

cut them off and they are left to fend for themselves without a
penny. When they leave school to earn enough money to be able
to go back, Libby becomes pregnant, and an abortion (to which
she submits most unwillingly and resentfully) wipes out their
meager savings. When, after spending a dismal year teaching in a
small college in Pennsylvania—where Libby develops kidney
trouble that makes it dangerous for her to have a child and where
Paul, in turn, develops a persistent case of impotence at the very
thought of sleeping with her—when, after all this, Paul finally
lands a good job in Chicago, he immediately antagonizes the
chairman of the department. When they decide to adopt a baby,
the waiting lists turn out to be too long, and Libby virtually
cracks up before the eyes of the social worker who is sent by the
adoption agency to look her over. When they do at last succeed
in adopting a baby, legal complications arise, and it is only at the
very end of the novel that we find out whether or not the child
will be taken from them.

There would, obviously, be gloominess enough here even if Roth
were less relentless in his insistence on rubbing our noses in the
grime and the muck of everyone's life. Yet he seems unable to
relax for even an instant. There is hardly a scene in *Letting Go*
that is not played out against a backdrop of squalor: not a room is
described but the floor must be strewn with soiled diapers and
empty bottles of Breck shampoo; not a bed is mentioned but it
must be messy and unmade; not a meal is eaten but it must be
unappetizing; not a conversation begins but it must end in a
squabble. Even when minor characters make their brief appearances, Roth's eyes will invariably light on the demeaning details:
the flaw in the beautiful woman's figure, the nasty-mindedness of
the pretty little child, the vindictive spite of the very old. And
where the major characters are concerned, he harps and harps and
harps—on Libby's anxieties, on Paul's priggishness, on Gabe's
coldness, on Dr. Wallach's foolishness, on Martha's bad temper.

The effect of this (except in the case of Martha, the only character Roth seems genuinely to like) is finally to make us lose all patience with these people and their nasty little woes. After watching Gabe in action for several hundred pages, who could conceivably care about the tiny bit of new and rather obscure self-knowledge that he so painfully acquires at the end? And after slogging through four or five years with Paul and Libby, who could possibly be interested in the great revelation he experiences at his father's funeral, or in the new occasion for anxiety and hysteria that she is bound to discover in becoming a mother? Roth would apparently like us to think that these things matter: certainly he describes them with the solemnity befitting important events. But the truth is that he also does everything in his power to prevent us from developing enough respect for his characters to see much meaning or significance in their climactic moments.

This, surely, is a curious way for a novelist to act: undercutting his own characters, subverting his own design and ultimately sabotaging his own book. How are we to account for such behavior? Part of the answer, I think, has to do with the nature of Roth's talent, which—on the evidence not only of *Letting Go* but of the stories collected in his first book, *Goodbye, Columbus*—is simply not suited to the kind of exploration in depth that he attempts with Gabe and Paul and Libby. Roth is so much the born satirist, so naturally driven by an instinct for seizing on those gestures and traits of personality by which people expose their weaknesses and make themselves ridiculous, that he has the greatest difficulty in seeing the world from any other point of view. He therefore runs into trouble whenever he tries to strike off a sympathetic character, as with the heroes of "Eli, the Fanatic" and "Epstein" in *Goodbye, Columbus*, and as with Gabe and Paul and Libby here. This limitation, it would seem, is the price that the Muses have required him to pay for the brilliance and authenticity of the satiric gift they have put into his hands. (In my opinion, Roth has it in him to develop into a satirist of the very first rank, but never the big tragic novelist he is struggling to be in *Letting Go*.)

But it is also possible, I think, to detect an element of ideology in Roth's impulse to subvert the basic scheme of *Letting Go*. Roth is on record—in a remarkable essay from which I have already quoted—as believing that something is radically wrong with American society. The whole country, he says in that essay, is insane: it is no place for a rational man to live, and it is beyond the poor powers of a novelist's imagination to apprehend. What, then, can the rational man do who is trying to write fiction in America? Roth never quite answers his own question, contenting himself instead with an analysis—and a very shrewd one—of the various strategies of evasion or retreat that writers have adopted in the face of this catastrophic "loss of subject matter." Nevertheless, an answer of sorts is implied in his concluding sentences of praise for Ralph Ellison's *Invisible Man*. Ellison, Roth tells us, is as convinced as most of his contemporaries that in an insane and corrupting world, the only way a man can hold on to his sanity and maintain himself in a state of moral and spiritual health is by withdrawing, by moving underground. But the fact that Ellison regards the necessity of withdrawal as a calamity makes *Invisible Man* a more honest response to "our distressing cultural and political predicament" than Saul Bellow's *Henderson the Rain King* or Herbert Gold's *The Optimist* or William Styron's *Set This House on Fire*—all of which, in one way or another, find "a cause for celebration" in the discovery that a man can survive and even flourish under such sorry conditions.

I think it is reasonable to suppose that *Letting Go* represents Roth's answer to Bellow and Gold and Styron. The very stridency of his insistence on the squalor and the muck and the grime of things suggests a polemical intent, as though he were less concerned with evoking a reality than with hammering home a thesis by bringing in every available scrap of evidence. Here, he seems to be saying, is what life is really like for those who have with-drawn into the interstices of American society; this what the life of personal relations and self-preoccupation really amounts to; see how mean it is, how narrow, how claustrophobic, how oppressive, and then tell me on what basis you can claim that it is possible for a man living such a life to survive, let alone to flourish? So bent is Roth on making this point that he finally succeeds in making it against his own characters. For if we are to believe that there is no hope for people like Gabe and Paul, why should we take any interest in what happens to them?

The upshot, it seems to me, is that Roth himself is caught in much the same intellectual confusion as the writers he has criti-cized for celebrating the possibilities of the life of withdrawal. He tells us in his essay that he cannot understand why the hero of Gold's *The Optimist*, having taken his lumps, should cry out at the end, "More. More. More! More! More!" Discussing Styron's *Set This House on Fire*, he expresses a similar bewilderment over the fact that the expatriate hero, Cass Kinsolving, "for all his disgust with what the American public life does to a man's private life," finally comes back to America, and that Styron sees this as a symptom of Kinsolving's moral regeneration. And in his discussion of Bellow's *Henderson the Rain King*, Roth comments wryly on the note of happy exuberance that rings through the last para-graph, when Henderson—on his way back to America from Africa—romps across the Arctic landscape with a child in his arms.

Now, it is enormously significant that the only explanation Roth is able to offer for these rather hollow gestures of affirmation is that the writers in question have found "joy, solace and muscle" in the vision of "self as the only real thing in an unreal environment." But, surely, there is more to it than that. Surely what is involved here is an idea about America—the idea that whatever may be wrong with our society is to be understood as the incarnation in modern dress of the flaw in the universe that originated with the expulsion of man from Eden. When Gold's hero asks for More! More! More!, he is saying that the lumps he has taken are the lumps of Life, not the lumps of bad social conditions or of a world gone mad; otherwise, why wish for more? When Styron's hero declares that "as for being and nothingness, the only thing I did know was that to choose between them was simply to choose being," he is identifying the imperfections of life in America with the imperfections of Being itself; otherwise, why return to America? And when Bellow's Henderson asserts that "The world of facts is real, all right, and not to be altered," he is referring not only to the world of physical facts but to the world of social facts as well; otherwise, why should Henderson restrict his new belief in man's power to make his own reality to individuals alone?

If America as we know it today is equivalent to Life or Being or Fate, then there is obviously no alternative to accepting it and there is nothing to complain about in the counsel of cheerful resignation that is urged upon us by so much contemporary fiction. As Carlyle said of the lady transcendentalist who announced that she had decided to accept the universe, "By God! she'd better." But if the troubles that Bellow and Gold and Styron and a host of other writers have chronicled—the malaise, the sense of purposelessness, the apathy, the boredom, the difficulty of communication between persons—are in fact the products not of Fate or of Life or of Being, but of a particular form of economic organization and a particular set of political arrangements, then to accept them as inexorable is to brand oneself a coward or a fool. "Each of us," C. P. Snow has observed, "is solitary: each of us dies alone: all right, that's a fate against which we can't struggle—but there is plenty in our condition which is not fate, and against which we are less than human unless we do struggle."

I would suggest in the light of all this that Roth's answer—both in his essay and in *Letting Go*—to the affirmative stance of Bellow and Gold and Styron is inadequate because he too endows the present condition of things in America with the status of an inexorable fate against which there is very little point in struggling. The only difference is that Roth refuses to be cheerful about the situation. It is a real difference, but not, I am afraid, a big enough one to matter very much in the end.

[1962]

In Defense of James Baldwin

Overpraising mediocre or merely passable or positively bad novels is a regular habit with American reviewers—so much so than anyone who takes literature seriously is forever finding himself in the tiresome position of having to cry Fraud at the latest masterpiece to be discovered by the papers. Yet when a truly important novel is either neglected (as was originally the case in this country with William Golding's *Lord of the Flies*) or gets a bad press (as, say, Norman Mailer's *The Deer Park* did), the process of correction seems to require an unconscionable length of time. The sooner the process begins, however, the sooner it is bound to end, and I would therefore like to venture a step or two in the direction of literary justice to a new novel that seems to me to have been maltreated in an appalling way: James Baldwin's *Another Country*.

In speaking of maltreatment, let me make it clear that I do not mean to introduce a note of pathos into the discussion. Mr. Baldwin is certainly a victim of injustice at the moment, but he is not a pathetic victim. For one thing, his two earlier novels, *Go*

Tell It On the Mountain and *Giovanni's Room*, were both praised beyond their proper deserts (especially the second), so that the general failure to appreciate *Another Country* can be taken as an ironic rectification of the balance. In addition to that, *Another Country* has been on the best-seller lists since it came out several months ago, so that Mr. Baldwin can at least read his bad reviews in comfort. Thirdly, far from being a perfect novel, *Another Country* is faulty to a degree that would wreck a work of lesser force and intensity and truthfulness, so that many of the charges that have been made against it are in themselves quite justified. Finally, the reviews were by no means uniformly hostile. Several pieces in scattered papers and magazines throughout the country —most notably Granville Hicks's moving and intelligent account in *The Saturday Review*—were enthusiastic, and many others, while finding fault with Baldwin's "lack of restraint," or his overly candid descriptions of sexual activity, or his use of dialogue, or his treatment of character, or his handling of plot, nevertheless acknowledged the novel's "power." All the reviewers, moreover (including those who detested the book), made sure to reserve enough space for an earnest tribute to Mr. Baldwin's talents, calling him one of our very best writers and voicing a pious confidence in his ability to do better in future.

But in spite of all this, I will stand by the word maltreatment. With few exceptions, the major reviewing media were very hard on *Another Country*. It was patronized by Paul Goodman in *The New York Times Book Review*, ridiculed by Stanley Edgar Hyman in *The New Leader*, worried over (with, it must be said, genuine distress) by Elizabeth Hardwick in *Harper's*, summarily dismissed by *Time's* anonymous critic, loftily pitied by Whitney Balliett in *The New Yorker*, and indignantly attacked by Saul Maloff in *The Nation*.

Three of these reviewers—Goodman, Hardwick, and Hyman—are first-rate critics, and I therefore find it hard to believe that their wrong-headed appraisals of *Another Country* can be ascribed to a simple lapse of literary judgment. How could anyone as sensitive and knowledgeable as Elizabeth Hardwick have been so led astray by Baldwin's occasional lapses into sentimentality in writing about love and sex as to call the book "conventional" and "uninspired"? How could a man of Stanley Edgar Hyman's sophistication have been so fooled by the large quantity of explicit erotic detail in *Another Country* as to accuse Baldwin of having cynically set out to fabricate a best seller? How could Paul Goodman, who most assuredly knows better, have taken the fact that all the characters are cut off from the main world of the city as a sign that this novel is a typical commercial product? My own guess is that all these critics disliked *Another Country* not because it suffers from this or that literary failing, but because they were repelled by the militancy and the cruelty of its vision of life. Granville Hicks was right when he called the book "an act of violence," and since it is the reader upon whom this violence is being committed, perhaps one ought to have expected that many reviewers would respond with something less than gratitude.

Another Country is about a crucial year in the lives of a group of people who inhabit a kind of underworld (for the most part physically located in Greenwich Village) of interracial and inter-sexual relations. Of the five main characters, two are Negroes—a famous jazz drummer, Rufus Scott, and his younger sister Ida, an aspiring singer—and the other three are white—Rufus's closest friend, a young, unpublished, and unmarried writer (Vivaldo Moore); a woman whose marriage is beginning to fail (Cass Silenski); and a homosexual actor who comes originally from the South (Eric Jones). Rufus—by far the most impressive character Baldwin has ever created—has a love affair with a pathetic white Southern girl named Leona which ends for him in suicide and for her in insanity. After Rufus's death, his sister Ida falls in love with Vivaldo, and while they are living together (less stormily than

Rufus and Leona had, but stormily enough), Ida is unfaithful to him with a television producer who promises to further her career, and he, though not a homosexual, spends a night in bed with Eric by whom, as Stanley Edgar Hyman delicately put it, he permits himself to be "rectally violated." By this time, we have already learned that Rufus, although not a homosexual either, had also had an affair with Eric. As for Eric, he too crosses over the line and enters into an affair with Cass, who is fed up with the kind of man her husband has become since producing a successful but trivial novel.

Whites coupled with Negroes, heterosexuals coupled with homosexuals, homosexuals coupled with women, none of it involving casual lust or the suggestion of neurotic perversity, and all of it accompanied by the most serious emotions and resulting in the most intense attachments—it is easy enough to see even from so crude a summary that Baldwin's intention is to deny any moral significance whatever to the categories white and Negro, heterosexual and homosexual. He is saying that the terms white and Negro refer to two different conditions under which individuals live, but they are still individuals and their lives are still governed by the same fundamental laws of being. And he is saying, similarly, that the terms homosexuality and heterosexuality refer to two different conditions under which individuals pursue love, but they are still individuals and their pursuit of love is still governed by the same fundamental laws of being. Putting the two propositions together, he is saying, finally, that the only significant realities are individuals and love, and that anything which is permitted to interfere with the free operation of this fact is evil and should be done away with.

Now, one might suppose that there is nothing particularly startling in this view of the world; it is, after all, only a form of the standard liberal attitude toward life. And indeed, stated as I have just stated it, and held with the mild attachment by which most liberal and enlightened Americans hold it, it is scarcely more shocking than the usual speech made at every convention of the American Society of Social Workers. But that is not the way James Baldwin holds it, and it is not the way he states it. He holds these attitudes with a puritanical ferocity, and he spells them out in such brutal and naked detail that one scarcely recognizes them any longer—and one is frightened by them, almost as though they implied a totally new, totally revolutionary, conception of the universe. And in a sense, of course, they do. For by taking these liberal pieties literally and by translating them into simple English, he puts the voltage back into them and they burn to the touch. Do you believe, he demands of you, that racial prejudice is wrong, that all men are created equal, that individuals must be judged on their own merits? Then you must dare to surrender the objections you are surely still harboring in your soul against miscegenation. You must acknowledge that there is no reason why whites and Negroes should not sleep together and marry and produce children with as little interference as members of the same race now encounter. And that this is impossible you must recognize as a momentous fact about American life, signifying a moral sickness that may end by destroying our capacity for any kind of human contact whatever. Do you believe, he demands of you again, that love is the supreme value and that sex is the most natural expression of love? Then you must dare to realize that the stifling of your own impulses toward a sexual articulation of the love you feel for members of your own sex is unnatural, signifying a warping of the instincts and of the body that may end by destroying your capacity for any kind of sexual experience whatever.

Another Country, then, is informed by a remorseless insistence on a truth which, however partial we may finally judge it to be, is nevertheless compelling as a perspective on the way we live now.

It is a cruel truth, and a demanding one, but it is not without an element of sweet spiritual generosity. For implicit in it is the idea that everyone carries his own burden, that every burden is ultimately as heavy as every other, and that a man is either brave enough or strong enough to stand up straight under the weight on his back or he isn't; and if he isn't, he will pay the price and no one else has the right to judge him harshly; and if enough people are found to be lacking in enough bravery or enough strength, then there must be something wrong with the conditions they are being forced to endure and the values these conditions have bred.

Wherever Baldwin manages to remain true to this vision—as in the magnificent opening section about Rufus, the account of the relations between Vivaldo and Ida, and scattered passages in every other part of the book—he is at his very best, achieving a unique blend of subtlety and forcefulness, anger and understanding. But there are situations and characters that tax Baldwin's power to sustain the burden of his moral attitudes to the breaking point. Thus, he is merciless on Cass Silenski's husband Richard, who is a bad writer and a success, while remaining infinitely charitable toward Vivaldo, who is also a bad writer but a failure; he inclines toward sentimentality in most of the erotic passages involving either a white and a Negro, or two men, or a homosexual and a woman, whereas he is visibly skeptical of the validity of the more standard varieties of sex; he can trace every nuance in the relations of an unmarried couple, but in writing about marriage he falls into something very close to philistinism; and in general he judges white characters (with the exception of the homosexual Eric) by more rigorous criteria than he is willing to apply to the Negroes in the book. All of which means that Baldwin, who speaks so passionately of the white man's need for the courage to know the Negro and the heterosexual's need to know the homosexual, is himself unable to summon the courage to know and respect those who live in that other country usually designated as normal.

But I do not wish to end on a negative note. Despite the lapses of which he is guilty here, what Baldwin has accomplished in *Another Country* is impressive and important. Within the context of his own development as a writer, I believe that *Another Country* will come to be seen as the book in which for the first time the superb intelligence of Baldwin the essayist became fully available to Baldwin the novelist, in which for the first time he attempted to speak his mind with complete candor and with a minimum of polite rhetorical elegance, and in which for the first time he dared to reveal himself as someone to be feared for how deeply he sees, how much he demands of the world, and how powerfully he can hate. Is that why so many of the reviewers disliked *Another Country?* The question is worth pondering.

[1962]

A Dissent on Updike

I have been puzzled by many things in the course of my career as a literary critic, and one of them is the high reputation of John Updike. When his first novel, *The Poorhouse Fair*, came out in 1958, I remember arguing about it at great length with Mary McCarthy and concluding after an hour or so of earnest give-and-take that one of us must be crazy. She insisted that Updike was an extraordinary stylist; I replied that his prose was overly lyrical, bloated like a child who had eaten too much candy. She thought that he had an interesting mind; I said that he had no mind at all. She wondered why I wasn't impressed by a writer in his twenties who was able to imagine what it must be like to be very old and dying; I answered that I wasn't altogether convinced by Updike's aged characters, and that in any case there was something that gave me the creeps about the way he had deliberately set out to reverse the usual portrait-of-the-artist-as-a-young-man pattern of the first novel. And so the conversation went, each of us after a while beginning to wonder what on earth could have gone wrong with the other.

Since *The Poorhouse Fair*, I have done my best to keep up with Updike. I have also done my best to understand why so many people I respect enjoy and admire his work. The results have not been good on either count. His short stories—which I usually find myself throwing away in disgust before I can get to the end— strike me as all windup and no delivery, and I am alternately bored and exasperated by the verbal pyrotechnics they specialize in. What, after all, is this display of rhetorical virtuosity for, if not to assure the reader that he is in the presence of a writer who is very sophisticated indeed and who therefore cannot possibly be as callow and sentimental as he seems to be and in fact is? The other side of the coin of sentimentality is, of course, cruelty—both qualities being expressions of the vacuum that occupies the place where feeling is supposed to be—and in his second novel, *Rabbit, Run*, it is a cruelty as callow as the sentimentality of the stories that is legitimized by the veneer of Updike's literary sophistication. I shall not soon get over the bad taste left in my mouth by the scene at the end in which the hero's wife—at the behest of Updike's "tragic" sense of retribution—accidentally drowns her newborn baby in the bath. Nor, whenever I think about Updike, can I forget my embarrassment at seeing him, all unknowingly, expose the adolescent level of his sexual attitudes in the fashionably audacious erotic passages that spice the action of *Rabbit, Run*.

And now we have a third novel, *The Centaur*, which might be described as an Updike show-case, so proudly does he exhibit his much-praised literary wares on every page. In the very first paragraph, for example, a character is wounded, and Updike's prose is off to the races: "The pain scaled the slender core of his shin, whirled in the complexities of his knee, and, swollen broader, more thunderous, mounted into his bowels. . . . The pain extended a feeler into his head and unfolded its wet wings along the walls of his thorax, so that he felt, in his sudden scarlet blindness, to be himself a large bird waking from sleep. . . . The pain seemed to be displacing with its own hairy segments his heart and lungs; as its grip swelled in his throat he felt he was holding his brain like a morsel on a platter high out of a hungry reach." Even leaving aside the question of whether writing that strains as self-consciously for brilliance as these sentences do can evoke anything for the reader but the author's desire to impress, how felicitous is Updike's description of the experience of a sudden shock of pain? I would say that it is a total falsification. Severe pain in one part of the body does not travel through the system, either on wet wings or dry; on the contrary, after the first flash of burning sensation, its effect is actually to focus one's entire consciousness on the hurt spot, as though the rest of the body had no existence at all. Consequently the appropriate images for rendering such an experience—those that would have occurred to a writer whose mind was struggling for precision rather than razzle-dazzle—would be images of immensely rapid contraction and tightening, not images of gradual unfolding and spreading.

The whole scheme of *The Centaur* is marked by a similarly self-conscious effort at brilliance, and it results in much the same violence to the job at hand. By the job at hand, I mean the story Updike is telling of a man named George Caldwell who apparently (one cannot be sure, since the last few sentences are literally written in Greek) commits suicide at the end for the sake of his fifteen-year-old son. It might be supposed that a proper telling of this story would involve an account of why Caldwell decides to commit suicide and in what sense his death can be of benefit to his son. But if we ask such questions of Updike, we are referred for answers not to the psychology of George Caldwell or to his situation in life or to some combination of both, but to Greek mythology, and specifically to the legend of Chiron, which—we are informed—is being translated here into modern dress. Chiron, the noblest of all the Centaurs, suffered great agony after being accidentally wounded by a poisoned arrow, and in order to be freed of his pain, he begged Zeus to relieve him of his immortality and to accept his death as the necessary expiation for the ancient sin that Prometheus had committed in stealing fire from the gods and bringing it to men. Zeus granted him his wish, and "set him among the stars as the constellation Sagittarius."

In *The Centaur*, Chiron, who taught wisdom to the gods on Olympus, becomes Caldwell, who teaches science at Olinger High School in Pennsylvania; Prometheus, whose punishment for the theft of fire was to be bound on a rock where a huge vulture came daily to peck away at his liver, becomes Peter Caldwell, who is plagued by a bad case of psoriasis; Zeus, whose attributes as King of Olympus included neither chastity nor a reliable sense of justice, becomes Zimmerman, the lecherous and rather sadistic principal of Olinger High; Hephaestus, the lame god of fire and the smith of Olympus, becomes Al Hummel, the lame garage mechanic of the town; Aphrodite (or Venus), the goddess of love, becomes Hummel's wife, Vera, who teaches physical education at Olinger and is notorious for her sexual escapades; Ceres, the goddess of grain, becomes Cassie Caldwell, George's wife and Peter's mother, who feeds him cereal every morning; Kronos, or Father Time, becomes Pop Kramer, Cassie's aged father; etc., etc., etc.

Half the time, these parallels are made explicit in phantas-magorical chapters where, for example, Caldwell will be called Chiron in one sentence and Caldwell in the next, and where Updike will speak of his four hooves, or of the rock on which Peter-Prometheus is bound. But in the chapters narrated by Peter himself, the scenes are consistently realistic, and the characters are all people living in rural Pennsylvania in 1947 and doing the things that people might do in that place and at that time. As we quickly discover, however, every single detail of these chapters is charged with a mythological parallel. Those we are not clever enough to detect ourselves, we can decipher with the help of the mythological index that Updike appended to the book at the suggestion, he says, of his wife—who, one imagines, was worried lest the full force of her husband's erudition and ingenuity be lost on the reader.

And indeed, without this index, I doubt that many readers could guess that Johnny Dedman playing the pinball machine on page 122 is Daedalus; that Ely, Pennsylvania is the Elysian Fields; or that the cheer of the student audience when a basketball game is tied is Pan's Shout. A fair number of readers might perhaps remember that Zeus avenged himself on mankind after Prometheus stole the fire by creating Pandora, and would therefore have no trouble in figuring out who Peter's girlfriend Penny represents. But I wonder how many readers left to themselves could catch the genuinely witty double entendre that we come upon by looking up the pages listed in the index under "Pandora's Box."

Apart from the crossword-puzzle-solving kind of pleasure such tricks can bring, I cannot see what purpose is served by the introduction of a mythological element into the story of George Caldwell's suicide other than a pretentious evasion of the requirements of the story itself. George Caldwell is a sweet, decent, anxious man doing a thankless job for inadequate pay and worrying constantly about the future. Feeling ill and suspecting that he may have cancer, he has some X-rays taken by Old Doc Appleton. While waiting for the results of the examination, he is further distressed by a mixed report on his teaching abilities that the principal has written after a visit to one of his classes. To make matters worse, he inadvertently catches a member of the school board coming out of the principal's office with her lipstick smeared, and this convinces him that they will look for some means of getting him fired, even though he has tenure. When the X-rays are finally developed and the doctor calls to say that he is not mortally ill but simply overworked and in need of a rest or a less taxing job, his despair grows even more acute, and he decides that death is his only hope of release.

In my opinion, the effect of seeing the story of George Caldwell as a re-enactment of the legend of Chiron is neither to illuminate his plight nor to enrich our understanding of his character; all it does is to surround *The Centaur* with a fake aura of profundity while at the same time permitting Updike to plug up holes of motivation and to impose a spurious significance on characters and events which have failed to earn any significance in their own right. "Chiron accepted death," Updike tells us at the end as George Caldwell stands in the snow of a Pennsylvania winter staring at his broken-down old Buick which, he understands, "is a chariot Zimmerman had sent for him." Well, we know why *Chiron* accepted death: the Greek myth in its own terms provides us with a wholly satisfactory explanation. There is no George Caldwell, however, in Greek mythology; the only George Caldwell we have is the George Caldwell of John Updike's imagination, and there is nothing in this character as Updike has created him that makes his suicide dramatically plausible, let alone inevitable. It doesn't help to be informed that the pain George Caldwell feels over his difficulty with teaching is comparable to the suffering Chiron felt after being wounded by a poisoned arrow, for he seems to be a very good teacher and beloved by his students. Nor does it help to be informed that he commits suicide for his son's benefit, as Chiron surrendered his immortality for the sake of Prometheus, for unless I have missed some subtle detail, no benefit could conceivably accrue to Peter as a result of his father's death.

We are left, then, with only one explanation: George Caldwell commits suicide because *The Centaur* is a re-telling of the Chiron legend whose intention (in the words of the jacket copy) is "to pierce the shadow-line that separates human experience from the mythical dimension." Such language would be pretentious gobble-degook even as applied to Joyce's *Ulysses*, where for the most part "the mythical dimension" supplements a fully realized and entirely self-contained fictional world. As applied to *The Centaur*, where the mythical dimension is mainly brought in to do the work of imaginative creation that Updike himself is incapable of doing, it is downright laughable.

In short, I am still as mystified by Updike's reputation as I was when he first burst forth onto the literary scene five years ago. I cannot for the life of me understand what there is about him that so impresses people like Mary McCarthy, Arthur Mizener, and Stanley Edgar Hyman—to mention only three critics who have spoken highly of Updike. To me he seems a writer who has very little to say and whose authentic emotional range is so narrow and thin that it may without too much exaggeration be characterized as limited to a rather timid nostalgia for the confusions of youth. So far as his famous brilliance as a stylist is concerned, the fact that prose as mandarin and exhibitionistic as Updike's can be universally praised seems to be an alarming sign of confusion in the general conception of how the English language functions best. *The Centaur* has only confirmed me in my feeling that in the list of the many inflated literary reputations that have been created in recent years, Updike's name belongs somewhere very near the top.
[1963]

Book Reviewing & Everyone I Know

Lately, it seems to me, everyone I know has been complaining about American foreign policy, President Kennedy, the cost of living—and the state of book reviewing in this country. Why, everyone I know wants to know, don't we have a good weekly Book Review—something like the *Times Literary Supplement*, only livelier, less stuffy, less academic? Of course, we *do* have *The New York Times Book Review*, but that, in the eyes of everyone I know, is exactly the trouble. (Everyone I know gave up long ago on *The Saturday Review*, and would probably also have given up on the *NYTBR* if not for the fact that it comes with the Sunday *Times* and can therefore scarcely be avoided.)

Now, there are, I must admit, moments when I feel inclined to defend the *NYTBR* against everyone I know. It is true, as everyone I know always says, that the *NYTBR* is generally bland and uncritical, that it caters to established reputations, that it rarely champions the unconventional, and that somewhere in its editorial mind there is lodged an unshakeable confusion between popularity and literary merit. But everyone I know usually forgets in talking about the *NYTBR* that some really good writers appear pretty often in its pages—writers like Alfred Kazin, Irving Howe, Kenneth Rexroth, and Harold Rosenberg—and I suspect that such writers would be used even more often if they themselves were willing. That they are not willing is at least partly attributable to the circumstance that among our most talented literary intellectuals (including just about everyone I know) reviewing is regarded as a job for young men on the make: you serve an apprenticeship as a reviewer and then you move on to bigger and more ambitious things. Money has been known to break this pattern, but the *NYTBR* doesn't pay quite enough to act as a genuinely effective counterforce. Besides, even with the best intentions and the most generous budget in the world, it would be extremely difficult to cover as many books as the *NYTBR* does from week to week and still turn out an interesting magazine. For the simple truth is that only a very small fraction of the books published every year in this country are worth the typewriter ribbons they have worn through, and consequently it is doubtful whether enough stimulus exists in a given week to generate two decent reviews, let alone twenty-two. This—rather than commercialism or venality—is probably the main reason for the *NYTBR*'s heavy reliance on cheerful mediocrities, claustrophobic specialists, and crippled hacks. Who else would want to waste his time on all that junk?

Still, there is no question that everyone I know is right: a good book-reviewing medium would be a lovely thing to have in this country, and given enough editorial imagination and energy, it might even be possible to overcome the problems that have defeated the *NYTBR* and to turn one out. At any rate, we shall soon see. Recently, two very imaginative and energetic editors indeed, Barbara Epstein and Robert B. Silvers, decided to take advantage of the New York newspaper strike to demonstrate concretely what they and everyone they know (who roughly coincide with everyone I know) think a good book-reviewing medium ought to look like. Since Mrs. Epstein and Mr. Silvers put together the demonstration issue of *The New York Review of Books* without any capital—costs were met by selling ads to the publishers, whose somewhat surprising eagerness to cooperate owed much to the fact that the strike left them with inadequate means of calling attention to their new books—it remains to be seen whether they will be able to continue, or whether they will only have produced what amounts to a brilliant implicit polemic against the assumptions behind the dullness and mediocrity of the *NYTBR*.

Just about everyone I know has contributed a piece to *The New York Review of Books*, but there are also a few contributors I don't know, and there is even one I never heard of before. His name is John Maddox (the editors have misspelled it, indicating that they probably never heard of him before either), and his piece, on Carleton Coon's *The Origin of Races*, is among the best in the whole collection. This is saying a great deal when you consider that Mrs. Epstein and Mr. Silvers have managed to smoke out a line-up of reviewers that includes W. H. Auden (on David Jones's *Anathemata*), Robert Lowell (on Robert Frost), Mary McCarthy (on William Seward Burroughs's *Naked Lunch*), Norman Mailer (on Morley Callaghan's memoir of Hemingway and Fitzgerald in the 20's), William Phillips (on Elias Canetti's *Crowds and Power*), Philip Rahv (on Alexander Solzhenitsyn's *One Day in the Life of Ivan Denisovich*), Alfred Kazin (on Olga Carlisle's *Voices in the Snow*), Irving Howe (on *The Partisan Review Anthology*), Dwight Macdonald (on Arthur Schlesinger, Jr.'s *The Politics of Hope*), Elizabeth Hardwick (on *The Ring Lardner Reader*), and about thirty other less famed but comparably sophisticated writers dealing with the latest offerings of such authors as

James Baldwin, J. D. Salinger, Edward Albee, Jean Genet, Robert Heilbroner, James MacGregor Burns, and John Updike.

All these reviewers inhabit much the same intellectual milieu, and what they have in common, apart from talent and intelligence, is an attitude toward books and an idea about the proper way to discuss them. This attitude might be characterized as one of great suspiciousness: a book is assumed to be guilty until it proves itself innocent—and not many do. It cannot be denied that a certain lack of generosity toward the fact of sheer effort is implicit here, but it should also be recognized that the major premise behind such suspiciousness is that books are enormously important events, far too important to be confronted lightly, and certainly too important to permit of charitable indulgence toward those who presume to write them without sufficient gift or seriousness. Taking exactly the opposite position from the *NYTBR*—which regards almost any book as ipso facto worth having—and working with the advantage of having the produce of about three months of publishing to choose from rather than only a week, *The New York Review* announces that it has spent neither time nor space "on books which are trivial in their intentions or venal in their effects, except occasionally to reduce a temporarily inflated reputation or to call attention to a fraud."

Strong language, this, and it bespeaks the inveterate preoccupation of everyone I know with the problems of mass culture and with the need for an embattled struggle against the deterioration of literary and intellectual standards. Clearly, *The New York Review* was conceived with the idea that a literary journal can be responsible to its function only if it commits itself without apology or diffidence to participating in that struggle.

But the struggle does not consist exclusively in discriminating between good books and bad books, in valuing the good and exposing the bad. Writers of the type who have come together to produce the demonstration issue of *The New York Review* have traditionally used the book review as a literary genre in its own right. Most of them, indeed, take the writing of reviews with the kind of seriousness that is ordinarily associated only with poets working at their verses, for on the whole they think of them-selves less as critics than as writers and intellectuals. And it is as writers and intellectuals responding to the issues raised by a book—often even a bad book—that they approach the job of reviewing. Their reviews are thus neither intended as a service to the potential consumer who wishes to know whether or not the book under consideration is likely to interest him (which is how the NYTBR conceives the function of a review), nor as a service to the author who wishes to know where he went right and where he went wrong so that he can do better next time (which is how no one but certain naive journalists and sanctimonious novelists conceives the function of a review). If writers like these are per-forming a service at all when they review a book, it is a service to consciousness: a book for them is, quite simply, an occasion to do some writing of their own.

This does not mean, however, that the writing will necessarily be "second-hand" stuff. On the contrary, one of the distinguishing marks of the literary intellectual is that to him a book is as real an experience as a raw event might be, and he therefore addresses himself to it with all the intelligence, knowledge, passion, grace, and style he can command. And so it is that some of the best writing done in America over the past ten or fifteen years, and some of the most illuminating discussion of the life of our times, can be found in the back files of magazines like *Partisan Review* and *Commentary*, in the small print of the book reviews con-tributed by many of the same people gathered together here in the *New York Review*, and others who have worked in the same tradition.

I would not go so far as to say that any of these writers has succeeded in bringing forth a masterpiece on this particular occasion; actually, most of them have appeared to better advantage before. Mary McCarthy, for instance, is decidedly coy about telling us just how good she thinks *Naked Lunch* really is, and for some incomprehensible reason insists on using scatological language to help her evade the issue. Dwight Macdonald's piece on Arthur Schlesinger, Jr. is characteristically charming and witty, but seems somewhat perfunctory, as do Philip Rahv's and Alfred Kazin's pieces. On the other hand, Macdonald, Rahv, and Kazin, even in their perfunctory moments, have more to say than most of us when we are trying hard, and therefore they do help to maintain the exhilaratingly high level of the issue in general.

But if no one I know has generated a masterpiece here, someone I know, F. W. Dupee, has come forward—in his lead article on James Baldwin's sensational essay *The Fire Next Time*—with a model of what a book review should be. Dupee, the author of an excellent biography of Henry James and as graceful a stylist as any we have today, manages in some 1500 words to define the role Baldwin has assumed in his polemical writings on the Negro problem ("Baldwin impresses me as being the Negro *in extremis,* a virtuoso of ethnic suffering, defiance and aspiration [who] wears his color as Hester Prynne did her scarlet letter, proudly"); to isolate and characterize the qualities of Baldwin's prose that paradoxically serve this role ("It suggests the ideal prose of an ideal literary community, some aristocratic France of one's dreams"); and to argue on the basis of his own reading of the Negro problem that Baldwin "manifestly weakens his grasp of his role, his style and his great theme itself" when he moves from criticism to prophesy. As it happens, I myself disagree with Dupee's final judgment of *The Fire Next Time,* whose faults—which he pinpoints with a precision that is as dazzling in its own unobtrusive way as Baldwin's lush passion can be—seem to me less damaging than they do to him. But that is another matter, and it is still a brilliant review.

If *The New York Review* were to succeed in establishing itself on a permanent footing—say as a bi-weekly or perhaps as a monthly*—everyone I know would certainly be happy, and the store of interesting and lively reading available to us would be increased by that much. But would any larger purpose be served? Would the existence of such a magazine have an *effect*? It is hard to say; even the people who were involved in putting out the demonstration issue find it hard to say. In fact, a tone of skepticism, a sense of doubt about the ultimate importance of the intellectual life and the critical intelligence, pervades *The New York Review,* introducing an oddly incongruous note into an enterprise which is, after all, dedicated to the belief that there is very great value indeed in the intellectual life and the critical intelligence. Mr. Dupee, for example, after expressing the fear that *The Fire Next Time* in its "madder moments" may have a bad effect both on the Negroes and on their enemies, ends his piece with the following sad sentence: "Assuming that a *book* can do anything to either." And Elizabeth Hardwick begins her touching little essay, "Grub Street: New York," on the same uneasy note: "Making a living is nothing; the great difficulty is making a point, making a difference—with words." (Dwight Macdonald, however, will have none of such doubts: he wishes that Arthur Schlesinger had never gone to work in the White House because the acquisition of political power has damaged him as a writer.)

But except for Dwight Macdonald and one or two others, everyone I know—indeed, everyone who writes—is often afflicted with the feeling that all he is doing is dropping stone after stone down the bottomless well of American culture. Who listens? Who cares? What differences does any of it make? There is no easy answer to questions like these, and in the end we are all thrown back, if we are lucky, upon a simple animal faith. As Paul Goodman once put it:

* As of September 1963, it seems to have done so, as a bi-weekly.

A man must believe that he and his peers, correcting one another's reasoning, and making it common and public, have finally as good a sampling of reality as there is. . . . And most important, a man must believe that the world is a world *for* him; if he exercises initiative and takes a step, his action will have an effect, however small, in the same real world. He will not suddenly be without ground underfoot. . . ; there is a human community that is thinking the same thoughts as himself and ready to act in concert.

A good motto, that, for *The New York Review of Books*—and for everyone I know.

[1963]

III

The World Out There

The World of Television Drama

At least fifty plays are produced on television every week. About a third of these are detective and mystery stories; another large portion is devoted to whimsical tales with surprise endings. But the remainder constitutes a genre peculiar to television. It has developed its own style, its own conventions, and to some extent its own subject matter.

These TV plays are theatrical rather than cinematic, taking their cue from Broadway, not Hollywood. Movie stars rarely appear in them, though prominent Broadway figures often do; the casts consist of extremely competent actors most of whom, I imagine, consider themselves theater people. The direction almost always betrays the influence of men like Kazan—which is to say that it tries to combine realism of surface with self-conscious, sometimes arty arrangements, movements, and overtones. Both dialogue and acting are more sophisticated than is usual in the movies. In general the productions are on a surprisingly high level, considering the number of plays turned out every week.

The tendency is toward low-key drama, a kind of domestic realism whose effect derives from its accuracy in reflecting the ordinary man's conceptions of the world. The very style of the acting—always plausible, always controlled, never permitting itself the least intimation of hamminess, rarely even admitting that it is artifice rather than actual conversation—restricts the drama to that level of reality which is easily accessible to common sense. A whole play may be based on a very trivial incident, chosen because everyone in the audience will have experienced something similar. For example, a teen-age boy takes the family car without his father's permission, gets involved in a minor accident, and doesn't come home until three in the morning. His parents wait up for him, anxiety-ridden, and when he finally returns, all is forgiven and the whole family goes to bed with the sense of having got through another crisis. This play is "true to life" in a way that popular culture seldom is: the audience has never had the stuff of its daily existence taken so seriously, and it responds with a new feeling of self-importance and dignity. Unlike the soap operas, which betray a masochistic relish in minor troubles, the point here is the relief people feel in being able to resume their usual routine: trouble teaches gratitude for the humdrum.

Depending for its effectiveness on its ability to remain content with the world perceived and comprehended by common sense, this kind of drama must resist appealing either to escapist fantasy or to the critical intelligence, never wandering above or below the staples of experience. Nowadays, to be sure, that can include a great deal of surprising matter. In a play about the relation between a mother and her son, suggestions of an Oedipus complex are offered in much the same way as characters appear wearing clothes: the writer, the director, the actors, take it completely for granted as an ordinary element in the family. It isn't a mysterious, sinister force (as it tends to be in the movies) but a tangible factor existing almost wholly on the surface and demanding to be observed. This means, of course, that it needn't have consequences; in this particular instance, it counted for nothing in the plot. That a son should be in love with his mother is an index of his normality, not of his monstrousness. This must imply, I suppose, that the audience has been trained to regard it thus, or is well on its way to doing so.

Life in these plays, then, is non-heroic: a world governed by common sense is a world where "everyone has his faults and his good points." No insuperable moral problems are recognized, for in a universe ruled exclusively by forces visible to the common-sense eye, there can be no dilemma which resists the touch of good will and a spirit of compromise. Often a play will open with a situation in which right seems to conflict with right, but in the end someone is proved wrong or neurotic or misguided, and the difficulty immediately resolves *itself*. A common-sense ethos must always hack its way through to the simple truths which are supposed to lie buried beneath the ugly and delusory overgrowths of experience.

Though everyone in these plays has weaknesses as well as virtues, we find the weaknesses far less in evidence. If a man sins, he does so almost accidentally, for sin is something that happens to people, not something they do. They make errors of judgment all the time, but they generally know nothing of pure or gratuitous malice. Only their virtues are essential to them; their sins are somehow external, reefs against which they have blundered in the fog. (The TV crime plays, on the other hand, become a repository of much that is omitted from domestic drama: crime is a violation of common-sense living, and therefore results in the criminal's exclusion from the sphere in which all slips can be made good.)

One would expect that a world made by common sense, ruled by common sense, and upheld by common sense, would be a pleasant world to live in. In many ways it is. It produces people whose passions are under control, who are well-bred, well-mannered, open, friendly, helpful, and above all, reasonable. More than anything else, they want to get along, they will do nearly anything to keep the peace.

And yet the optimism we find here is gray rather than flaming; it is overcast with a sadness that seems a new element in American popular culture. There is a distinct feeling that life is tough even for those who aren't harassed by the landlord and the grocer; and there is a shade of disillusion over the discovery that human possibility is not infinite—reverberations of Korea are in the air. The mood is more sober than what used to be called American optimism, and, as we shall see, far more honest.

Before the dislocations caused by 3D, Hollywood had been gravitating in several full-dress productions toward a similar form of drama. But the features characterizing the new genre—an insistent interest in domestic life, a *dramatis personae* entirely composed of ordinary people, a strict fidelity to the appearance of things, a quiet tone (everything is underplayed), a paucity of plot, and much discussion and debate—made it apparent that its real home was in television. Going to the movies is still more or less an occasion for most people, and on occasion demands something extraordinary. Even the size of the cinema screen insures that the movie world shall be larger than life (indeed, in answer to the small television screen, movie screens have become larger); perhaps for this reason, movies reproduced on television lose their bite. Watching television, on the other hand, has become an integral part of domestic routine, and the new genre serves an impulse to make the program a relevant and appropriate presence in the living room.

The living room, in fact, is the favorite setting of these plays, just as the favorite cast is a family. It is a middle-class family, neither unusually happy nor (as in the soap operas) continually besieged with trouble. Its most remarkable quality as a group is a negative one—fear is absent from the relations of its members and power thus becomes a corollary of love: it can only be had by free consent. The father guides and administers his household; he does not rule it. The plot always turns on some crisis that has suddenly developed, often in the family relations themselves: as in any family, its members are continually in the process of losing their illusions about one another, and the effort at readjustment is constant. Ultimately they emerge from their difficulties as more of a family, having restored a workable balance of power.

Almost always the father comes through as a sharper figure than the mother, who is supposed to have her being in and through her husband and children. A good woman is not so much *by* as *on* the side of her husband. If she asserts her personality too forcefully, we may be sure that calamity will result. Evil, when it makes one of its rare visits to these plays, is likely to come in the shape of a domineering wife or an overly possessive mother. As for the father, he is an earnest man, but his earnestness is mellow compared with the fierce unyielding grimness of his children or his wife's firm, uncritical loyalty to her feelings. Soft-spoken, controlled, never glamorous-looking, but always carrying himself with great dignity and self-assurance, he exhibits the palpable scars of a long combat with life. His humility, patience, and sadness are the products of many frustrations, and he is thus extremely skeptical of any comprehensive schemes or over-ambitious plans. Sometimes he is portrayed as a great disappointment to his children—for we live in an era where parents rather than children are perennially on trial—and in such cases the guilt and bitterness he feels are tempered by his pity for the son who will soon learn that all human beings are disappointing to those who make excessive demands on them.

We practically never see this new American father (as we used to in the movies and as we still do in television soap operas) involved in the big business deal, or embroiled in the problems of earning money: a comfortable income is taken for granted, while his career is merely a shadowy presence in the background. The great reality of his life, the sphere in which things happen to him, is his family. He carries his responsibilities willingly, without a sense of oppression, and the fact that they occupy him so fully, challenging all his resources of character and mind, never allowing him to get bored, is his most powerful proof to his son that the ordinary life is worth living. For this is the great lesson he is intent upon teaching. We find him telling his daughter that marriage, children, and love are far more important than fame and wealth; we find him insisting to his son that there is no disgrace in compromise. He represents reasonableness, tolerance, and good will: the image of American maturity.

Preserving the family from disruption is the role he is most often called upon to play. One species of disruption is conflict with his children. The conflict never takes the form of youth's rebellion against parental authority because the father's authority over his children is not given in the nature of things. Since he is a constitutional leader rather than an absolute monarch, his authority must constantly be reaffirmed at the polls. Nor can he assert it forcefully or arbitrarily: he must win the right to participate in his son's problems by making himself sufficiently attractive in the boy's eyes—good "public relations" is essential to his position. Interference with his son's private affairs being a matter of the greatest delicacy, he only presumes to speak in crucial matters. Otherwise he is there, looking on, setting an example, communicating through the silent power of his personality.

In an encounter with his children, he confronts them with a flexibility that often seems to be weakness but in reality turns out to be a wisdom based on the knowledge that human beings cannot afford to be too hard either on themselves or others. One play (already mentioned above) was about a young man of twenty who discovers his mother committing adultery while his father is away on a business trip. After wandering around the streets all night, the son staggers into his house, dishevelled, distraught, and looking a little drunk; to his amazement, he finds his father waiting for him. "Now listen, son, I know everything; your mother wired me and I took the next plane back. She told me the whole story."* The boy covers his face with his hands, unable to speak. "What are you going to do?" asks his father. "What do you mean, what am *I* going to do? What are *you* going to do?" "Well, what do you expect me to do—leave your mother and break up our home because she made a mistake?" At this suggestion that his father wants to forget the whole thing, the boy stares at him incredulously; it is impossible to go on living with an immoral mother and a weak-kneed father. Patiently and sympathetically, the father persists in trying to convince his son that their family is too important to be destroyed by a mistake. His wife, he explains, is going through a difficult phase; her son is grown up, she has nothing left to do, she thinks she isn't needed. Now she's upstairs suffering more than her son would believe, terrified that he may turn away from her. "Our job is to help her, not to kill her. I've got to be more loving, you've got to show that you understand her side of things. Will you do it?" And, of course, the play ends with the boy going upstairs to comfort his mother. This is an atmosphere in which adultery and betrayal breed not hatred, but new responsibility. Yet all this understanding disturbs one: is there no breaking point?

Occasionally there is, as when the father's worldliness becomes irrelevant (or worse) to his son's problems. A young man, caught violating the Honor System in his pre-graduation exams at college, is about to be expelled by a committee of his peers when he offers to turn in the names of the others who had cheated with him. The list of names is confided to the chairman of the committee, a brilliant student who is planning to marry a sweet young classmate and go into his father's business. On the list he finds his fiancée's name. Should he, before handing it in to the Dean, strike

---

* I quote from memory throughout this article.

off her name? His father, guessing the boy's trouble, persuades him to do so: "You're going out into a tough world where nobody will care about you and your interests. You have to look out for yourself and the people you love. This is a small town, son; they never forget a scandal, they'll never let you forget that your wife was once expelled from college for cheating. Everybody cheats; the only difference between a respectable man and a cheater is that the cheater has been caught. Son, don't let your 'principles' destroy your happiness. Use your head, boy!" At first the boy takes this advice, but later, to the consternation of his father, confesses while delivering his valedictory address, and proclaims his own expulsion. The two young people leave the small university town together to begin a new life.

Though repudiated, the father in this play is not unsympathetically portrayed. He realizes that the Honor System places too great a burden on young people, and that there is something absurd—something that violates common sense—in allowing a trivial matter to ruin a life. He does not, as his own father might have done, advise his son to give up this girl who will disgrace him: the highest value is still preservation of the family, even if it hasn't quite been formed yet. And in this play the idea of family takes on special significance. The world outside is assumed to be hostile (like the outraged student body demanding the expulsion of the cheaters), or, like the kindly Dean, helpless in the face of circumstances and the Rules. The world outside is mechanical, rigid, governed by cold standards of no one's making: even the Dean can't protect the students he would like to forgive. Within the family, however, a man has resources, for the family rests on love and reasonableness, and it is in the nature of love to persist despite circumstances, while reasonableness provides flexibility to liberate the spirit from the tyranny of Rules. A person is most a person to those who love him; otherwise he is judged and disposed of.

That understanding and flexibility should be the father's greatest qualities is not surprising. What does surprise us, however, is that he rarely feels ambition for his children, merely wishing them to lead normal, contented lives. The only ambitious father I remember seeing is the one in the play just discussed, and he is also the only father who comes off badly in the end—as if ambitiousness were an act of *hubris* to be avenged. The drive for extraordinary achievement has always been considered notoriously American. An identity is something that must be earned, not inherited, and once earned it remains precarious and must be vigilantly maintained: if you lose your money, you also lose your name. This compulsion to prove that we are "saved" is probably a consequence of being born into a Puritan culture—many marks of status in America are simply secularized versions of what once were the symptoms of grace.

We seem, however, under the influence of psychoanalysis, to have reached a point where the most important mark of status has become not money, power, or fame, but a reasonably happy family life. Play after play insists that everyone is saved, that all are granted grace if they are but willing to accept it: adjustment is supposed to be available to all.

The way to justify the space you take up in the world is—as one father puts it—not to be *somebody*, but just to *be*. An adaptation of Dos Passos's *The Big Money* is used as a vehicle for showing the disastrous consequences of the pursuit of wealth; a young boxer who had been a foundling realizes that he needn't be compulsive about becoming a champion in order to give his infant son a "name"; a great soprano feigns the loss of her voice because she has learned that happiness lies in raising children and being supported by a responsible husband; a distinguished (divorced) actress gives up her career because she falls in love with a man who teaches her that what she really wants is a husband and family; a potentially great pianist is forced to admit that he is incapable

of performing on the concert stage, and finds that being released
from an immature ambition allows him for the first time to feel
content in his marriage.

A particularly interesting example is a play about a widower,
father of a fifteen-year-old daughter, who falls in love with a
formerly great concert pianist. We are given to understand that
some sort of illness interrupted her career, but now she is working steadily to stage a comeback. The woman is in her thirties,
completely dedicated to music, living in a room which is stuffed
with busts of great composers and that suggests the atmosphere of
a mausoleum. Pressured into a date with the widower by a friendly
neighbor, she reveals herself as socially inept. Her behavior is
awkward, she can't dance, and she commits the great crime of
being a killjoy by leaving the country club at midnight. ("I'm so
sorry to have ruined your evening," she apologizes pathetically. "I
knew I shouldn't have come. I'm just no good at this sort of thing.
And now I have to get some sleep, because I have a long day of
practice ahead of me.") The widower was an extremely good representative of his type: equable, quiet, observant (the camera kept
finding excuses for giving us close-ups of his intently serious eyes),
sensible, understanding, and completely at his ease in the many
different situations the play showed him in. We soon discover that
the widower's young daughter fancies herself a pianist too. Against
the tactful urging of her father, she breaks a date for the junior
prom in order to prepare for a high-school concert. Eventually, of
course, the daughter and the ex-concert pianist become great
friends. Father is disturbed, but for the moment does nothing, allowing her to study with the older woman. As soon as the high-
school concert is over, he intends to be firm. The night before the
concert, however, he is horrified to learn that great plans are being made for his daughter. "She reminds me so much of what I
was like at her age. And she has talent. You can't stand in her
way. I've sent for the Great Maestro to hear her tomorrow night.

He'll convince you." After the concert, the Great Maestro tells his ex-pupil that her protegée is extremely talented, but that she'll never be anything more than a competent performer: the divine spark is missing. Father is pleased, but the woman refuses to accept this judgment as final. "There are other teachers. We'll get them to hear her. I *know* she has talent. She'll work hard, oh it will be very hard, but she'll make it, I know she will." The father shakes his head sadly. "Why did you stop giving concerts?" "Because I was ill." "No, you weren't ill. I know because I looked up the reviews. They said you had lost your genius, that you were a great child prodigy who never developed." "No, no, it's not true!" "But it is true, my darling. Why can't you face reality? Why won't you move out of this tomb and live?" Through her tears she whimpers, "But don't you understand? I have to be somebody." Then comes the clinching line of the play: "Why do you have to be *somebody*? Why can't you just *be*?" And she collapses into his arms. In the last act, the young girl tells her idol that she has to be somebody, but the redeemed artist repeats father's epigram, adding that "there are so many things in life for you. There's your first dance, and the first time you fall in love, and marriage and children." The child weeps hysterically and rushes out of the room, but father and stepmother-to-be embrace. "Don't worry. She'll be all right now."

The play hardly entertains the suggestion that there are circumstances in which a normal life is worth sacrificing, nor does the writer admit that there may be more than one way of finding happiness, or that there may be other forms of the good life which take place outside the family circle. All this is typical of serious television drama. It would be a mistake, however, to think that "conformity" is being urged, if we mean by that imposing a specific model of behavior. On the assumption that everyone really wants the same kind of things out of life, these plays argue, quite plausibly, that only childishness or neurosis (both of which are characterized by the excessive demands they foster) will prevent people from taking advantage of their inalienable right to pursue happiness. Nor is there any uncertainty about the content of happiness; the only problem is finding the surest, swiftest, and safest means to a predetermined end.

Yet, curiously enough, the most salient feature of this ethos remains its sadness. It presents itself as making a modest demand upon life, a demand so modest that life would be guilty of the cruelest perversity to deny it. Bearing in its countenance the lines and wrinkles of maturity, it is always opposed to the presumptuous, enthusiastic "idealism" of Youth. Yet what could be more optimistic than the belief that contentment and security are within everyone's reach? When success is measured by money or fame, failure can be chalked up to bad luck; the whole man is rarely in the balance, for a certain distinction will be maintained between the private and public selves: the private self is there to fall back upon if the other turns out treacherous. But when success is conceived as an attribute of the personality rather than of the wallet, failure becomes the tenth circle of Hell. A new fortune can be made, but a man's personality is his essence—personality, in fact, is the modern word for soul—and if that proves befouled, then no good can come of it. In these plays personality itself figures as the goal of all striving; the object of ambition becomes not success but "successful living." The type of all failures is the neurotic, pictured writhing under his burdens like one of the damned; and appropriately so, for in this view of things, a failure of the personality is the last and most refined torture of the Devil. Perhaps some perception of this accounts for the resignation that overcomes the intrinsic cheeriness of the new ethos.

It would be foolish at this point to make any simple judgments on television drama as a whole. Its most notable achievements, I think, are the sharpness with which it has distinguished itself from the movies, the effort it has made to be honest, the success with which it has managed to be serious without being objectionably pretentious. Most important, perhaps, it gives pleasure as so many "serious" movies have failed to do—Hollywood's great fault is its inability to see any connection between "entertainment" and "significance." Apart from a few comic strips, television drama seems the only area of American popular culture that refuses to distinguish finally between the two. Because it isn't imitative, it gives a picture of American life whose accuracy may be difficult to measure but whose honesty is sometimes astonishing: there was a time when the play about the mother's adultery would have ended with the discovery that she hadn't really committed adultery at all.

It may be that this drama reflects the values and aspirations of the newly emerged middle class, now large enough to constitute a mass audience and powerful enough to set the stamp of its attitudes on an important segment of popular culture. Formed by psychoanalysis and nourished by the concepts of social work, this class show a conspicuous distaste for violence and a remarkable lack of interest in the ungovernable passions of young love. It puts a very high value on the family, though not in order to retreat from the community. The family here is an expanding rather than a restrictive entity, the nucleus of community; it comes to mean all decent, sensible, and understanding people, "people like us," people, that is, who act *as* people and not as "forces." The retreat to the home, then, means a retreat from "environment"—from the competitive world of business and politics, which menaces amiable human relations and does not yield easily to compromise and good will.

Finally, this drama has contributed a new figure to the popular imagination. Attractive and disturbing as he is, the father may turn out to be a summation of the postwar ethos. In his benign firmness, in his mature sobriety, in his sad but determined sense of responsibility, in his unceasing efforts to keep the peace, we can detect the traces of the contemporary political climate. He reflects the feeling that the only safe oasis in a dangerous cold-war world is our own home, a home which, though it may once have been taken lightly, must now be preserved at all costs if the battle is not to be lost everywhere. And in the long series of plays which turn on a rediscovery of the father by his son, we find, perhaps, the mark of a generation which has moved out of rebellion and skepticism into a patient and humble acquiescence; and we may here discover the role the new middle class seems to have marked out for its own.

[1953]

Gallipoli: Romance and Reality

Though it probably will not be judged an important contribution to historical scholarship, Alan Moorehead's *Gallipoli* is an impressive contribution to historical literature. The book gives one a very vivid sense of what it was like to be in the trenches at Gallipoli during those nine months in 1915 when the Allies, largely British forces, tried to storm the Dardanelles, getting nothing for their pains but a quarter of a million casualties (only a thousand less than they inflicted on the Turks) and a lesson in how not to conduct an amphibious operation. Mr. Moorehead's account of the tactics of the campaign could not be more lucid, and his portraits of the leading figures involved are done with the touch of a professional novelist. He tells the whole story with an eye on its dramatic value and an awareness of the workings of destiny on the ambitions of men, for his purpose, I suspect, is not only to relate what "really" happened at Gallipoli but to create a Gallipoli as worthy of an epic poem as the Trojan War. Indeed, *The Iliad* is no further from Mr. Moorehead's mind when he writes of

Gallipoli than it was from the minds of some of the men who fought there, in particular the commander-in-chief, General Sir Ian Hamilton. In the preface to his *Gallipoli Diary*, addressed to the soldiers who had served under him, Hamilton declared:

> Already you form part of that great tradition of the Dardanelles which began with Hector and Achilles. In another few thousand years the two stories will have blended into one, and whether when "the iron roaring went up to the vault of heaven through the un-harvesting sky," as Homer tells us, it was the spear of Achilles or whether it was a hundred-pound shell from Asiatic Annie won't make much odds to the Almighty.

Mr. Moorehead quotes this passage as an epigraph to his last chapter, and it obviously expresses one side of his own feelings about Gallipoli.

Yet what are the facts of this story that is supposed to have the stuff of heroic legend in it? In September of 1914, Turkey, after some hesitation, entered the war on the side of Germany. Neither the British nor the French were much concerned by this development, but Russia was seriously affected. The Turks controlled the Dardanelles and the Bosporus, Russia's major trade route, so the Russians were now cut off from England and France. It was Winston Churchill, then First Lord of the Admiralty, who conceived the idea of dispatching a fleet of old battleships and mine-sweepers to attack the Dardanelles. He believed that the Turkish fortifications on the Gallipoli Peninsula could be destroyed by naval action alone and that the fleet could then move through the Dardanelles to capture Constantinople, reopen the way for Russian shipping, and perhaps make it possible for the Allies to launch a flanking attack on Germany through Turkey and the Balkans. Using all his persuasive power, Churchill managed to convince the War Council of the soundness of this scheme. In a few weeks, and at the cost of a few ships that were ready for scrapping anyway, Turkish resistance was practically eliminated. The available evidence indicates that one more all-out assault would have eliminated it altogether. But suddenly the admirals in London lost heart, and neither Churchill's eloquence nor reports from optimistic officers on the scene could reassure them. It was decided that the Navy needed military support after all.

From that point on, the Gallipoli campaign became a marvel of futility, in which every plan miscarried and every step was a blunder. It was a war such as Tolstoy, who sneered at strategy and saw only chaos and blind will at work on the battlefield, would have understood. By the time the Allied army arrived, the Turks, led by a German commander, had been reorganized, but they still would have been no match for the British, French, and Anzac troops had not the Allied campaign been so mismanaged. The first landings were begun without maps, without intelligence reports, and without an adequate system of communication between detachments:

> While their senior officers strolled about through the scrub inspecting the position the men sat down to smoke and brew themselves a cup of morning tea. And so the morning was whiled away. Less than an hour's march to the south their comrades at Sedd-el-Bahr and Tekke Burnu were being destroyed, but they knew nothing of this. They heard the distant sounds of firing through the clear sunlit air, but they made no move in that direction.

And so it proceeded, for nine months of suffering and slaughter. At last, the War Council decided to pull the troops out, even though it had been estimated that the evacuation would cost forty thousand casualties. But the War Council was wrong again; the evacuation turned out to be the only successful phase of the campaign, and it was accomplished with almost no loss of life.

This, then, is the story that General Hamilton thought belonged with the heroic legends of the ancient world, and that Mr. Moorehead seems intent on associating with *The Iliad*. But if one's first impulse is to ridicule Hamilton, it is only fair to remember that the General, who often exposed himself to enemy fire and denied himself any comforts that his men did not have, was never unaware of the horrors of war; nor is Mr. Moorehead insensitive to them—his most effective pages are those in which he describes the day-to-day life of the troops in the trenches. Their assertion of the nobility and dignity of Gallipoli is made in full consciousness of the sordid realities of Gallipoli. It represents the belief that war— again in Hamilton's words—is "the only exercise in devotion on the large scale existing in this world." We must also remember that Hamilton was an Englishman, and the self-dramatizing impulse that came so easily to him was a traditional habit of mind with the British, who once had a great capacity for seeing their history as continuous with the world of epic. It used to be thought that Aeneas had been the founder of Britain; he presumably came upon the island in his wanderings after the Trojan War. Then, throughout the 18th century, Englishmen were forever comparing themselves with the ancients, believing that between the light of Homer and the light of Pope stretched one vast shadow of barbarous night. And with the growth of the British Empire in the 19th century, it was inevitable that England should identify herself with Rome. Moreover, one recognizes in Hamilton's remark the peculiarly British ability to speak without embarrassment of national disasters, no less than national triumphs, in the extravagant language of legend and romance. A political compromise between the Whigs and the Tories in 1688 is known to English historians as the Glorious Revolution. Similarly, while the Crimean War was still going on, Tennyson glorified the slaughter of six hundred men at Balaclava in "The Charge of the Light Brigade," convinced that his readers would consider it appropriate for Balaclava to be exalted into the "Valley of Death" and for their brothers and cousins to be transformed overnight into warriors in a saga.

But even apart from all this, Gallipoli readily lent itself to romantic enthusiasm. Troy was just a few miles from the peninsula, and the Dardanelles was once the Hellespont, the "river" that separated Hero and Leander (about whom Marlowe had written a long poem) and that Byron had made a special point of swimming a century earlier. Then, too, there was the object of the expedition, the fabulous Constantinople. Rupert Brooke, whom Mr. Moorehead considers "the symbolic figure in the Gallipoli campaign" and who died of sunstroke before firing a shot, wrote as he was setting out:

> I had not imagined Fate could be so kind. . . . Will Hero's Tower crumble under the fifteen-inch guns? Will the sea be polyphloisboic and wine-dark and unvintageable? Shall I loot mosaics from St. Sophia, and Turkish Delight and carpets? Should we be a Turning Point in History? Oh God! I've never been quite so happy in my life I think. . . . I suddenly realize that the ambition of my life has been—since I was two—to go on a military expedition against Constantinople.

It would be a mistake to regard this as merely the naïve exuberance of a young poet; Mr. Moorehead has enough evidence to persuade us that Brooke's sentiments were more typical than extraordinary. Frequently, the rank-and-file soldier at Gallipoli behaved in ways that suggest that Hamilton and Brooke were not alone in their attitude. During a particularly bloody battle, offers of money were made in the ranks for a chance to get to the front lines. And when it was announced that two hundred men had to be left behind until the very last minute to keep up a barrage of deceptive rifle fire while their comrades were being evacuated, there were hordes of volunteers. It almost seems that the troops fought harder and with greater spirit as they became aware of the uselessness of their efforts. If Gallipoli was a fiasco, it was also a display of magnificent human perversity in an irredeemable situation.

And yet, having said all this, one must still rebel at speaking of Gallipoli in Homeric terms. The First World War has receded far enough into history to acquire an archaic air, to exist in a world utterly unlike our own, but the fact remains that it was a *modern* war, the beginning of an era in which it would no longer be possible to regard armed conflict between nations as an opportunity for adventure and glory, or as the occasion for exultant paeans to heroism. Partly, this was brought about by the appalling efficiency of modern weapons, but a fundamental cause was the gradual erosion of the attitudes that had nourished the heroic view of war. The spread of liberalism and internationalism in the 20th century made it increasingly difficult for the Western world to accept the advantage of one's own country simply as an end in itself. This was true even of the British, who in the age of Gladstone had been notorious for their inability to detect any distinction between the dictates of morality and the requirements of national interest. But above all it was the impersonality of modern war that rendered obsolete the traditional spirit in which battles had always been fought. Achilles's encounter with Hector on the plains of Troy has something in common with the British square holding tight against the Fuzzy-Wuzzies in the Sudan several thousand years later, but rifle and artillery fire raging anonymously in no-man's-land is the voice of another universe. The true pathos of Gallipoli is that the sacrifice and heroism exhibited there seem quixotic and meaningless in this new universe, which is also why the words of Hamilton and Brooke today appear so at variance with the realities of the campaign.

Mr. Moorehead, of course, is aware of these things, but he appears reluctant to admit them. At moments, his book sounds like a eulogy of a dead world; at others, like a desperate insistence that the corpse still has life in it. But to most of his readers, I think, it will be clear that Gallipoli was no Trojan War. It was a cruel joke played by history on the illusions of men who had not yet had time to notice that they were living in the 20th century. Many more such jokes were to follow, and they became ever more cruel and ever more sordid as the century wore on.

[1956]

Truman and the Common Man

The Truman memoirs (*Year of Decisions* and *Years of Trial and Hope*) are devoted mainly to Truman's political career, which of course is as it should be. But this is not strictly a political autobiography. Truman tells us a good deal about his life apart from politics—and we must remember that he was thirty-eight years old before he got involved even in local politics. Some of his more personal reminiscences are unconvincing. For example, in writing about his childhood (which he does "without any introspective trimmings") he sees himself as a less mischievous, untroubled Tom Sawyer, a carefree, rough-and-tumble American farm boy who was forever having the time of his life:

> I pulled the wagon with the two boys in it into the hole and upset it. It seemed a good thing to do, and it was repeated several times, taking turn about. When my mother found us, we were plastered with mud and dirty water from head to foot. What a grand spanking I got as the ringleader!

I would sit in the judges' stand with Grandpa and watch the races, eat striped candy and peanuts, and have the best time a kid ever had.

My mother and grandmother dried a lot of peaches and apples, and what fine pies they would make in the winter.

My mother's older sister, Aunt Sally, was a lovely person, as were all my aunts.

There were four children in [Aunt Emma's] family, and we really had a grand time when we spent the day with them.

Those were wonderful days and great adventures. My father bought me a beautiful black Shetland pony and the grandest saddle to ride him with I ever saw.

We had an old Negro woman who washed for us every week and sometimes cooked for us. She had three boys and two girls, and what a grand time we had.

I do not remember a bad teacher in all my experience. They were all different, of course, but they were the salt of the earth. They gave us our high ideals. . . .

In Independence we made a number of new acquaintances, and I became interested in one in particular. She had golden curls and has, to this day, the most beautiful blue eyes. We went to Sunday school, public school from the fifth grade through high school, graduated in the same class, and marched down life's road together. For me she still has the blue eyes and golden hair of yesteryear.

The fact that the whole picture is a little too sweet, a little too conventional in its healthy, old-fashioned Americanness gives us no warrant to doubt its truth. On the contrary, it is very important to understand that this is how Truman has genuinely come to see his childhood. But it is also impossible not to feel that all those grand times he had must be partly the product of a rather wilful memory. At the age of eight he was fitted with thick glasses which kept him out of games (he had to content himself with umpiring in baseball "because I couldn't see well enough to bat"); he was probably more delicate as a child than he lets on, for at ten he had difficulty in recovering from a case of diphtheria ("my legs, arms, and throat were paralyzed for some months after the diphtheria left me, but [my brother] Vivian made a rapid and complete recovery"); and he was enough of a solitary to have read "all the books in the Independence Public Library and our big old Bible three times through" by the time he was thirteen or fourteen. No wonder, then, that history and biography were his favorite reading matter and that "the lives of great men and famous women intrigued" him: "I wanted to know what caused the successes or the failures of all the famous leaders of history. . . . Reading history, to me, was far more than a romantic adventure. It was solid instruction and wise teaching which I somehow felt that I wanted and needed."

At this point Truman teeters on the edge of complete honesty and one waits for him to admit simply that he was an ambitious, perhaps lonely boy who dreamed of greatness. But no. He read history because "I felt that I ought to know the facts about the system of government under which I was living, and how it came to be. . . . [It was] a valuable part of the total education which I hoped to have some day." Not only was he ambitious, but he lived under the tyranny of a need which is crucial to an understanding of his later development as President:

> I used to watch my father and mother closely to learn what I could do to please them, just as I did with my schoolteachers and playmates. Because of my efforts to get along with my associates I usually was able to get what I wanted. It was successful on the farm, in school, in the Army, and particularly in the Senate.

But, he might have added, it was not necessary in the Presidency. Truman flowered in the Presidency, as perhaps no man

except Lincoln has ever done, possibly because the office liberated
him for the first time in his life from the eternal compulsion to
please those around him. From the moment he fired Byrnes as
Secretary of State, there is a kind of exhilarating quality—as of a
man who has suddenly lost his fear on the battlefield and become
daring through the sheer joy of fearlessness—in the way Truman
the President slashed about him with what often seemed highly
impolitic vigor, culminating, of course, in the dismissal of Mac-
Arthur. He had only to please an abstraction now—the "people"—
not those "associates" who nagged and pressed their demands on
him and may have been skeptical of his abilities. And pleasing the
people turned out to be a means of self-realization for him: he
identified himself so completely with the people that he was unable to distinguish between his feelings, his needs, and theirs.

To please the people was to please himself, for he *was* the
people, he was good old "give 'em hell" Harry Truman, the ex-
haberdasher, "plain folks" in the White House. But this affec-
tionate character he developed only gradually. By now the name
of Truman has grown so resonant with intimations of the colorful
and the spirited that it takes an effort of the imagination to remember what he looked like to the world at the moment of
Roosevelt's death. In 1945 when people said that Truman was
an ordinary little man, they said it with dismay and condescension.
Of course he was "solid"—everyone remembered the Truman
Committee as a courageous and honest investigating body that
went after all the corrupt contractors who were growing fat on
the war effort, and everyone knew that Truman (despite his uncomfortable associations with the Pendergast machine) had a
fine New Dealing record in the Senate. But with the death of
Roosevelt, the nation turned its eyes to the bespectacled, sharp-
faced little fellow and saw prose where before there had been
poetry, it listened to the stumbling, wooden delivery of his
speeches where before it had heard the most mellifluous oratory in

living American memory, and it mourned, like Shakespeare's Cleopatra at the death of Antony: "The odds is gone and there is nothing left remarkable beneath the visiting moon."

And indeed the truth is that at the beginning he *was* prosaic, though never "ordinary"—it is absurd how we get trapped by our own metaphors. He came into the Presidency with no big ideas or new conceptions—yet one guesses from hints dropped here and there in the memoirs that he was not altogether surprised to find himself President and had been preparing for it; instead, he stated his determination to continue the policies of his "great predecessor" (what else could he do, after all?). The first matters he addressed himself to were problems of detail and administration:

> When there is a change in administration, there are bound to be some changes in the Cabinet, but I knew how necessary it was for me to keep an open mind on all the members of the Cabinet—until we had had an opportunity to work together. Their experience with President Roosevelt and their knowledge were necessary to me in this crisis. I intended, also, to maintain a similar attitude toward the heads of all the federal agencies. But I had some mental reservations about the heads of certain temporary war agencies.

These he records as his thoughts just a few minutes after he was sworn in, only two hours after Roosevelt died, and they suggest not merely that he had been thinking about the Presidency, but also how he intended to feel his way into his new job.

There is no question that he took over in the White House almost immediately. But he had to exercise a certain tact:

> President Roosevelt's belongings were numerous in the room. Ship models and ship prints were especially obvious, and the desk was laden with mementos. Everywhere were signs of the man who had labored there so long. I had no wish to change the room as yet, but I was forced to use the desk, and so I asked an aide to put away

the former President's belongings. Except for the objects on the desk, I carefully avoided disturbing the late President's possessions.

The symbolic drama in which Truman was involved vis-à-vis Roosevelt is enacted in that passage. He tells us that he had never been very close to Roosevelt, and in his eighty days as Vice-President he saw him only once or twice. Now he had to move through the magic presence of Roosevelt into a job, and move he did—by clearing away the desk. He immediately had reports submitted to him by each executive department on the policies of the government; and he studied them late into the night, with the same earnest diligence that marked those boyhood days when he pored over Plutarch and Abbott, and when he made it his business in school to look up the background of "each great event in history . . . to find out who brought them about." This is the same man, too, who, before leaving for Washington after his election to the Senate, "read the biographies of every member of the Senate and studied every piece of information I could find on our chief lawmaking body." This was also the man who as a freshman Senator served on two of the busiest committees in the Senate— Appropriations and Interstate Commerce—and never missed a meeting. This was the man who in addition requested to serve on a subcommittee that was formed to study the railroad system and who then "began at once to read all of the records I could locate of earlier testimony concerning the railroads. I read past newspaper accounts of the industry's financial tangles. I ransacked the Library of Congress for every book on the subject of railroad management and history, and at one time had fifty volumes sent by the Library to my office in the Senate Office Building." In short, this was a methodical, hard-working, almost pedantic man who felt most at home with details and who was clearly uncomfortable with any but the simplest abstractions: a personality indeed antithetical to Roosevelt's.

But perhaps the most revealing touch in either of the two volumes of the memoirs is this letter Truman wrote to his mother toward the end of his first week as President. After telling her the story of how he found out that he had become President, he goes into the domestic arrangements:

> This afternoon we moved to this house, diagonally across the street (Penn. Ave.) from the White House, until the Roosevelts have had time to move out of the White House. We tried staying at the apartment, but it wouldn't work. I can't move without at least ten Secret Service men and twenty policemen. People who lived in our apartment couldn't get in and out without a pass. So— we moved out with suitcases. Our furniture is still there and will be for some time. . . . But I've paid the rent for this month and will pay for another month if they don't get the old White House redecorated by that time.

Now even allowing for the fact that this is the kind of thing a man might feel would interest his old mother, it is nevertheless astonishing that Truman, who had just been through the most overwhelming five days of his life, who had just had the "most momentous, and the most trying time anyone could possibly have," who had just inherited "the most terribly responsible job a man ever had," who "felt like the moon, the stars, and all the planets had fallen" on him—it is astonishing that this man could have had *rent* on his mind. Astonishing and yet wonderful. Truman is blessed with what can only be called a limited imagination which never allows him to make an unnecessary fuss or to go beyond the strictly relevant considerations of a given problem. "By nature not given to making snap judgments or easy decisions," he tells us, "I required all available facts and information before coming to a decision. But once a decision was made, I did not worry about it afterward." Only a man of limited imagination could have said of the atomic bomb, "Let there be no mistake about it.

I regarded the bomb as a military weapon and never had any doubt that it should be used." Only a man of limited imagination could have said, on seeing the rubble of Hitler's Reich Chancellery, "That's what happens when a man overreaches himself."

And only a man of limited imagination could have been so little awed at Potsdam, confronted by the two greatest figures in world politics when he himself had only just succeeded to the position of the hero who had been the third. Of course he represented the United States, but he was still Harry Truman of Missouri facing Winston Churchill and Joseph Stalin, and still he was undaunted. "I told them frankly that I did not wish to waste time listening to grievances but wanted to deal with the problems which the three heads of government had come to settle. I said that if they did not get to the main issues I was going to pack up and go home. I meant just that. Stalin laughed heartily and said he did not blame the President for wanting to go home; he wanted to go home too." He also chides Churchill no less than three times for not liking the same kind of music that he and Stalin enjoyed ("Chopin, Liszt, Tchaikowsky and all the rest"). And again he writes to his mother:

> Stalin gave his state dinner night before last, and it was a wow. Started with caviar and vodka and wound up with watermelon and champagne, with smoked fish, fresh fish, venison, chicken, duck and all sorts of vegetables in between. There was a toast every five minutes until at least twenty-five had been drunk. I ate very little and drank less, but it was a colorful and enjoyable occasion. . . . It was a nice dinner.

Of course, we must beware of taking some of these remarks too much at face value. What we have here is another example of Truman's disposition to regard himself as the typical Midwestern American, Tom Sawyer grown up, the prissy Innocent Abroad who is disappointed when princes drink beer like "us common folk" and who finds the Folies Bergère a "disgusting" spectacle, but whose innocence is in the last analysis an assertion of moral superiority. Moreover Truman is not above coyness in this regard. He knows very well that if Churchill and Stalin condescended slightly to him, the joke was on them, just as he knows that in the end his methodical way of doing things was a match for the Churchillian brilliance. When he met Churchill for the first time at Potsdam, he showed the Prime Minister his detailed agenda for the meeting and asked to see his. "I don't need one," said Churchill. (Did Roosevelt need one, we wonder?) Truman lets Churchill's laconic reply pass without comment, but later he makes this observation. "He always found it necessary . . . to make long statements . . . and then agree to what had already been done. . . . On several occasions when Churchill was discussing something at length, Stalin would lean on his elbow, pull on his mustache, and say, 'Why don't you agree? The Americans agree, and we agree. You will agree eventually, so why don't you do it now?' Then the argument would stop. Churchill in the end would agree, but he had to make a speech about it first."

And Truman knows what the impact will be on the reader when he tells the story of how his old schoolmate Charlie Ross, upon being appointed as Truman's press secretary, telephoned Miss Tillie Brown (who had been their teacher in Independence). "You and Harry have made good," Miss Brown said, "and I am very proud of you." What else Miss Brown might have said is difficult to imagine; nevertheless she neither fainted nor shrieked when Truman got on the phone to "report" to his old teacher. Ladies like Miss Brown (not to mention his mother) obviously had an enormous influence on his character and their matter-of-fact refusal to make too much even of the Presidency symptomized an attitude that Truman absorbed. Though fascinated by power and greatness, he is genuinely unimpressed with high position *per se*. A job is a job to him and the main thing is to do it well.

Truman's development in the public mind from the colorless "ordinary man" into the symbolic "common man" is one of the major political facts of our time. It would have been fascinating to hear from Truman himself how the revision was accomplished, but on this point he is completely silent. Indeed, he takes such pains to demonstrate the consistency of his political principles over the years as to make it appear that the Presidency changed him not one whit. By his own account he has always been an internationalist in foreign affairs, but there is very little in his background to explain the dramatic burgeoning of a Senator from Missouri who had been mainly interested in taxes and railroads into one of the most responsible international statesmen of history. Similarly he claims always to have been "a Jefferson Democrat living in modern times," the latest representative of a "tradition" that includes Jackson, Wilson, and Franklin Roosevelt, and whose distinguishing mark is that it fights for the welfare of "all the people" against "the special crew who has the inside track." From the memoirs it would be impossible to tell that Roosevelt chose Truman as his running mate in 1945 primarily because Truman, as a border-state Senator of reputedly moderate views, was a more acceptable candidate to the conservative wing of the party than Wallace. The only indication Truman gives of the surprise that greeted his twenty-one point Fair Deal message to Congress in September 1945 (from which, incidentally, he dates his assumption of the Presidency in his own right) is this comment made to him by Judge Rosenman:

"You know, Mr. President, this is the most exciting and pleasant surprise I have had in a long time. . . I suppose I have been listening too much to rumors about what you are going to do—rumors which come from some of your conservative friends, and particularly from some of your former colleagues up on Capitol Hill. They say . . . that a good part of the so-called 'Roosevelt nonsense' is now over . . . that the conservative wing of the party has now taken charge."

Truman could not have had this reputation on Capitol Hill for nothing, though it must have been based on his privately voiced opinions and an estimate of his character, rather than on his voting record (which was consistently New Deal, including support of the measure to pack the Supreme Court).

But the fact is that he believed it to be the President's duty under the Constitution to represent "all the people," as against Congress, which mainly provides a voice for special and regional interests. This is one reason why in the White House he came to identify himself more and more closely with the "common people," and, by extension, with minorities like the Jews and Negroes. But his conception of the Presidency was not the only reason for the changes in Truman.

Neither his liberalism nor his increasingly strong anti-Communist foreign policy made him very popular with the most vocal elements in the nation. The press hated him for his reconversion program and for the Fair Deal; many liberals hated him simply for not being Roosevelt (who, they were sure, would have known how to live in peace with the Russians); and, one guesses, many of those associates whom Truman had been trying to please all his life refused to acknowledge that he was the boss and could make all the decisions. Byrnes in particular (like "those striped pants boys in the State Department") seems to have been rather insolent:

[Secretary of State Byrnes's] message told me very little that the newspaper correspondents had not already reported from Moscow.

This was not what I considered a proper account by a Cabinet member to the President. It was more like one partner in a business telling the other that his business trip was progressing well and not to worry.

And there are other indications that a good number of the people around Truman were not ready to do him justice.

In any case, Truman's real virtues—his conscientious attention to detail, his ability as an administrator, and most important, his decisiveness—did not form a style calculated to excite anyone to rabid admiration, and least of all a nation still enthralled by the spell of Roosevelt's "brilliance." But at some point Truman began to believe that he was *vox populi*, not merely in his Constitutional position, nor even merely in his political principles, but in his very soul. He may not have been brilliant, but he was something better: the salt-of-the-earth American writ large—plucky, loyal to his friends, devoted to fair play, outspoken, competent, honest, strong but never bullying. Even his foreign policy (the Marshall Plan, Point Four, and the Truman Doctrine) he saw as a reflection of the American character, *his* character: generosity combined with a principled toughness ("The American people have accomplished much and attained greatness not by the use of force but by industry, ingenuity, and generosity").

The process by which Truman came to regard himself as the quintessential embodiment of the average American is impossible to trace in the memoirs. But there can be no doubt that it was in the 1948 election campaign that he finally succeeded in crystallizing this image and projecting it onto the public mind. In his whistle-stop tour of the country, that "one-man circus" during which he addressed millions and sometimes made a dozen or more speeches a day, he threw away the prepared manuscripts whose stilted rhetoric he always had such trouble mouthing, and spoke extemporaneously for the first time. And the new Truman, the grinning, cocky, vernacular, "give 'em hell" Harry began to emerge for all to see:

> I simply told the people in my own language that they had better wake up to the fact that it was their fight. If they did not get out and help me win this fight, I emphasized, the Republicans would soon be giving the farmers and the workers the little end of the stick again. I spoke bluntly and sincerely, and warned the people that if they were fools enough to accept the little end again, they deserved it.

It was often vulgar and at times demagogic, but Truman's portrayal of his own character was reinforced by the drama of the campaign itself. How completely he seemed the little man, forsaken and alone, with the newspapers solidly against him, with the public opinion polls insistently predicting his defeat, with the Dixiecrats on the right and the Wallace Progressives on the left agitating against him from out of his own ranks! And when the miracle came to pass and he had won, it seemed to the whole country that his morality-play picture of American political life had been vindicated, that the Good in the person of the average man had triumphed over the clever and the powerful.

A politician's relation to his own public image can be very complicated, and by now it must be impossible for Truman to disentangle the man he "really" is from the figure he has created in our minds. For example, the one image of Truman that is missing almost entirely from the memoirs is that of the shrewd politician dominating the smoke-filled room, in love with the camaraderie of the political game, not to mention the excitements of the poker game. And what of the Truman who seems to have averted his eyes—like the Jacksonian he is—from shady financial dealings in his own administration? How does Truman fit this side of himself into the Mark Twain character he has assumed? By a theory, it would seem. What he appears to see today as he looks back over his career is a peculiarly American success story. He is the poor farm boy who made good by dint of healthy ambition, hard work, faithful service, luck, and mastery of the political craft. But the craft of politics, he reminds us, is two-sided, involving principles on the one hand, and on the other, the ability to muster the support that makes it possible for a politician to realize his principles and become a statesman.

No one can deny that there is an important truth in such a representation of his life, and it would be true even if he was indeed half-aware of the dubious practices of some of his appointees. But we can see quite another moral significance in his career when we contemplate the fact that this extraordinary man who has probably done more than anyone else to keep the world alive on the edge of an apocalypse, was able to emerge into greatness only by becoming, in his own eyes and in the eyes of the nation, a perfect symbol of the average American.

[1956]

Anthony Eden's 30's

After stepping down as Prime Minister in 1957 thanks to the combined effects of illness and the disastrous Suez campaign, Sir Anthony Eden (now Earl of Avon) naturally set out to write his memoirs, but instead of starting with an account of his entry into public life, he decided that it would be best to get the most sensitive part of the story out of the way first. Accordingly, the first volume, which appeared in 1960 under the title *Full Circle,* was devoted to the period 1951–7, when for the third time in his career, Eden (always the bridesmaid) became Foreign Secretary and then, upon Churchill's resignation in 1955, Prime Minister at last—an office that took him thirty-two years in Parliament to attain and that he was only able to hold for the poignantly brief span of twenty-two months. Now, in the second volume, *Facing the Dictators,* Eden has gone back to the beginning of his story: his election in 1923 to the House of Commons as Conservative member for Warwick and Leamington; his apprenticeship in the early 30's as a precociously brilliant diplomat negotiating with the likes of Hitler, Mussolini, and Stalin; and his first stretch as Foreign Secretary, originally under Stanley Baldwin and then under the infamous Neville Chamberlain. *Facing the Dictators* ends with his resignation in 1938 from the Chamberlain cabinet over his disagreement with the policies that would soon result in the Munich Pact; and in as many subsequent volumes as are necessary, Eden will proceed chronologically to fill in the gap between this event and the one with which *Full Circle* opens (the Tory ouster of the post war Labor government in 1951).

Facing the Dictators is a more interesting book than *Full Circle*, if only because England played a more central role in the history of the 30's than it could possibly do during the Washington-dominated 50's. Yet both volumes suffer in about equal measure from the colorlessness of Eden's personality—a colorlessness of such dimension that after a few hundred pages it begins to assume the character of a positive attribute. Eden is so completely the public figure in these memoirs that one is startled to come upon an occasional reference to "my wife" or "my two sons": when in the world did *they* happen on the scene? It is even more startling to discover from time to time that Eden is capable of strong personal feelings—though fortunately for his claim to the title of perfect British diplomat, he manages on the whole to keep these intrusively ill-bred elements well under control. "At last I have climbed to the top of the greasy pole," said Benjamin Disraeli, another Tory politician who waited many years to become Prime Minister and finally made it. Here is Eden commenting (in *Full Circle*) on his arrival at the top of the greasy pole:

> No two men have ever changed guard more smoothly. In these words Sir Winston Churchill afterwards described his resignation from the office of Prime Minister and my summons from Her Majesty to succeed him. Here was a movement which, on personal as well as political grounds, called for delicacy in execution. It was

not made easier by Sir Winston's stature, nor by the fact that I had been so long his second in command. . . . My own reflections were mixed.

But it is not only in speaking of himself that Eden is so flat and ungiving. His portraits of the great historical figures who parade through the pages of *Facing the Dictators* are marked by the same correct reticence, the same unimaginative blandness. Except for Neville Chamberlain (against whom Eden's bitterness still rankles enough to inspire one or two moments of vivid recollection), none of the actors in the awful drama that culminated in World War II ever succeeds in breaking his way through the thick fog of Foreign Office prose in which these memoirs are written. Hitler "was essentially the man who would pass in the crowd," and Mussolini (no need to be overly polite toward him) had "the mentality of a gangster." On Stalin, Eden is a little better. "Though I knew the man to be without mercy, I respected the quality of his mind and even felt a sympathy which I have never been able entirely to analyse." This curious affection for Stalin is one of the few redeemingly human touches in *Facing the Dictators* (the others being the grudge against Chamberlain and the readiness Eden displays to get in a dig at the Labor party whenever the opportunity presents itself). Despite the unexpectedness of his attitude, however, all Eden can tell us about Stalin is that his manners were good ("perhaps a Georgian inheritance"), that his mind was pragmatic rather than doctrinaire (big surprise), and that he was "the quietest dictator I have ever known, with the exception of Dr. Salazar."

But if Eden's colorlessness makes *Facing the Dictators* something less than a pleasure to read, it also results in the compensating advantage of allowing us a glimpse into how the history of the 30's actually looked as it unfolded from day to day, month to month, and year to year. Or so, at any rate, it seems. The reason

we cannot be sure that this is *really* how it looked at the time is
that Eden believes there are lessons here which are directly relevant to the international situation of our own day, and he has
therefore written *Facing the Dictators* with an eye toward suggesting a number of implicit parallels. How much distortion of
emphasis this may have created is a question that only a specialist
in the history of the 30's would be competent to answer. But even
if we take Eden's account as fairly accurate, we are still left wondering whether a wise policy for dealing with the Communists
today can be framed more or less by inverting the mistakes that
were made in dealing with Hitler and Mussolini during the 30's.

These mistakes, of course, go by the collective name of "appeasement," which has become such a dirty word in the contemporary
political vocabulary that by now something close to a heroic
effort is required simply to understand the rationale that supported
it. Essentially, appeasement was based on the idea that both
Mussolini and Hitler had legitimate claims and grievances which,
if satisfied, would ensure the stability of Europe and hence prevent
the outbreak of a major war. Eden was almost alone among his
colleagues in the government in disagreeing with this view, but if
Facing the Dictators makes anything clear, it is that the grounds
of his disagreement were specific rather than general. That is to
say, he believed that the two dictators had larger ambitions than
Chamberlain and the other appeasers thought they had, that their
word could not be trusted, and that they could better be stopped
by resisting their demands than by giving in to them.

He was, of course, right, but it is important to recognize that if
his judgment had prevailed, World War II would almost certainly
have come about anyway. It might perhaps have been won more
easily and allied lives might have been saved—which is saying a
lot—but if the objective was peace, Eden's policy could no more
have achieved it than Chamberlain's. Was Eden aware of this? So
far as we can tell from *Facing the Dictators*, he was not—or at

least not perfectly. What he seems to have thought was that Hitler could be "restrained" by a show of determination on the part of the democracies (i.e., a stepped-up rearmament program); as for the rest, it could be taken care of by the ordinary processes of negotiation. In other words, Eden in pursuing peace wanted to hedge his bets, while the appeasers—this was the main difference between them—dogmatically saw no need for a hedge.

So thoroughly discredited were the appeasers by subsequent developments that there was no danger of the same mistakes being made over again in the postwar period, when Stalin began to look like a threat comparable in kind to the one Hitler had been in the 30's. By 1948, it seemed clear that Stalin's word could no more be trusted than Hitler's (he had broken his promise about free elections in the countries occupied by the Soviet armies during the latter part of the war); that his ambitions were boundless (the whole of Europe felt menaced by the Czechoslovak coup, while Greece and Turkey worried about invasion); and that he was motivated by an ideology which envisioned its own extension over the face of the globe (whereas no one in the foreign ministries of Europe seems to have paid much attention to *Mein Kampf* in the 30's, everyone in Washington had boned up on Marx and Lenin). The steps taken by the United States in response to all this—the Truman Doctrine, the Marshall Plan, the formation of NATO, etc.—were obviously taken with the memory of Munich very firmly in mind. Stalin was to be halted by a build-up of military strength, and by speeding the economic reconstruction of Western Europe.

Assuming that Stalin was in fact the kind of threat that the Western powers believed him to be in 1948, it would seem eminently reasonable to conclude that the lesson of Munich was well applied. After all, Stalin *was* stopped from advancing westward by American power—no doubt about that. But would he have been stopped by anything short of *nuclear* power? Certainly Hitler would not have been, if only because he saw war as a necessary consummation of the revolution he had wrought and therefore wanted it for its own sake. Stalin had no such notions about war and neither, of course, does Khrushchev. And yet it is entirely possible that either of the two Russian leaders would have been willing to engage in a conventional war with the West if it had struck them as necessary. For that matter, if not for the Bomb, we ourselves would undoubtedly have seized the opportunity to "roll back" Soviet power by going into Hungary in 1956. The Bomb, then, makes nonsense of all analogies between this period and the 30's, for it has given both sides something that neither side had then and that only one side mistakenly thought it had—an overriding interest in preventing the outbreak of a major war.

So far as the Russians are concerned, all of this means that they can be expected to behave less and less like a messianically inclined revolutionary power, and more and more like a traditional nation-state, to be dealt with in what we might call here the Eden manner: a combination of strength and the readiness to negotiate. Consequently, if the problem were only one of establishing international stability through agreements with the Soviet Union, there would be very little to trouble our sleep. But, of course, the Soviet Union qua nation-state is not the whole story; there is also the matter of Communism and its relation to the so-called "revolution of rising expectations" now taking place all over the world. To say a word about Communism first: just as the Bomb (acting in cooperation with their own internal evolution and their own growing prosperity) dampens the Russians' revolutionary fervor, whether they like it or not, so their commitment to Communism requires them to express a risky degree of such fervor—again whether they like it or not. To the extent that they do *not* like it, they have the Chinese to prod them along, forcing them—on pain of losing their position of leadership in the Communist world—to make dangerous demonstrations of their toughness and of their enthusiasm for "wars of national liberation" (Castro is a case in point).

Ironically, then, the very success of the Communists in turning Russia into a great modern super-power has helped to unleash a world-wide revolution over which they have as little control as we do and for which no precedent can be found in the 30's. As David Bazelon has put it in a recent article: "The world revolution is simplicity itself to define: the members of the human race have decided that they don't want any longer to live miserably and die young. They are convinced that the means are available to achieve this objective. This is quite a decision: it is, from here on out, the alpha and omega of world politics." To which it may be added that small countries have also decided that they do not wish to be pushed around any longer by big ones, and they will not hesitate to play the big ones off against each other to prevent this from happening. It was because Anthony Eden failed to understand the operations of the revolutionary dynamic of our time that he committed the huge blunder of trying to topple Nasser in 1957 by the simple 19th-century expedient of sending in a few troops to put the insolent fellow down. Eden was not, it should be remembered, stopped by Khrushchev; he was stopped by Eisenhower. Such are the weird complications of international life today.

In short—to return to *Facing the Dictators*—the 30's, Eden to the contrary notwithstanding, had little to teach the 50's and they have even less to teach the 60's. To think that they have can only distract our minds from the problems that history has saddled us with and that the 30's knew nothing about. For, on the one hand, the fear of appeasement leads to losing chances for useful negotiations, and on the other hand, the reliance on military strength to hold the Russians in check leads to a neglect of the political struggle which, from a long-run perspective, is the real struggle, the decisive struggle. The outcome of the recent Cuban crisis is a good illustration. Having triumphed over Khrushchev by a show of force and determination, the President is now back to where he was before the Russians tried to upset the status quo, but the conditions that produced Castro in the first place are still present throughout Latin America. How are they to be dealt with, and is enough being done about them to make sure that the revolutionary thrust they have created will develop along democratic rather than Communist lines? And what about Asia and Africa? Is enough being done there? On these questions, the crucial ones for us, neither the experience of the 30's, nor the essentially 19th-century mind of Anthony Eden, Earl of Avon, is capable of shedding very much light.

[1963]

Herman Kahn and the Unthinkable

Herman Kahn's massive treatise *On Thermonuclear War* has been called the Bible of the Pentagon, and Kahn himself has been widely extolled as the master military strategist of our time, the Clausewitz of the nuclear age. There are, however, circles in which the name of Herman Kahn, far from being venerated, is habitually pronounced with a virulence so intense that one might think the Devil himself were being discussed. "This evil and tenebrous book," said one reviewer of *On Thermonuclear War* when it appeared in 1960, "is a moral tract on mass murder: how to plan it, how to commit it, how to get away with it, how to justify it." The rhetoric of another reviewer was milder, but the outrage no less superb: "I can understand and respect career military officers who have chosen the 'honorable profession of arms' as a way of life, often at a sacrifice in comfort and emoluments and who are subsequently assigned the duty of formulating war plans to meet all eventualities. But Mr. Kahn is a physicist, a scholar and a civilian.

To be blunt, his book makes me ashamed that we are fellow countrymen."

Strong charges, these—strong enough to have provoked Kahn into writing a new book, *Thinking About the Unthinkable*, to defend himself against them and others of a similar nature by arguing for the moral and intellectual necessity of speculating on such questions as how a nuclear war might start, how it might be fought, how long it might last, how much damage it might do, and how it might be won or lost. These were the main questions he discussed in *On Thermonuclear War*, much of whose doctrine is repeated here in simpler and less technical form, along with a fascinating description of the methods of analysis that he and his fellow researchers in the RAND Corporation and the Hudson Institute have used in arriving at their answers.

While Kahn spends a good deal of time—both here and in his earlier volume—on the subject of how to deter a nuclear war between the United States and the Soviet Union, his mind always seems to be magnetized by the idea that deterrence, or the "balance of terror," might very well fail. Indeed, so fascinated is he by this idea that he is endlessly fertile in imagining situations—accidents, miscalculations, unauthorized behavior, cold-blooded or desperate aggressions—in which the balance of terror simply could not be relied upon to prevent an "exchange" of missiles. This is why he continually stresses the need for facing up to the possibility that a nuclear war may actually occur—a possibility, he tells us, that most people (including even strategists and highly placed military men) refuse to accept because they take it for granted that such a war would inevitably result in mutual annihilation. But mutual annihilation, according to Kahn, is the least likely of all the possible results of a nuclear war, at present levels of weapons technology. Everything, he says, depends on how the war starts (by accident, by miscalculation, by calculation); how it is fought (rationally or punitively); and the kinds of preparations that have been made to reduce the damage and to hasten recuperation (civil defense, active defense, stockpiling of food and medical supplies and records, training in methods of decontamination, etc.).

In other words, Kahn's position is that while a thermonuclear war may be different in degree from all past wars, it is no different in *kind*: someone would win and someone would lose. Under certain circumstances that Kahn considers not altogether implausible, the victor might even emerge with fewer casualties and less damage to his resources than either Germany or Russia suffered in World War II. Yet even in the case of a more ferocious war, there are "tragic but distinguishable" computations to be made: a hundred million dead is twice as bad, says Kahn, as fifty million dead —though most people seem unable to grasp the distinction. But "would the survivors envy the dead?" he asks, and the answer is a fairly emphatic No, especially if sensible preparations for recovery have been made in advance. "What evidence there is," reads one of his more notorious pronouncements, "suggests that relatively normal and happy lives would not be impossible even under the harsh conditions that might prevail after a nuclear war, and in spite of the personal and social traumas that would have been experienced."

Kahn's insistence on treating nuclear war as a war like any other—potentially more destructive but still very far from the absolute holocaust that it is widely imagined to be—goes a long way toward explaining the hatred he has brought down upon his head. His critics have not only charged him with being wrong in his reasoning and in his predictions; they have even accused him of helping to bring about a nuclear war by painting a "rosy" picture of what the postwar world would look like. The idea behind this astonishing accusation is that thermonuclear war has so far been avoided only because neither side has believed in the possibility of surviving, let alone winning; therefore in underestimating the damage a nuclear war would do, Kahn is contributing to the erosion of a major restraint.

I myself find it hard to accept the notion that Kahn's ideas have increased the danger of war, even though I hear on good authority that they have influenced American military thinking to the point where they can be held responsible for crucial changes in our whole strategic "posture." In any event, I suspect that the people who hate Kahn and call him a monster are responding more to certain qualities of his imagination than to his special line as a military analyst. For one thing, Kahn does seem to take a visible delight in thinking about the unthinkable; in reading him you can feel the pleasure and excitement he experiences at his own intellectual daring in having crossed over a line beyond which no one else has had the courage to look with such brutal clarity. He sees himself, obviously, as an intellectual pioneer who has had the will, the discipline, and the scientific integrity to cast off the inhibiting pieties, the squeamishness, and the somnolent apathy that have prevented others from exploring the dark terrain of nuclear war: from coolly discussing the wiping out of whole cities, the slaughter of many millions of people, the breeding of deformed infants, and all the other horrors that the military planner must face today. "It does indeed," he remarks, "take an iron will or an unpleasant degree of detachment to go about this task," by which he means us to understand that he has had to teach himself to be callous and cold-blooded for the sake of a job that has to be done. Yet there is no denying that he enjoys the job, and while this in itself is irrelevant to the question of whether the kind of thing he is doing ought to be done at all, whether he in particular has been doing it well, it has nevertheless served to arouse passionate hostility and resentment against him.

But even greater than the delight Kahn takes in the boldness and depth of his own mind is the fun he gets out of exposing the shallowness and timidity of other people's minds. I don't mean to imply that he is a nasty or vicious polemicist. On the contrary, he is extremely good-natured in dealing with opponents (including those who have attacked his moral character), he is always ready to concede the force of a point or an argument on the other side, and he is forever one-upping his antagonists by admitting the weaknesses in his own position before they have the chance to do so themselves. But the fun comes in when he begins using his phenomenally rich imagination of disaster to think up situations which might arise to defeat the intentions of any given policy, whether it be one aimed at enhancing our ability to fight and win a nuclear war, or one calculated to enhance the possibilities of disarmament and world government. Often these situations are simply incredible, but just as often they look more incredible than they actually turn out to be on reflection, for they are always constructed for the purpose of exposing the hidden implications of our present position. For example, one such "scenario"—as Kahn calls these little excursions into "future history"—describes a deliberate attack by the Russians (which Khrushchev, incidentally, has great difficulty in launching, since the officer who is supposed to fire the missiles refuses to believe the order he has heard on the phone), and the ensuing negotiations between Moscow and Washington. Bizarre, implausible, and grossly exaggerated though some of the details of this scenario are, it does nevertheless make us aware of the enormous complexities that anyone who wants to think responsibly about military policy must be prepared to consider. And I suspect that Kahn is right when he suggests that much of the hatred he has inspired is a consequence of the problems he has created for those who, on the one hand, do not wish to think about nuclear war at all, and those who, on the other, wish to take refuge in easy slogans and pious sentiments.

But if Kahn has made nuclear war "thinkable" by demonstrating that it is *possible*, he has also—and by the same token—cast even more serious doubt than the most ardent pacifists have yet been able to do on the ability of a strong military establishment to deter a nuclear war. Kahn's critics within the "peace movement" have been so busy venting their indignation at him and trying to prove that a nuclear war would be far more horrible than he says it would be, that they have missed an opportunity to claim him as one of their own. If I wanted to convince a skeptic that there is no security in the balance of terror which American policy is committed to maintaining, I would send him to the works of Herman Kahn far sooner than to the writings of the unilateralists and the nuclear pacifists who have done their best to refute him. Even though it is true that Kahn voices grave doubts as to the feasibility of disarmament, the case he makes against disarmament is rather less devastating—at least to my mind—than the case he makes against deterrence. So devastating, indeed, is his critique of deterrence that it would scarcely be an exaggeration to say that he, the great theorist of deterrence, does not believe in it at all. Has he not made fun of the kind of general whose motto is: "If these buttons are ever pushed, they will have completely failed in their purpose"? Has he not indicated in a thousand ways that war is virtually inevitable unless some form of disarmament treaty is worked out soon? And has he not warned over and over again that if we fail to arrive at an adequate measure of arms control within the next decade or so, we will almost certainly have the mutually annihilating war on our hands that he so firmly denies we are confronted with today?

It would seem, then, that many advocates of a hard line in American foreign policy have derived comfort from Kahn's arguments only by reading him as selectively in their own way as his enemies have in theirs. There is no question that Kahn's conception of a nuclear war as a war like any other has been useful to those who believe in being tough with the Communists. Being tough—as Kahn has repeatedly pointed out—necessarily involves a willingness to go to war in the event of an extreme provocation, and there are very few people whose anti-Communism is so great that they would be ready to blow up the whole world rather than see the Russians take it over. (Kahn himself has declared that while he would consider it an act of cowardice for a man to say, "I would rather be red than dead," he would agree with the proposition that it is better for *everyone* to be red than for everyone to be dead.) If, however, a nuclear war need be no worse, or only somewhat worse, than World War II, anyone who thinks that the Communists are at least as bad as the Nazis can contemplate World War III with a relatively untroubled conscience—while hoping, of course, that deterrence will work well enough to maintain us indefinitely in a state of troubled peace.

Yet it is just here that the more sensible and humane advocates of a hard line run into difficulties. Since such people are genuinely appalled by the prospect of a nuclear war (which they are honest enough to realize would be sufficiently horrible even at best), they must rely on the tremulous conviction that our military might *will* deter the Communists both from attacking us and from provoking us to the point where the only choice we have is between war and surrender. But if I am right in my reading of Kahn, he is in effect telling us that it is naïve to suppose that deterrence can be relied upon to work for very much longer. The arms race, he says in *Thinking About the Unthinkable*, has so far resembled a walk more closely than a race: neither side has been moving as far or as fast as it could. But failing an adequate system of arms control, we can expect—and within the next twenty years—the spread of nuclear weapons to many other countries (including small ones), and we can also expect the development of what he calls "doomsday machines" which would indeed be capable of destroying the whole planet.

Kahn's doctrine thus contains within itself the seeds of its own obsolescence, and this—if I understand him correctly—is what he is hinting at in the extraordinary chapter, "Thinking About the Future," with which he ends his new book. After having in the previous two chapters sketched out the absurd dangers that are involved in the "game of chicken" that is being played by the United States and the Soviet Union, and then having shown why he believes that the system of autonomous national sovereignties has been rendered obsolete by the technology of the nuclear age, Kahn goes on in "Thinking About the Future" to discuss fourteen alternative policies that this country might follow, ranging from "renunciation" (or unilateral disarmament) to preventive war. This summary is worth the price of the whole book: I doubt that a better picture of the alternatives before us exists anywhere. Of the fourteen strategies he discusses, two he dismisses as counsels of despair: unilateral disarmament and preventive war. Of the rest, about half are programs calling in various ways for greater aggressiveness and belligerence than we have yet exhibited, while the other half consists of strategies which aim at the development of a non-military approach to the problems of international life. Kahn concludes by emphasizing the importance of research into the implications of all these positions, but since he and his colleagues have been taking pretty good care of the military side of things, one can only suppose that he is now preparing to devote an equivalent amount of energy to the possibilities of a non-military solution. If this is so, it would be immensely valuable, for the kind of thinking that Kahn has applied with such startling effect to the unthinkable might be turned on the thinkable with even more startling results.

[1962]

The Most Essential of All Possible Lippmanns

A great many tributes have been paid to Walter Lippmann in the course of his extraordinary career, but I doubt that anyone has ever made such large claims for him as are put forward by Clinton Rossiter and James Lare in the introduction to their anthology of his work, *The Essential Lippmann*. Lippmann, they tell us, is "one of the few truly 'essential' men of private station in the past fifty years." (Among the others they mention are John Dewey, Thorstein Veblen, Frank Lloyd Wright, Eugene O'Neill, and Robert Frost—quite a list.) It is not, however, Lippmann the journalist who seems to them "the most 'essential' of all possible Lippmanns," but rather Lippmann the political philosopher, "the man who speaks in general terms about ethical and social problems that have been with us in the West from the beginning and will be with us to the end, and thus who speaks not only to the living but also to generations unborn." So far as his work in journalism is concerned, they quote Lippmann himself as saying that it has provided the "laboratory" in which he has tested his philosophy from day to day to "keep it from becoming too abstract." The philosophy, then, is the "wheat," and the columns of comment on passing events the "chaff"; it is as a political thinker—"perhaps the most important American political thinker of the twentieth century"—that Lippmann will be remembered and honored by posterity.

Not having by a long shot read everything Lippmann has written (some two dozen books, hundreds of magazine articles, and about four thousand newspaper pieces), I cannot say with complete assurance that Rossiter and Lare are wrong in their overall view of him. On the basis of what is presented in this book, however, I think the conclusion is inescapable that they have done him a disservice by judging his theoretical reflections on politics and society to be more "essential," or even of greater permanent value, than the running observations he has been making for the past thirty years in the New York *Herald Tribune* and elsewhere on the daily public business of America and the world. Lippmann the columnist is an irreplaceable glory, no doubt about that. But about Lippmann the philosopher there is room for considerable doubt, and it seems unfair that the case for his greatness should be hung on so slender a reed when it could have been set unshakeably on his massive accomplishment as a journalist.

This accomplishment has very little to do with the particular positions he has taken on specific issues, and even less with the philosophical assumptions that lurk rather uneasily behind his thinking. It lies, rather, in the incredibly high level of discourse on which he has been able to operate, consistently and for so long, while writing at breakneck speed on events pouring hot from the busy history of our time. What I am suggesting is that Lippmann's real distinction is less philosophical than literary: he shows us what a writer of the very first rank can do in a field that is largely barren of educated literary talent. Who else among our regular political commentators approaches him in cultivation, sensibility, or grace? Who else, for example, would be capable of the precision and felicity of a passage like the following?

> There is nothing in the teachings of Jesus or St. Francis which justifies us in thinking that the opinions of fifty-one per cent of a group are better than the opinions of forty-nine per cent. The mystical doctrine of equality ignores the standards of the world and recognizes each soul as unique; the principle of majority rule is a device for establishing standards of action in this world by . . . adding up voters. Yet owing to a confusion between the two, the mystical doctrine has been brutalized and made absurd, and the principle of majority rule has acquired an unction that protects it from criticism.

As it happens, I find the ideological implications of this passage repugnant. Nevertheless, I cannot help admiring and taking pleasure in the exquisite feel for language it reveals, especially in the use of the words "brutalized" and "unction" in the last sentence. No one but a really good writer could have hit upon images of such surprising inevitability; no one but a really good writer could have achieved the rich rhetorical drama they generate.

Of course, Lippmann is not always as lucky as this in his formulations. Even so, I have never read anything by him that was not at least tasteful and lucid in phrasing, elegantly shaped and sharply stated. His main fault, I think, is a tendency toward pomposity which showed itself even in his most youthful efforts and which, if anything, has been encouraged by the veneration that his advancing years (he is now 74) have brought upon him. Presidents come and go; Congressmen and Senators come, and even they eventually go; but Walter Lippmann stays on in Washington forever—the last articulate representative of the political ambience of an older America, our last remaining link to the ethos of the Federalist Papers. He is, apparently, heeded and feared in Washington in a way that no other writer is, for his judgment of a government official, or of a policy, or of a bill seems to carry with it all the authority of the basic intentions of the American political system. When he speaks, it is as though the true Constitution were speaking, or as though Jefferson and Madison and Hamilton were communicating a mystical consensus through him—so thoroughly has he steeped himself in their spirit, and with such authenticity is he sometimes capable of recapturing the accents of their intellectual style. This, I suspect, is the secret source of his unique power to make the mighty listen: Walter Lippmann's opinion is the closest they can ever come to the judgment of history upon them. Under these circumstances, it is no wonder that Lippmann should occasionally be given to delivering himself of portentous platitudes without being aware that platitudes are what they are. The wonder is that he should still be capable of anything else at all.

But pomposity is not the only price Lippmann has had to pay for his success in holding the ears of the mighty. There is also the narrowing of perspective that he has had to impose upon his beautiful intelligence in order to squeeze it into the terms in which political questions are always discussed in Washington. In one sense, of course, these are the most relevant terms, for they reflect the realities of power and they set the limits to any program of action. Yet the truth is that the great national "debates" that the New York *Times* daily calls upon us to consider are invariably puerile from an intellectual point of view and far beneath the consideration of any sophisticated mind. The prime example is the argument over federal deficits that goes on endlessly in Washington and on all the editorial pages, though the issue under dispute has been settled on the theoretical plane for many years and there is no longer anything to argue about except who gets what. This is, to be sure, a terribly important matter, but it is a mere contest of brute force that cannot seriously be accorded the dignity of a rational debate between two opposing principles. The fact that politicians are obliged to pretend that it can be accorded such dignity is one of the reasons why politics is so boring in America, and it is also one of the reasons why those who speak in public for the ears of politicians will be ignored unless they humor the same delusion.

And so you get the sorry phenomenon of a man like Walter Lippmann judiciously suggesting in the year 1963 that the so-called conventional wisdom in economic theory—which, as he well knows, was exploded beyond all repair ages ago—may perhaps be in need of some slight revision in the light of changing conditions. So, too, you can pick up the *Herald Tribune* these days to find Lippmann telling you that in his considered opinion the time has come for Negroes to be granted their full rights as American citizens. (In 1949, ironically, he was willing to justify the filibuster on the ground that it was a mechanism for preventing the majority from coercing the minority—which is as telling an illustration as one could wish of the kind of trap that lies in wait for anyone who confines his thinking to the given terms of the Washington moment.)

Curiously enough, however, Lippmann is less prone to this sort of thing when he is talking about a concrete issue than when he dons his philosopher's cap and gets down to exploring "essentials." It is true that he often confers a false dignity on the sordid squabbles of our political life, but just as often his entry into the going terms of discussion results in the refinement and purification of those terms. And sometimes it can do better than that: it can result in the voicing of noble imperatives that—Walter Lippmann being who he is—are not easy for the practical to dismiss as the idle chatter of a woolly-minded dreamer.

Thus, while many writers have argued that the nuclear stalemate has made an accommodation with Communist power necessary and that there is no alternative to coexistence, Lippmann is probably the only one who has been able to do so in a manner that is forcefully persuasive to the practical political mind. And this is because at his best he speaks in what may be called the ideal language of that mind: he is never cavalier about the immense difficulties under which it labors, yet he continually holds up the realistic possibility of transcending these difficulties. Lately, for instance, he has been urging the President to stop being intimidated by the tiny margin of his victory in 1960 and to behave like the leader he promised to be during the campaign. One feels sure that this call to action, coming from Lippmann, will have an effect where similar calls have disappeared down the bottomless well of Washington inattention.

When he talks about the problems of modern democracy in the abstract, Lippmann enters into a wholly different and more sophisticated set of terms: those of theorists and social critics like Hobbes, Burke, Hamilton, Carlyle, and Matthew Arnold, who in one form or another and on the basis of one group of assumptions or another said everything there is to be said about the dangers of government by popular rule. It is these dangers—at least to judge by *The Essential Lippmann,* which draws on all his philosophical writings of the past fifty years—that have preoccupied him from the beginning, and that in some cases have continued to bother him long past the time when they had any relevance to anything happening in the real world.

One of his obsessive themes, for example, is the necessity for guarding against the tyranny of the majority. Over and over again he praises the Founding Fathers for understanding that absolute rule by the majority is no better than absolute rule by a king, and he harps incessantly on the safeguards against the coercion of minorities that they in their infinite wisdom built into the American constitutional system. Yet there is not a single word in *The Essential Lippmann* to indicate that these safeguards have worked so well that by now the urgent problem to be dealt with is the coercion of *majorities* by minorities. The Southern minority rules out the civil rights legislation clearly desired by the majority; the rural minority frustrates a serious attack on the problems of the majority who live in the cities; the "fiscally responsible" minority prevents the enactment of the welfare and public-works programs willed by the majority in electing a President who promised to carry them out. And so on and on into the night of our present state of Gallic immobilism.

For the rest, the particular Lippmann whom Professors Rossiter and Lare consider to be "essential" is ideologically interchangeable with a dozen other neo-conservative critics (including Professor Rossiter himself) who are over-impressed with the evil propensities of man and under-impressed with the possibility of political and social arrangements that would encourage the development of the human potentiality for good instead of concentrating on restraint of the bad. In short, Lippmann the political thinker, as presented by Rossiter and Lare, seems to me inferior to Lippmann the journalist—less flexible, less open, less in tune with the pulse of the times, and less moved (to paraphrase a favorite document of his) by a decent respect for the aspirations of mankind.
[1963]

Genocide?

For what, I suppose, are fairly obvious reasons having to do with the general apprehensiveness over the possibility that a nuclear war may yet have to be endured, a large number of books have been written in recent years about the great disasters of the past— events like the sinking of the *Titantic*, the Gallipoli campaign and the opening battles of World War I. To this list we can now add the Irish famine of the 1840's, which forms the subject of Cecil Woodham-Smith's *The Great Hunger*. Mrs. Woodham-Smith, like her nearest American equivalent, Barbara Tuchman, writes with one eye on the general reader and the other on the experts. Her prose is cleaner than Mrs. Tuchman's, more homely and energetic, less given to splashes of color and melodramatic flourishes: on the whole, a style perfectly suited to the job of popular historical writing on a high intellectual level. As for her scholarship, it seems both meticulous and broad: her documentation is extensive, and—what is more important—her judgments are restrained at every point by an awareness of the total play of forces on the actors in the terrible drama she is describing.

Nevertheless, she *does* make judgments; and there is passion in her telling of the story and an urgency that leads one to suspect her of having chosen to deal with the Irish famine less for its own sake than for what it exemplifies. Interestingly enough, much the same note of urgency has also been present in some of the earlier contributions to this new genre of disaster studies—Mrs. Tuchman's *The Guns of August* and Alan Moorehead's *Gallipoli*, for instance, which further resemble *The Great Hunger* in the view they implicitly take of how and why such disasters come about. What fascinated Mrs. Tuchman about the first 30 days of World War I, and Mr. Moorehead about the conduct of the Gallipoli campaign, was the immense discrepancy between the confident expectations of the generals and the realities as they came to pass: in short, the extent to which stupidity and dogmatism can operate in high places when the lives of millions are at stake. (And if then, the question suggests itself, why not now?) This is precisely the kind of thing that astonishes and angers Mrs. Woodham-Smith in *The Great Hunger*, and it is what gives an edge of contemporary relevance to her account of how the British government went about the task of coping with a calamity that was to cause unimaginable suffering and that was finally to claim the lives of at least a million and a half people.

Even before the famine struck in 1845, Ireland was in a wretched condition. According to Disraeli, the population (close to 9,000,-000 at the time) was denser on arable land than that of China; and, according to the Duke of Wellington, "There never was a country in which poverty existed to the extent it exists in Ireland." Roughly half the rural population lived in windowless mud cabins of a single room, often without furniture. With no industry to speak of, the towns offered very little employment, and since the land (much of it owned by callous absentee landlords) was broken up into tiny parcels and rented out to tenant farmers who just about managed to support themselves, there was no agricultural employment to be had either. "Unless an Irish laborer could get hold of a patch of land and grow potatoes on which to feed himself and his children," Mrs. Woodham-Smith tells us, "the family starved." Thus "the possession of a piece of land was literally the difference between life and death." Not only were rents high— between 80 and 100 per cent higher than in England—but the tenant had no legal protections against his landlord. Any improvements made on the property belonged to the landlord, and eviction, which amounted to a death warrant, was a matter of the landlord's whim.

Under this system, dependence on the potato in Ireland became virtually absolute. The potato was easy to grow (only a spade was required), great quantities of it could be produced cheaply from a small plot of ground, it provided a good diet both for animals and humans, it was simple to cook and it did not pall. Yet, as Mrs. Woodham-Smith points out, "it was the most dangerous of crops. It did not keep, nor could it be stored from one season to another. Thus, every year, the nearly two and a half million laborers who had not regular employment more or less starved in the summer, when the old potatoes were finished and the new had not come in." Worse still, if the potato did fail, nothing could replace it, for no other food existed that was equally cheap, and it would have taken a long time to prepare the soil for the cultivation of any other crops.

Fail the potato did before, but never on such a scale as between 1845 and 1849, when a hitherto unknown disease called blight invaded Europe from North America and destroyed the potato crop, either partially or wholly, for four successive years. The British government, with masses of starving people before its eyes and the prospect of worse to come, reacted with such extraordinary inadequacy that some historians—and many Irishmen—firmly believe that it was pursuing a deliberate policy of genocide against the Irish, no less certainly than Nazi Germany pursued a policy of genocide against the Jews. British hostility to Ireland, rooted in long-standing religious and political differences, was so deep and bitter that Sydney Smith, the famous 19th-century wit, could remark, "The moment the very name of Ireland is mentioned, the English seem to bid adieu to common feeling, common prudence and common sense, and to act with the barbarity of tyrants and the fatuity of idiots." And, indeed, as one follows Mrs. Woodham-Smith's highly detailed account of the schemes and counter-schemes developed in London for the presumed purpose of relieving Irish distress during the famine years, one begins to wonder whether there may not in fact have been some half-conscious evil design at the bottom of all this cruel bungling and administrative callousness.

For example, an ostensibly generous system of public works was set up to provide employment, but at the same time it was turned over to corrupt or inept officials, and the scale of wages was kept so low that purchase of enough food to prevent a family from starving became impossible in a great many cases. Food in the form of Indian corn imported from North America was distributed in some parts of the country, but in ridiculously small quantities—and even then it did next to no good, for it was difficult to digest and failed to provide proper nourishment. So, too, with the soup that was later handed out and that slaked hunger momentarily, only to collaborate with the dysentery to which the starving are always a prey and therefore to hasten the progress of death.

As the famine entered its third year, the British government, irritated by the failure of such measures (which had cost the Treasury more than 8,000,000 pounds), decided to throw the burden of relief on Ireland itself. This meant that the starving masses were to become the responsibility of the local Poor Law "unions" or workhouses—those 19th-century British institutions of which it has been said that their purpose was not to help the destitute but to make relief so unattractive that a man would rather die than throw himself onto the benevolence of the public. The Irish workhouses were in an even filthier and more disorganized condition than their counterparts in England. Many of them, as the British government well knew, were bankrupt (property owners were taxed for their support and even in normal times it usually took troops and warships to collect these taxes). Nevertheless, in the summer of 1847, the government, pleading the excuse of a financial crisis, in effect washed its hands of the Irish famine, while starvation and typhus were claiming thousands of lives with every passing month, and while the country was being further depleted by the emigration of almost a million ignorant, emaciated and disease-ridden creatures who were to endure miseries in the slums of Liverpool, Montreal, Boston, and New York, scarcely less hideous than those from which they had fled.

In addition to the murderous inadequacy of the measures it did take, the government was also guilty of huge crimes of omission. Despite the fact that everyone in London understood that a nation living on potatoes was doomed to a state of constant peril, nothing was done to wean the people away from their absolute dependence on this treacherous crop. Nor was anything done to reform the vicious system of land tenure to which so many of Ireland's troubles could be traced. In consequence, as Mrs. Woodham-Smith puts it, "The famine was never 'over,' in the sense that an epidemic occurs and is over. The poverty of the Irish people continued, dependence on the potato continued, failures of the potato, to a greater or lesser extent, continued, and hunger continued."

Was it genocide? Mrs. Woodham-Smith thinks not. She points out that although the government was parsimonious in dealing with the Irish famine, it is doubtful whether any European government in the 1840's would have done even as much under similar circumstances. The main villain of the story, in Mrs. Woodham-Smith's view, is the fanatical commitment of mid-19th century politicians to the idea that government must not interfere with the operations of the free market and must refrain from any action that would stifle the virtues of "self-reliance and industry." Out of this belief had sprung the incredibly punitive Poor Laws, and out of it, too, came the self-righteous attitudes which dictated British policy in relation to the famine. Charles Trevelyan, the Treasury official who was in charge of the situation, who was as able an administrator as any in England and who worked with untiring energy and devotion, reluctantly admitted rather early on that "this is a real famine, in which thousands and thousands of people are likely to die"—an admission which did not, however, prevent him from adding that help must be given with the utmost caution. For, he wrote, "if the Irish once find out there are any circumstances in which they can get free government grants . . . we shall have a system of mendicancy such as the world never saw." This in the midst of what Mrs. Woodham-Smith, who is not in the habit of offering exaggerated characterizations, calls "one of the major famines of history."

Reading *The Great Hunger* is an experience rather like reading about the Nazi concentration camps. The horrors—descriptions of little children bloated from starvation, of dogs feeding on half-naked corpses, of smells issuing from typhus-infested huts—pile up with such unrelenting force that after a while the mind refuses to take them in any longer. At some point, a certain guilty impatience with the victims even begins to stir in one, as though they could be blamed for the unspeakable things happening to them —the eternally helpless victims, the poor, miserable, wretched creatures forever at the mercy of nature on the one side and power on the other, why can't they *stop* being victims for once? But this impatience is as nothing compared with the fury that any reader of *The Great Hunger* is bound to feel at the fact that *a million and a half* people were allowed to die of starvation and disease because to have fed them would have resulted in a drop of prices, and because they could only be kept alive at the cost of impairing their capacity for self-reliance. If the British government had indeed been deliberately aiming at the extinction of the Irish people, it could scarcely have done a better job than it actually succeeded in doing by treating the famine as an abstract problem, the elements of which were not human beings in desperate need, but such factors as the rights of property and the demands of economic stability. The main objective of everything the British government did in coping with the famine was not to feed the hungry —nothing would have been easier to accomplish if anyone had wanted to accomplish it—but to make certain that private enterprise would be protected. To the extent that protecting it was compatible with feeding the hungry, but not an inch further than that, the hungry were fed. And so they starved. And as they starved, troops with bayonets at the fix stood on the piers, and warships stood in the harbors whence merchant vessels laden with grain sailed forth from Ireland on the export trade.

Today, in the advanced industrial countries, death by starvation is no longer permitted. What is still very much in evidence among us, however, is the kind of political mentality that attacks problems of human need as though the element of need were the least important consideration to be taken into account in framing a solution. At this very moment, for example, untold numbers of migratory farm laborers throughout the United States are as close to starvation as anyone in America is allowed to get, and yet the government granaries are stuffed to bursting with surpluses which are acquired and stored at an annual cost of more than three billion dollars so that food prices can be maintained at an artificially high level. But there is an even better example to hand than that, and a morbidly ironic one in this context. Only recently, the descendant of a famine Irish immigrant who now sits in the White House signed a long-awaited Executive Order banning discrimination in federally subsidized housing. This order is a political masterpiece worthy of Sir Robert Peel and Lord John Russell themselves, for it simultaneously covers the problems of the realtors, the objections of Southern Congressmen and the demands of the liberal pressure groups. As a result, Negroes and Puerto Ricans—the protection of whose rights and the satisfaction of whose needs should have been the uppermost objective of the order—will actually be saved from discrimination in a mere fraction of the housing that is going to be built with government aid in the coming years, while very little will be done to ensure their relocation when they are evicted from their homes to make room for the new high-rent apartment buildings into which they will be unable to move.

In such situations, elaborate explanations always abound. Yet even when the explanations seem plausible, the fact remains that food is expensively stored while deprivation exists nearby, and that private real estate ventures are subsidized by the government in the familiar name of incentive while masses of people are forced to live in conditions of crowdedness, filth and decay. Besides, after reading a book like *The Great Hunger* and being exposed to the assurance with which explanations that seemed eminently plausible at the time were proffered, it becomes more difficult than ever to believe in *any* justification for a political solution to a problem of human need that satisfies every condition except the one that created the problem in the first place.

[1963]

Hannah Arendt on Eichmann: A Study in the Perversity of Brilliance

One of the many ironies surrounding Hannah Arendt's book on the Eichmann trial* is involved in the fact that it should have been serialized in the *New Yorker* so short a time after the appearance in the same magazine of James Baldwin's essay on the Black Muslims. A Negro on the Negroes, a Jew on the Jews, each telling a tale of the horrors that have been visited upon his people and of how these horrors were borne; and each exhorting the prosperous, the secure, the ignorant to understand that these horrors are relevant to them. The two stories have much in common and they are both, in their essentials, as old as humankind itself—so old and so familiar that it takes a teller of extraordinary eloquence, or else of extraordinary cleverness, to make them come alive again. Baldwin is all eloquence; there is nothing clever in the way he tells the story of the Negro in America. On the one side are the powerless victims, on the other the powerful oppressors; the only sin of the victims is their powerlessness, the only guilt is the guilt of

* *Eichmann in Jerusalem: A Report on the Banality of Evil.*

the oppressors. Now, this black-and-white account, with the traditional symbolisms reversed, is not the kind of picture that seems persuasive to the sophisticated modern sensibility—the sensibility that has been trained by Dostoyevski and Freud, by Nietzsche and Kierkegaard, by Eliot and Yeats, to see moral ambiguity everywhere, to be bored by melodrama, to distrust the idea of innocence, to be skeptical of rhetorical appeals to Justice. And indeed, not even Baldwin's eloquence, which forced many of his readers to *listen* for once, could overcome the dissatisfaction many others felt at the moral simplicity of the story as he told it. For as he told it, the story did not answer to their sense of reality; it was an uninteresting story and a sentimental one.

Precisely the reverse is true of Hannah Arendt's telling of the story of how six million Jews were murdered by the Nazis. If Baldwin is all eloquence and no cleverness, Miss Arendt is all cleverness and no eloquence; and if Baldwin brings his story unexpectedly to life through the bold tactic of heightening and playing exquisitely on every bit of melodrama it contains, Miss Arendt with an equally surprising boldness rids her story of melodrama altogether and heavily underlines every trace of moral ambiguity she can wring out of it. What she has done, in other words, is translate this story for the first time into the kind of terms that can appeal to the sophisticated modern sensibility. Thus, in place of the monstrous Nazi, she gives us the "banal" Nazi; in place of the Jew as virtuous martyr, she gives us the Jew as accomplice in evil; and in place of the confrontation between guilt and innocence, she gives us the "collaboration" of criminal and victim. The story as she tells it is complex, unsentimental, riddled with paradox and ambiguity. It has all the appearance of "ruthless honesty," and all the marks of profundity—have we not been instructed that complexity, paradox, and ambiguity are the sign manifest of profundity?—and, in addition, it carries with it all the authority of Miss Arendt's classic work on *The Origins of Totalitarianism.*

Anyone schooled in the modern in literature and philosophy would be bound to consider it a much better story than the usual melodramatic version—which, as it happens, was more or less the one relied upon by the prosecution at the Eichmann trial, and which Miss Arendt uses to great effect in highlighting the superior interest of her own vision. But if this version of hers can from one point of view be considered more interesting, can it by the same token be considered truer, or more illuminating, or more revealing of the general situation of man in the 20th century? Is the gain she achieves in literary interest a matter of titillation, or is it a gain to the understanding?

Let us be clear about these questions: they cannot be answered by scholarship. To the extent that *Eichmann in Jerusalem* parades as history, its factual accuracy is of course open to critical examination. But it would be unwise to take the scholarly pretensions of the book at face value. This is in no sense a work of objective historical research aimed at determining "the way things really were." Except in her critique of the trial itself, which she attended, Miss Arendt's sources are for the most part secondary ones (she relies especially on Raul Hilberg's *The Destruction of the European Jews*), and her manipulation of evidence is at all times visibly tendentious. Nevertheless, a distorted or exaggerated picture drawn in the service of a suggestive thesis can occasionally bring us closer to the essential truth than a carefully qualified and meticulously documented study—provided that the thesis accords reasonably well with the evidence. The point to begin with, then, is Miss Arendt's thesis, and the problem to settle is whether it justifies the distortions of perspective it creates and the cavalier treatment of evidence it impels.

According to Miss Arendt, the Nazis, in order to carry out their genocidal plan against the Jews, needed Jewish cooperation and in fact received it "to a truly extraordinary degree." This cooperation took the form of "administrative and police work," and it was extended by "the highly assimilated Jewish communities of Central and Western Europe" no less abundantly than by "the Yiddish-speaking masses of the East." In Amsterdam as in Warsaw, in Berlin as in Budapest, Miss Arendt writes,

> Jewish officials could be trusted to compile the lists of persons and of their property, to secure money from the deportees to defray the expenses of their deportation and extermination, to keep track of vacated apartments, to supply police forces to help seize Jews and get them on trains, until, as a last gesture, they handed over the assets of the Jewish community in good order for final confiscation.

All this has long been known. What is new is Miss Arendt's assertion that if the Jews (or rather, their leaders) had not co-operated in this fashion, "there would have been chaos and plenty of misery but the total number of victims would hardly have been between four and a half and six million people."

So much for the Jews. As for the Nazis, carrying out the policy of genocide required neither that they be monsters nor pathological Jew-haters. On the contrary: since the murder of Jews was dictated by the law of the state, and since selfless loyalty to the law was regarded by the Germans under Hitler as the highest of virtues, it even called for a certain idealism to do what Eichmann and his cohorts did. Miss Arendt in this connection quotes the famous remark attributed to Himmler: "To have stuck it out and, apart from exceptions caused by human weakness, to have remained decent, that is what has made us hard." Eichmann, then, was telling the truth when he denied having been an anti-Semite: he did his duty to the best of his ability, and he would have performed with equal zeal even if he had loved the Jews. Thus also, the Israeli prosecutor Gideon Hausner was absurdly off the point in portraying Eichmann as a brute and a sadist and a fiend: Eichmann was in actual fact a banal personality, a nonentity whose evil deeds flowed not from anything in his own character, but rather from his position in the Nazi system.

This system is, of course, known as totalitarianism, and it is totalitarianism that brings the two halves of Miss Arendt's thesis together. Long ago, David Rousset, Bruno Bettelheim, and Miss Arendt herself taught us that securing the complicity of the victim is one of the distinguishing ambitions of totalitarian states, and her tale of Jewish complicity here is offered (at least on the surface) as yet another illustration of this point. Long ago, too, she and her colleagues taught us that totalitarian states aim at the destruction of common-sense reality and the creation of a new reality moulded to the lineaments of the official ideology, and her conception of Eichmann as an ordinary man whose conscience was made to function "the other way round " is similarly set forth in illustration of the more general point. Obviously, though, this ordinary man could not have been turned into so great and devoted a perpetrator of evil if the system had not been so tightly closed—if, that is to say, there had been voices to protest or gestures of resistance. Such voices as existed, however, were in Miss Arendt's judgment pathetically small and thin, and such gestures of resistance as were displayed she finds relatively insignificant. Not only did "good society everywhere" accept the Final Solution with "zeal and eagerness," but the Jews themselves acquiesced and even cooperated—as we have seen—"to a truly extraordinary degree." Here, then, is the finishing touch to Miss Arendt's reading of the Final Solution, and the explanation she gives for dwelling on Jewish complicity: this chapter of the story, she says, "offers the most striking insight into the totality of the moral collapse the Nazis caused in respectable European society— not only in Germany but in almost all countries, not only among the persecutors but also among the victims."

An interesting version of the story, no doubt about that. But let us look at it a little more closely. Assuming for the moment that Jewish leadership did in fact cooperate with the Nazis "to a truly extraordinary degree" (the degree is the point under contention), why did the Nazis *want* their cooperation? A reader of *The Origins of Totalitarianism* might have expected Miss Arendt to reply that they wanted it for their own sake. And indeed, she does quote David Rousset to this effect in dealing with the "cruel and silly question," as she calls it, that Hausner kept putting to his witnesses at the trial ("Fifteen thousand people were standing there and hundreds of guards facing you—why didn't you revolt and charge and attack?"). The passage from Rousset is crucial and worth quoting again:

> The triumph of the S.S. demands that the tortured victim allow himself to be led to the noose without protesting, that he renounce and abandon himself to the point of ceasing to affirm his identity. And it is not for nothing. It is not gratuitously, out of sheer sadism, that the S.S. men desire his defeat. They know that the system which succeeds in destroying its victim before he mounts the scaffold . . . is incomparably the best for keeping a whole people in slavery. In submission. Nothing is more terrible than these processions of human beings going like dummies to their deaths.

Yet when Miss Arendt arrives a hundred pages later at the matter of "Jewish help in administrative and police work," considerations of a strictly mundane and thoroughly utilitarian nature suddenly enter as the decisive ones. The Nazis wanted Jewish help, for without it, "there would have been either complete chaos or an impossibly severe drain on German manpower."

Coming from Miss Arendt, this is surprising—"to a truly extraordinary degree," we might say. It is surprising because one of the major points she makes in *The Origins of Totalitarianism* is that the Nazi will to murder every Jew in Europe was so powerful that resources badly needed at the front in 1944 and early 1945 were tied up so that the ovens of Auschwitz could be kept working at full capacity. Certainly it was more *convenient* for Eichmann that the Jews took some of the burdens upon themselves that would otherwise have fallen to him. But to contend that such burdens would have put enough strain on German resources to force the Nazis to ease off on the Jews is ridiculous by Miss Arendt's own account.

For by her own account, the Nazis were determined at almost any cost to "cleanse" Europe of the Jews; nothing in their program had higher priority. But was there no possibility of stopping them? Miss Arendt now argues that there was. Whenever they encountered determined opposition, she says, they backed down, and she cites France, Italy, Belgium, Bulgaria, and (most glorious of them all) Denmark, where the Nazis succeeded in deporting only a comparatively small proportion of the resident Jews. In Holland, Rumania, Hungary, Poland, and the Ukraine, on the other hand, the slaughter was near complete. Looking at all these countries, one can readily agree that the determining factor in the number of Jews murdered was the amount of resistance (either active or passive) offered to the Final Solution. The important question to be decided, however, is: resistance by *whom?* Miss Arendt knows, of course, that it was the attitude of the local populace that made the main difference—where they were willing to co-operate in the rounding up and deportation of Jews, most Jews were deported, and where they were unwilling to cooperate, fewer Jews were deported. But since Miss Arendt wishes us to believe that the Nazis could never have killed as many as six million Jews without Jewish help, she tries very hard to convey the impression that what the Jews themselves did in any given country mattered significantly too. And it is here that she becomes most visibly tendentious in her manipulation of the facts. In explaining, for example, why not a single Belgian Jew was ever deported (though thousands of stateless Jews living in Belgium were), she tells us how the Belgian police and the railwaymen quietly sabotaged deportation operations, and then adds: "Moreover, among those who had fled were all the more important Jewish leaders . . . so that there was no Jewish Council to register the Jews—one of the vital prerequisites for their seizure." But there *was* a Jewish Council in Belgium. There was also one in France, and Miss Arendt simply neglects to mention it. Quite right, too, for the U.G.I.F. made no more difference to the situation in France than the *Association des Juifs en Belgique* made to the situation in Belgium, or than any other *Judenrat* made to the situation in any other country.

So far as the *Judenräte* were concerned, the chief difference between Western countries like Belgium and France on the one hand, and the Eastern territories on the other, was that the Germans did not set up ghettos in the West. The reason is suggested in Léon Poliakov's account of the role of the French *Judenrat*: "In France you never had a situation where Jews were systematically presiding over the deportation of other Jews. [For] *the attitude of the French population, which strenuously opposed the policy of segregation and isolation of the Jews, made such degradation impossible*" (my italics). In any case, the Nazis may indeed have backed down somewhat when they encountered opposition from the Danish king or the Italian army or the Bulgarian people, but even there only somewhat. (Hilberg: "The increasing recalcitrance of the French administration . . . finally resulted in a German decision to employ all the available forces of the Security Police for an all-out drive against the remaining Jews.") As for Jewish opposition, all *it* ever did was bring out more German troops. Certainly the Nazis showed little concern over the drain on their manpower when the Warsaw Ghetto revolted.

But not only is Miss Arendt wholly unwarranted in emphasizing Jewish cooperation as a significant factor in the number of victims claimed by the Final Solution; the irony is that her insistence on doing so also involves her in making the same assumption about the Nazis that lay behind Jewish cooperation itself. This assumption was that the Nazis were rational beings and that their aims must therefore be limited and subject to negotiation. When one of the most notorious of the Jewish leaders—Jacob Gens of Vilna —declared that "with a hundred victims I save a thousand people, with a thousand ten thousand," he was saying precisely what the heads of all the major European governments had said about Hitler. "Herr Hitler," as the London *Times* always referred to him in the 30's, was after all a statesman; he had grievances, some of them legitimate; if a few of these grievances were satisfied, his anger would be "appeased," and war could be averted. As many historians have pointed out, the policy of appeasement was not in itself foolish or evil; it was a perfectly traditional diplomatic tactic, and its foolishness in this case lay in the fact that it was being applied to an aggressor who was *not* politically prudential and whose aims were *not* of the traditionally limited kind. The mistake of the appeasers, in other words, stemmed from their failure to recognize the unprecedented and revolutionary character of the Nazi regime.* Almost every Jewish leader in Europe made the same mistake regarding the intentions of the Nazi toward them and their people—a mistake that the Nazis incidentally did everything they could to encourage.

If, then, we ask why Jewish leadership cooperated with the Nazis, the answer would seem to be that they were following a policy of appeasement, and that there was nothing in the least "extraordinary" about this. That, however, is not the answer we get from Miss Arendt; her answer is more interesting and complicated and paradoxical. A distinction must be made, she argues, between the Jewish masses and the Jewish leaders. It was "cruel and silly" of Hausner to ask why the masses went passively to their deaths, "for no non-Jewish group or people had behaved differently." But it is apparently compassionate and intelligent to ask

* Even Anthony Eden was guilty of this failure. See pp. 307–8 above.

much the same question of the Jewish leaders, even though no non-Jewish leaders had behaved differently. In any event, having raised the issue, Miss Arendt finds herself afflicted for the only time in the book with an attack of speculative diffidence and tells us nothing—literally nothing—about why so many Jewish leaders should have cooperated in the destruction of their own people and (since hardly any of them managed to survive) in their own ruin as well. "Wherever Jews lived, there were recognized Jewish leaders, and this leadership, almost without exception, cooperated in one way or another, for one reason or another, with the Nazis." *In one way or another, for one reason or another.* Period. ". . . we can still sense how they enjoyed their new power. . . . We know how the Jewish officials felt when they became instruments of murder. . . . We know the physiognomies of the Jewish leaders during the Nazi period very well." Do we, now? Then pray, Miss Arendt, what did they look like? Give her exactly thirteen lines— four and a bit each for the incredible Chaim Rumkowski of Lodz, the many-sided Leo Baeck of Berlin, and the tortured Adam Czerniakow of Warsaw—and her picture is complete. And why not? The Jews in Miss Arendt's interesting and complicated and paradoxical and ruthlessly honest version of the story are a people curiously without psychology (except of the darker sort, leading to self-destruction), and a people curiously without a history (except of the disabling sort, leading to hopeless inadequacy). When they act—whether it be going to their death, or running a country, or prosecuting a trial—a mere glance at them is enough to produce a confident judgment. And again, why not, when the judgment will almost invariably be adverse?

For what is Miss Arendt really saying when she tells us that "if the Jewish people had . . . been unorganized and leaderless, there would have been chaos and plenty of misery but the total number of victims would hardly have been between four and a half and six million people." Why, she is saying that if the Jews had not been Jews, the Nazis would not have been able to kill so many of them—which is a difficult proposition to dispute. I do not think I am being unfair to Miss Arendt here. Consider: the Jews of Europe, even where they were "highly assimilated," were an organized people, and in most cases a centrally organized people. This was a fact of their condition no less surely than sovereign nationhood was a fact of the French condition. Yet I doubt that Miss Arendt would ever take it into her head to declare that if the French people had not been organized into a nation-state, they could never have been sold out to the Nazis by Pétain and Laval. Throughout this book, Miss Arendt is very nasty about Zionists and Zionism, but the only sense one can glean from her argument is a grain of retroactive Zionist sense. The Jews, she is implying, should have known that anti-Semitism rendered their position in the Diaspora untenable, and they should therefore either have set up a state of their own or renounced their communal existence altogether. She does not explain how such renunciation could have saved them from the Nuremberg Laws. Nor does she tell us why the slaughter of Jews in occupied Russia should have been so complete even though there was no central Jewish leadership or communal organization in the Soviet Union.

But it is unnecessary to pursue the absurdities of Miss Arendt's argument on this issue, just as it is unnecessary to enter once again into the endless moral debate over the behavior of the Jewish leaders—the endless round of apology and recrimination. They did what they did, they were what they were, and each was a different man. None of it mattered in the slightest to the final result. Murderers with the power to murder descended upon a defenseless people and murdered a large part of it. What else is there to say?

In stark contrast to the Jews, whose behavior in Miss Arendt's version of the story self-evidently explains and condemns itself, the

Nazis—or anyway Adolf Eichmann—need the most careful and the most imaginative attention before they can be intelligently judged. The irony here is of course obvious, and even the Eichmann trial to some extent fell victim to it. As Harold Rosenberg once put it:

> Why should this self-styled nobody who had hurled into silence so many of the subtlest and most humane intellects of Europe have been permitted to elaborate on each trait of his character, his opinions on all sorts of matters, including Kant's categorical imperative, and his conception of himself as Pontius Pilate and as a "romantic," his reaction to his wife's reading the Bible, his drinking of mare's milk and *schnapps*? One question would have sufficed to complete the formulation of his culpability: "Weren't you the head of Sec. IV B4 of RSHA charged with the extermination of the Jews of Europe, and did you not carry out the function assigned to you to the best of your ability?"

This, in Rosenberg's view, was the main defect of the trial, and it flowed from Gideon Hausner's persistent efforts to prove that Eichmann was subjectively vicious, as well as a perpetrator of objectively criminal deeds. Miss Arendt also disapproves of these efforts by Hausner, but her complaint is against Hausner's particular conception of Eichmann's character and not against the opportunity he gave him to speak. Far from being offended at the idea that *this self-styled nobody who had hurled into silence so many of the subtlest and most humane intellects of Europe* should have been permitted to discourse himself at such great length, Miss Arendt helps the discourse along, develops it, refines it, and in the end virtually justifies it. By this I do not mean that she defends Eichmann, as some of her critics have stupidly charged: she does nothing of the kind anywhere in her book, and she says plainly in the closing chapter that he was guilty of participation in mass murder and deserved to hang. What she does do, however, is accept Eichmann's account of himself and of his role in the Final Solution as largely true. In some sense, he *was* an "idealist"; in some sense, he was *not* an anti-Semite; and the degree of his responsibility for the murder of the six million, while sufficient to hang him, *was* relatively insignificant, and certainly nowhere near what the prosecution claimed. By building Eichmann up into a fiendish Jew-hater and a major Nazi figure, Miss Arendt believes, the prosecution missed the whole point of his crimes, of the system which made them possible, and of the lessons to be drawn for the future.

Taking Eichmann pretty much at his own word, then (except when his own word conflicts with her reading of his character), Miss Arendt treats us to a genuinely brilliant portrait of the mind of a middle-echelon Nazi and, by extension, of the world that produced him and gave him the power to do the things he did. And around this theme of Eichmann's "banality" other themes gather: the almost universal complicity of Christian Europe, and especially of the German people, in Nazism (for in diminishing Eichmann's personal responsibility for the Final Solution, she enlarges the area of European responsibility in general); and the almost total consequent unwillingness of the Federal Republic to prosecute and mete out adequate punishment to Nazi war criminals still at large and in many cases flourishing (Miss Arendt, it should be noted, presents perhaps the most severe indictment of Adenauer's Germany that has yet been seen this side of the Iron Curtain, and whatever comfort the book may bring to the Germans in some respects, it is bound in the main to infuriate them).

The brilliance of Miss Arendt's treatment of Eichmann could hardly be disputed by any disinterested reader. But at the same time, there could hardly be a more telling example than this section of her book of the intellectual perversity that can result from the pursuit of brilliance by a mind infatuated with its own agility and bent on generating dazzle. The man around the corner who makes ugly cracks about the Jews is an anti-Semite, but not Adolf Eichmann who sent several million Jews to their death: *that* would be uninteresting and would tell us nothing about the Nature of Totalitarianism. Similarly, the behavior of the Jewish leaders under the Nazis was "extraordinary," but Adolf Eichmann was ordinary, even unto banality; otherwise, he tells us nothing about the Nature of Totalitarianism. Did he have no conscience? Of course he had a conscience, the conscience of an inverted Kantian idealist; otherwise he tells us nothing about the Nature of Totalitarianism. But what about his famous statement that he would die happy because he had sent five million "enemies of the Reich" to their graves? "Sheer rodomontade," sheer braggery—to believe it is to learn nothing about the Nature of Totalitarianism. And his decision to carry on with the deportations from Hungary in direct defiance of Himmler's order that they be stopped? A perfect example of the very idealism that teaches us so much about the Nature of Totalitarianism.

No. It finally refuses to wash; it finally violates everything we know about the Nature of Man, and therefore the Nature of Totalitarianism must go hang. For uninteresting though it may be to say so, no person could have joined the Nazi party, let alone the S.S., who was not at the very least a *vicious* anti-Semite; to believe otherwise is to learn nothing about the nature of anti-Semitism. Uninteresting though it may be to say so, no person of conscience could have participated knowingly in mass murder: to believe otherwise is to learn nothing about the nature of conscience. And uninteresting though it may be to say so, no banality of a man could have done so hugely evil a job so well; to believe otherwise is to learn nothing about the nature of evil. Was Hausner right, then, in repeatedly calling Eichmann a liar? Yes, he was right, however successfully Eichmann may have deceived himself by then, and however "sincere" he may have thought his testimony was.

And the Nature of Totalitarianism? What Miss Arendt's book on the Eichmann trial teaches us about the Nature of Totalitarianism is that the time has come to re-examine the whole concept. Apart from the many other weaknesses it has revealed since the days when it was first developed to distinguish between the "simple" dictatorships of the pre-modern era and the ideologically inspired revolutionary regimes of Stalin and Hitler, the theory of totalitarianism has always been limited in its usefulness by the quasi-metaphysical and rather Germanic terms in which it was originally conceived. For what the theory aimed at describing was a fixed essence, not a phenomenon in flux, and the only changes it saw as possible within the totalitarian structure were those leading toward a more perfect realization of the totalitarian idea itself. (One consequence of this—and it speaks worlds about the limitations of the theory in general—was that many students of Soviet society refused for a long time to credit the significance of the liberalizing tendencies that were so obviously becoming manifest under Khrushchev: once a totalitarian state always a totalitarian state, unless, of course, it could be overthrown by force.)

But since the perfect totalitarian state did not yet exist, how did the theorists of totalitarianism know what it would look like in a fully realized condition? The answer is that they knew from the Nazi concentration camps, which, as they rightly understood, had in part been set up to serve as models and as "laboratories" for experimenting with techniques of absolute domination. Here was where totalitarianism stood nakedly revealed; here was its essential meaning; here was what the system was really all about.

So far, so good. The trouble began with a tendency to speak of Nazi Germany and Soviet Russia as though they had already attained to the perfection of vast concentration camps, and as though the Nazis in their style and the Communists in theirs had already been transformed into the new men of the transvalued totalitarian future. Yet on the basis of a somewhat more optimistic view of human nature than is implicit in the theory of totalitarianism (which substitutes for the naïve liberal idea of the infinite perfectibility of man the equally naïve idea of the infinite malleability of man), one may be permitted to doubt that the whole world could under any circumstances ever be made over into a concentration camp. As it is, Soviet Russia seems to be moving in the other direction. And so far as the Third Reich is concerned, it lasted for less than thirteen years and conquered only a small section of the globe, with the result that: (1) Nazi Germany never had a chance to seal itself off completely from outside influences; and (2) the people who participated actively in Nazism *knew* they were being criminal by the standards under which they themselves had been raised and that also still reigned supreme in the "decadent" culture of the West.

This is why it is finally impossible to accept Miss Arendt's conception of Eichmann's role and character. Eichmann was not living in the ideal Nazi future, but in the imperfect Nazi present, and while we can agree with Miss Arendt that, as a mere lieutenant-colonel, he probably did not enjoy the importance that the Israeli indictment attributed to him, neither can he have been quite so banal as she makes him out to be. After all, there *was* enough opposition to the Final Solution to have persuaded him that not everyone looked upon the murdering of Jews as a fine and noble occupation, and after all, he *was* a first-generation Nazi and an important enough one to have been trusted with a large measure of administrative responsibility for a top-priority item in the Nazi program. Now, if we are not to lose our own minds in the act of trying to penetrate into the psychology of the Nazi mind, we must be very careful to keep it clear that this item of the Nazi program—the "cleansing" of Europe, and ultimately the whole world, of Jews—was literally insane. It is one thing to hate Jews, but it is quite another to contemplate the wholesale slaughter of Jews; it is one thing to believe that no nation-state can be healthy when it contains "alien" elements, but it is quite another to decide upon the murder of eleven million people (the estimated target of the Final Solution) as a means of achieving ethnic homogeneity. Ponder the difference between the Germans and the Rumanians in this connection. The Rumanians were the worst anti-Semites in Europe and were delighted to join in the butchering of Jews, until they discovered that there was money to be made from the saving of Jews, whereupon they began saving Jews: this is pathological anti-Semitism bounded by rational limits. The Germans, on the other hand, regarded the Jews, whom they had rendered utterly helpless with a stroke of the pen, as dangerous enemies, and they were so convinced of the necessity to do away with these enemies that they were willing to let the war effort suffer rather than let up: this is pathological anti-Semitism bounded by no rational limits. Insanity, in short.

It is in this insanity, I believe, and not in the pedestrian character of Adolf Eichmann, that whatever banality attaches to the evil of the Final Solution must be sought. And because Hitler and his cohorts were madmen on the Jewish question, there is probably little of general relevance we can learn from the Final Solution beyond what the Nuremberg trials established concerning the individual's criminal accountability when acting upon superior orders, even within a system guided by insane aims. There is, however, much to be learned from the Final Solution about other matters, and principally about anti-Semitism. When Miss Arendt speaks of the amazing extent of the moral collapse that the Nazis caused "everywhere," she must be referring specifically to the Jewish question. The will to fight the German armies did not collapse everywhere, and the will to defend democracy against the Nazi onslaught stood up well enough to triumph in the end; the only collapse that took place "everywhere" was a collapse of the will to prevent the Nazis from wiping the Jews off the face of the earth. Here again, Miss Arendt can be refuted out of her own mouth, for acquiescence in the Final Solution (as she demonstrates) was far from universal in Europe (though it may well have been nearly universal in Germany). The fact remains, however, that there was acquiescence enough to allow this insane Nazi ambition to come very close to succeeding. Nobody cared about the Gypsies because nobody ever thinks about the Gypsies—except the police. But how did it happen that nobody cared about the Jews when everyone seems always to be thinking about the Jews? The question surely answers itself, and the answer incidentally provides the justification for Ben Gurion's statement that one of the purposes of the Eichmann trial was to make the nations of the world ashamed.

Miss Arendt dislikes that statement, but no more than she dislikes every other statement Ben Gurion made about the trial. She is also unhappy with the trial itself—the fact that Eichmann was tried before an Israeli court instead of an international tribunal, the substance of the indictment, the way Hausner handled the prosecution, the way Servatius conducted the defense. The only aspect of the trial that pleases her is that the judges behaved with scrupulous regard for the interests of Justice: she is as unstinting in her praise of them as she is relentless in her contempt for Hausner and Ben Gurion ("the invisible stage manager of the proceedings"). A few of Miss Arendt's criticisms of the trial seem reasonable, but given the animus she exhibits from the very first sentence of the book, it becomes extremely difficult to look upon these criticisms as anything other than further instances of the inordinate demands she is always making on the Jews to be better than other people, to be braver, wiser, nobler, more dignified—or be damned.

This habit of judging the Jews by one standard and everyone else by another is a habit Miss Arendt shares with many of her fellow-Jews, emphatically including those who think that the main defect of her version of the story is her failure to dwell on all the heroism and all the virtue that the six million displayed among them. But the truth is—*must* be—that the Jews under Hitler acted as men will act when they are set upon by murderers, no better and no worse: the Final Solution reveals nothing about the victims except that they were mortal beings and hopelessly vulnerable in their powerlessness. And as with the victims, so with those who were lucky enough to survive the holocaust. There is no special virtue in sheer survival, whatever Bruno Bettelheim may say, and there is no martyrdom in sheer victimization, whatever certain sentimentalists among us may think.

The Nazis destroyed a third of the Jewish people. In the name of all that is humane, will the remnant never let up on itself?

[1963]

My Negro Problem—And Ours

If we—and . . . I mean the relatively conscious whites and the relatively conscious blacks, who must, like lovers, insist on, or create, the consciousness of the others—do not falter in our duty now, we may be able, handful that we are, to end the racial nightmare, and achieve our country, and change the history of the world.

—James Baldwin

Two ideas puzzled me deeply as a child growing up in Brooklyn during the 1930's in what today would be called an integrated neighborhood. One of them was that all Jews were rich; the other was that all Negroes were persecuted. These ideas had appeared in print; therefore they must be true. My own experience and the evidence of my senses told they were not true, but that only confirmed what a day-dreaming boy in the provinces—for the lower-class neighborhoods of New York belong as surely to the provinces as any rural town in North Dakota—discovers very early: *his* experience is unreal and the evidence of his senses is not to be trusted. Yet even a boy with a head full of fantasies incongruously synthesized out of Hollywood movies and English novels cannot altogether deny the reality of his own experience—especially when there is so much deprivation in that experience. Nor can he alto-gether gainsay the evidence of his own senses—especially such evidence of the senses as comes from being repeatedly beaten up, robbed, and in general hated, terrorized, and humiliated.

And so for a long time I was puzzled to think that Jews were supposed to be rich when the only Jews I knew were poor, and that Negroes were supposed to be persecuted when it was the Negroes who were doing the only persecuting I knew about—and doing it, moreover, to *me*. During the early years of the war, when my older sister joined a left-wing youth organization, I remember my astonishment at hearing her passionately denounce my father for thinking that Jews were worse off than Negroes. To me, at the age of twelve, it seemed very clear that Negroes were better off than Jews—indeed, than *all* whites. A city boy's world is contained within three or four square blocks, and in my world it was the whites, the Italians and Jews, who feared the Negroes, not the other way around. The Negroes were tougher than we were, more ruthless, and on the whole they were better athletes. What could it mean, then, to say that they were badly off and that we were more fortunate? Yet my sister's opinions, like print, were sacred, and when she told me about exploitation and economic forces I believed her. I believed her, but I was still afraid of Negroes. And I still hated them with all my heart.

It had not always been so—that much I can recall from early childhood. When did it start, this fear and this hatred? There was a kindergarten in the local public school, and given the character of the neighborhood, at least half of the children in my class must have been Negroes. Yet I have no memory of being aware of color differences at that age, and I know from observing my own children that they attribute no significance to such differences even when they begin noticing them. I think there was a day—first grade? second grade?—when my best friend Carl hit me on the way home from school and announced that he wouldn't play with me any more because I had killed Jesus. When I ran home to my mother crying for an explanation, she told me not to pay any attention to such foolishness, and then in Yiddish she cursed the *goyim* and the *schwartzes*, the *schwartzes* and the *goyim*. Carl, it turned out, was a *schwartze*, and so was added a third to the categories into which people were mysteriously divided.

Sometimes I wonder whether this is a true memory at all. It is blazingly vivid, but perhaps it never happened: can anyone really remember back to the age of six? There is no uncertainty in my mind, however, about the years that followed. Carl and I hardly ever spoke, though we met in school every day up through the eighth or ninth grade. There would be embarrassed moments of catching his eye or of his catching mine—for whatever it was that had attracted us to one another as very small children remained alive in spite of the fantastic barrier of hostility that had grown up between us, suddenly and out of nowhere. Nevertheless, friendship would have been impossible, and even if it had been possible, it would have been unthinkable. About that, there was nothing anyone could do by the time we were eight years old.

Item: The orphanage across the street is torn down, a city housing project begins to rise in its place, and on the marvelous vacant lot next to the old orphanage they are building a playground. Much excitement and anticipation as Opening Day draws near. Mayor LaGuardia himself comes to dedicate this great gesture of public benevolence. He speaks of neighborliness and borrowing cups of sugar, and of the playground he says that children of all races, colors, and creeds will learn to live together in harmony. A week later, some of us are swatting flies on the playground's inadequate little ball field. A gang of Negro kids, pretty much our own age, enter from the other side and order us out of the park. We refuse, proudly and indignantly, with superb masculine fervor. There is a fight, they win, and we retreat, half whimpering, half with bravado. My first nauseating experience of cowardice. And my first appalled realization that there are people in the world who do not seem to be afraid of anything, who act as though they have nothing to lose. Thereafter the playground becomes a battle-ground, sometimes quiet, sometimes the scene of athletic compe-tition between Them and Us. But rocks are thrown as often as baseballs. Gradually we abandon the place and use the streets instead. The streets are safer, though we do not admit this to our-selves. We are not, after all, sissies—that most dreaded epithet of an American boyhood.

Item: I am standing alone in front of the building in which I live. It is late afternoon and getting dark. That day in school the teacher had asked a surly Negro boy named Quentin a question he was unable to answer. As usual I had waved my arm eagerly ("Be a good boy, get good marks, be smart, go to college, become a doctor") and, the right answer bursting from my lips, I was held up lovingly by the teacher as an example to the class. I had seen Quentin's face—a very dark, very cruel, very Oriental-looking face —harden, and there had been enough threat in his eyes to make me run all the way home for fear that he might catch me outside.

Now, standing idly in front of my own house, I see him ap-proaching from the project accompanied by his little brother who is carrying a baseball bat and wearing a grin of malicious anticipa-tion. As in a nightmare, I am trapped. The surroundings are secure and familiar, but terror is suddenly present and there is no one around to help. I am locked to the spot. I will not cry out or run away like a sissy, and I stand there, my heart wild, my throat clogged. He walks up, hurls the familiar epithet ("Hey,

mo'f——r"), and to my surprise only pushes me. It is a violent
push, but not a punch. Maybe I can still back out without entirely
losing my dignity. Maybe I can still say, "Hey, c'mon Quentin,
whaddya wanna do *that* for? I dint do nothin' to *you*," and walk
away, not too rapidly. Instead, before I can stop myself, I push
him back—a token gesture—and I say, "Cut that out, I don't
wanna fight, I ain't got nothin' to fight about." As I turn to walk
back into the building, the corner of my eye catches the motion
of the bat his little brother has handed him. I try to duck, but the
bat crashes colored lights into my head.

The next thing I know, my mother and sister are standing over
me, both of them hysterical. My sister—she who was later to join
the "progressive" youth organization—is shouting for the police
and screaming imprecations at those dirty little black bastards.
They take me upstairs, the doctor comes, the police come. I tell
them that the boy who did it was a stranger, that he had been
trying to get money from me. They do not believe me, but I am
too scared to give them Quentin's name. When I return to school
a few days later, Quentin avoids my eyes. He knows that I have
not squealed, and he is ashamed. I try to feel proud, but in my
heart I know that it was fear of what his friends might do to me
that had kept me silent, and not the code of the street.

Item: There is an athletic meet in which the whole of our junior
high school is participating. I am in one of the seventh-grade rapid-
advance classes, and "segregation" has now set in with a vengeance. In the last three or four years of the elementary school
from which we have just graduated, each grade had been divided
into three classes, according to "intelligence." (In the earlier
grades the divisions had either been arbitrary or else unrecognized
by us as having anything to do with brains.) These divisions by
IQ, or however it was arranged, had resulted in a preponderance
of Jews in the "1" classes and a corresponding preponderance of

Negroes in the "3's," with the Italians split unevenly along the spectrum. At least a few Negroes had always made the "1's," just as there had always been a few Jewish kids among the "3's" and more among the "2's" (where Italians dominated). But the junior high's rapid-advance class of which I am now a member is overwhelmingly Jewish and entirely white—except for a shy lonely Negro girl with light skin and reddish hair.

The athletic meet takes place in a city-owned stadium far from the school. It is an important event to which a whole day is given over. The winners are to get those precious little medallions stamped with the New York City emblem that can be screwed into a belt and that prove the wearer to be a distinguished personage. I am a fast runner, and so I am assigned the position of anchor man on my class's team in the relay race. There are three other seventh-grade teams in the race, two of them all Negro, as ours is all white. One of the all-Negro teams is very tall—their anchor man waiting silently next to me on the line looks years older than I am, and I do not recognize him. He is the first to get the baton and crosses the finishing line in a walk. Our team comes in second, but a few minutes later we are declared the winners, for it has been discovered that the anchor man on the first-place team is not a member of the class. We are awarded the medallions, and the following day our home-room teacher makes a speech about how proud she is of us for being superior athletes as well as superior students. We want to believe that we deserve the praise, but we know that we could not have won even if the other class had not cheated.

That afternoon, walking home, I am waylaid and surrounded by five Negroes, among whom is the anchor man of the disqualified team. "Gimme my medal, mo'f——r," he grunts. I do not have it with me and I tell him so. "Anyway, it ain't yours," I say foolishly. He calls me a liar on both counts and pushes me up against the wall on which we sometimes play handball. "Gimme my mo'f——n' medal," he says again. I repeat that I have left it home. "Le's search the li'l mo'f——r," one of them suggests, "he prolly got it *hid* in his mo'f——n' *pants*." My panic is now unmanageable. (How many times had I been surrounded like this and asked in soft tones, "Len' me a nickel, boy." How many times had I been called a liar for pleading poverty and pushed around, or searched, or beaten up, unless there happened to be someone in the marauding gang like Carl who liked me across that enormous divide of hatred and who would therefore say, "Aaah, c'mon, le's git someone else, *this* boy ain't got no money on 'im.") I scream at them through tears of rage and self-contempt, "Keep your f——n' filthy lousy black hands offa me! I swear I'll get the cops." This is all they need to hear, and the five of them set upon me. They bang me around, mostly in the stomach and on the arms and shoulders, and when several adults loitering near the candy store down the block notice what is going on and begin to shout, they run off and away.

I do not tell my parents about the incident. My team-mates, who have also been waylaid, each by a gang led by his opposite number from the disqualified team, have had their medallions taken from them, and they never squeal either. For days, I walk home in terror, expecting to be caught again, but nothing happens. The medallion is put away into a drawer, never to be worn by anyone.

Obviously experiences like these have always been a common feature of childhood life in working-class and immigrant neighborhoods, and Negroes do not necessarily figure in them. Wherever, and in whatever combination, they have lived together in the cities, kids of different groups have been at war, beating up and being beaten up: micks against kikes against wops against spicks against polacks. And even relatively homogeneous areas have not been spared the warring of the young: one block against another, one gang (called in my day, in a pathetic effort at gentility, an "S.A.C.," or social-athletic club) against another. But the Negro-white conflict had—and no doubt still has—a special intensity and was conducted with a ferocity unmatched by intramural white battling.

In my own neighborhood, a good deal of animosity existed between the Italian kids (most of whose parents were immigrants from Sicily) and the Jewish kids (who came largely from East European immigrant families). Yet everyone had friends, sometimes close friends, in the other "camp," and we often visited one another's strange-smelling houses, if not for meals, then for glasses of milk, and occasionally for some special event like a wedding or a wake. If it happened that we divided into warring factions and did battle, it would invariably be half-hearted and soon patched up. Our parents, to be sure, had nothing to do with one another and were mutually suspicious and hostile. But we, the kids, who all spoke Yiddish or Italian at home, were Americans, or New Yorkers, or Brooklyn boys: we shared a culture, the culture of the street, and at least for a while this culture proved to be more powerful than the opposing cultures of the home.

Why, *why* should it have been so different as between the Negroes and us? How was it borne in upon us so early, white and black alike, that we were enemies beyond any possibility of reconciliation? Why did we hate one another so?

I suppose if I tried, I could answer those questions more or less adequately from the perspective of what I have since learned. I could draw upon James Baldwin—what better witness is there?—to describe the sense of entrapment that poisons the soul of the Negro with hatred for the white man whom he knows to be his jailer. On the other side, if I wanted to understand how the white man comes to hate the Negro, I could call upon the psychologists who have spoken of the guilt that white Americans feel toward Negroes and that turns into hatred for lack of acknowledging itself as guilt. These are plausible answers and certainly there is truth in them. Yet when I think back upon my own experience of the Negro and his of me, I find myself troubled and puzzled, much as I was as a child when I heard that all Jews were rich and all Negroes persecuted. How could the Negroes in my neighborhood have regarded the whites across the street and around the corner as jailers? On the whole, the whites were not so poor as the Negroes, but they were quite poor enough, and the years were years of Depression. As for white hatred of the Negro, how could guilt have had anything to do with it? What share had these Italian and Jewish immigrants in the enslavement of the Negro? What share had they—downtrodden people themselves breaking their own necks to eke out a living—in the exploitation of the Negro?

No, I cannot believe that we hated each other back there in Brooklyn because they thought of us as jailers and we felt guilty toward them. But does it matter, given the fact that we all went through an unrepresentative confrontation? I think it matters profoundly, for if we managed the job of hating each other so well without benefit of the aids to hatred that are supposedly at the root of this madness everywhere else, it must mean that the madness is not yet properly understood. I am far from pretending that I understand it, but I would insist that no view of the problem will begin to approach the truth unless it can account for a case like the one I have been trying to describe. Are the elements of any such view available to us?

At least two, I would say, are. One of them is a point we frequently come upon in the work of James Baldwin, and the other is a related point always stressed by psychologists who have studied the mechanisms of prejudice. Baldwin tells us that one of the reasons Negroes hate the white man is that the white man refuses to *look* at him: the Negro knows that in white eyes all Negroes are alike; they are faceless and therefore not altogether human. The psychologists, in their turn, tell us that the white man hates the Negro because he tends to project those wild impulses that he fears in himself onto an alien group which he then punishes with his contempt. What Baldwin does *not* tell us, however, is that the principle of facelessness is a two-way street and can operate in both directions with no difficulty at all. Thus, in my neighborhood in Brooklyn, *I* was as faceless to the Negroes as they were to me, and if they hated me because I never looked at them, I must also have hated them for never looking at *me*. To the Negroes, my white skin was enough to define me as the enemy, and in a war it is only the uniform that counts and not the person.

So with the mechanism of projection that the psychologists talk about: it too works in both directions at once. There is no question that the psychologists are right about what the Negro represents symbolically to the white man. For me as a child the life lived on the other side of the playground and down the block on Ralph Avenue seemed the very embodiment of the values of the street—free, independent, reckless, brave, masculine, erotic. I put the word "erotic" last, though it is usually stressed above all others, because in fact it came last, in consciousness as in importance. What mainly counted for me about Negro kids of my own age was that they were "bad boys." There were plenty of bad boys among the whites—this was, after all, a neighborhood with a long tradition of crime as a career open to aspiring talents—but the Negroes were *really* bad, bad in a way that beckoned to one, and made one feel inadequate. *We* all went home every day for a lunch of spinach-and-potatoes; *they* roamed around during lunch hour, munching on candy bars. In winter *we* had to wear itchy woolen hats and mittens and cumbersome galoshes; *they* were bareheaded and loose as they pleased. *We* rarely played hookey, or got into serious trouble in school, for all our street-corner bravado; *they* were defiant, forever staying out (to do what delicious things?), forever making disturbances in class and in the halls, forever being sent to the principal and returning uncowed. But most important of all, they were *tough*; beautifully, enviably tough, not giving a damn for anyone or anything. To hell with the teacher, the truant officer, the cop; to hell with the whole of the adult world that held *us* in its grip and that we never had the courage to rebel against except sporadically and in petty ways.

This is what I saw and envied and feared in the Negro: this is what finally made him faceless to me, though some of it, of course, was actually there. (The psychologists also tell us that the alien group which becomes the object of a projection will tend to respond by trying to live up to what is expected of them.) But what, on his side, did the Negro see in me that made me faceless to *him*? Did he envy me my lunches of spinach-and-potatoes and my itchy woolen caps and my prudent behavior in the face of authority, as I envied him his noon-time candy bars and his bare head in winter and his magnificent rebelliousness? Did those lunches and caps spell for him the prospect of power and riches in the future? Did they mean that there were possibilities open to me that were denied to him? Very likely they did. But if so, one also supposes that he feared the impulses within himself toward submission to authority no less powerfully than I feared the impulses in myself toward defiance. If I represented the jailer to him, it was not because I was oppressing him or keeping him down: it was because I symbolized for him the dangerous and probably pointless temptation toward greater repression, just as he symbolized for me the equally perilous tug toward greater freedom. I personally was to be rewarded for this repression with a new and better life in the future, but how many of my friends paid an even higher price and were given only gall in return.

We have it on the authority of James Baldwin that all Negroes hate whites. I am trying to suggest that on their side all whites— all American whites, that is—are sick in their feelings about Negroes. There are Negroes, no doubt, who would say that

Baldwin is wrong, but I suspect them of being less honest than he is, just as I suspect whites of self-deception who tell me they have no special feeling toward Negroes. Special feelings about color are a contagion to which white Americans seem susceptible even when there is nothing in their background to account for the susceptibility. Thus everywhere we look today in the North we find the curious phenomenon of white middle-class liberals with no previous personal experience of Negroes—people to whom Negroes have always been faceless in virtue rather than faceless in vice—discovering that their abstract commitment to the cause of Negro rights will not stand the test of a direct confrontation. We find such people fleeing in droves to the suburbs as the Negro population in the inner city grows; and when they stay in the city we find them sending their children to private school rather than to the "integrated" public school in the neighborhood. We find them resisting the demand that gerrymandered school districts be re-zoned for the purpose of overcoming de facto segregation; we find them judiciously considering whether the Negroes (for their own good, of course) are not perhaps pushing too hard; we find them clucking their tongues over Negro militancy; we find them speculating on the question of whether there may not, after all, be something in the theory that the races are biologically different; we find them saying that it will take a very long time for Negroes to achieve full equality, no matter what anyone does; we find them deploring the rise of black nationalism and expressing the solemn hope that the leaders of the Negro community will discover ways of containing the impatience and incipient violence within the Negro ghettos.*

But that is by no means the whole story; there is also the phenomenon of what Kenneth Rexroth once called "crow-jimism."

---

* For an account of developments like these, see "The White Liberal's Retreat" by Murray Friedman in the January 1963 *Atlantic Monthly*.

There are the broken-down white boys like Vivaldo Moore in Baldwin's *Another Country* who go to Harlem in search of sex or simply to brush up against something that looks like primitive vitality, and who are so often punished by the Negroes they meet for crimes that they would have been the last ever to commit and of which they themselves have been as sorry victims as any of the Negroes who take it out on them. There are the writers and intellectuals and artists who romanticize Negroes and pander to them, assuming a guilt that is not properly theirs. And there are all the white liberals who permit Negroes to blackmail them into adopting a double standard of moral judgment, and who lend themselves—again assuming the responsibility for crimes they never committed—to cunning and contemptuous exploitation by Negroes they employ or try to befriend.

And what about me? What kind of feelings do I have about Negroes today? What happened to me, from Brooklyn, who grew up fearing and envying and hating Negroes? Now that Brooklyn is behind me, do I fear them and envy them and hate them still? The answer is yes, but not in the same proportions and certainly not in the same way. I now live on the upper west side of Manhattan, where there are many Negroes and many Puerto Ricans, and there are nights when I experience the old apprehensiveness again, and there are streets that I avoid when I am walking in the dark, as there were streets that I avoided when I was a child. I find that I am not afraid of Puerto Ricans, but I cannot restrain my nervousness whenever I pass a group of Negroes standing in front of a bar or sauntering down the street. I know now, as I did not know when I was a child, that power is on my side, that the police are working for me and not for them. And knowing this I feel ashamed and guilty, like the good liberal I have grown up to be. Yet the twinges of fear and the resentment they bring and the self-contempt they arouse are not to be gainsaid.

But envy? Why envy? And hatred? Why hatred? Here again the

intensities have lessened and everything has been complicated and qualified by the guilts and the resulting over-compensations that are the heritage of the enlightened middle-class world of which I am now a member. Yet just as in childhood I envied Negroes for what seemed to me their superior masculinity, so I envy them today for what seems to me their superior physical grace and beauty. I have come to value physical grace very highly, and I am now capable of aching with all my being when I watch a Negro couple on the dance floor, or a Negro playing baseball or basketball. They are on the kind of terms with their own bodies that I should like to be on with mine, and for that precious quality they seemed blessed to me.

The hatred I still feel for Negroes is the hardest of all the old feelings to face or admit, and it is the most hidden and the most overlarded by the conscious attitudes into which I have succeeded in willing myself. It no longer has, as for me it once did, any cause or justification (except, perhaps, that I am constantly being denied my right to an honest expression of the things I earned the right as a child to feel). How, then, do I know that this hatred has never entirely disappeared? I know it from the insane rage that can stir in me at the thought of Negro anti-Semitism; I know it from the disgusting prurience that can stir in me at the sight of a mixed couple; and I know it from the violence that can stir in me whenever I encounter that special brand of paranoid touchiness to which many Negroes are prone.

This, then, is where I am; it is not exactly where I think all other white liberals are, but it cannot be so very far away either. And it is because I am convinced that we white Americans are— for whatever reason, it no longer matters—so twisted and sick in our feelings about Negroes that I despair of the present push toward integration. If the pace of progress were not a factor here, there would perhaps be no cause for despair: time and the law and even the international political situation are on the side of the Negroes, and ultimately, therefore, victory—of a sort, anyway— must come. But from everything we have learned from observers who ought to know, pace has become as important to the Negroes as substance. They want equality and they want it *now*, and the white world is yielding to their demand only as much and as fast as it is absolutely being compelled to do. The Negroes know this in the most concrete terms imaginable, and it is thus becoming increasingly difficult to buy them off with rhetoric and promises and pious assurances of support. And so within the Negro community we find more and more people declaring—as Harold R. Isaacs recently put it in an article in *Commentary*—that they want *out*: people who say that integration will never come, or that it will take a hundred or a thousand years to come, or that it will come at too high a price in suffering and struggle for the pallid and sodden life of the American middle class that at the very best it may bring.

The most numerous, influential, and dangerous movement that has grown out of Negro despair with the goal of integration is, of course, the Black Muslims. This movement, whatever else we may say about it, must be credited with one enduring achievement: it inspired James Baldwin to write an essay which deserves to be placed among the classics of our language. Everything Baldwin has ever been trying to tell us is distilled in *The Fire Next Time* into a statement of overwhelming persuasiveness and prophetic magnificence. Baldwin's message is and always has been simple. It is this: "Color is not a human or personal reality; it is a political reality." And Baldwin's demand is correspondingly simple: color must be forgotten, lest we all be smited with a vengeance "that does not really depend on, and cannot really be executed by, any person or organization, and that cannot be prevented by any police force or army: historical vengeance, a cosmic vengeance based on the law that we recognize when we say,

'Whatever goes up must come down.'" The Black Muslims Baldwin portrays as a sign and a warning to the intransigent white world. They come to proclaim how deep is the Negro's disaffection with the white world and all its works, and Baldwin implies that no American Negro can fail to respond somewhere in his being to their message: that the white man is the devil, that Allah has doomed him to destruction, and that the black man is about to inherit the earth. Baldwin of course knows that this nightmare inversion of the racism from which the black man has suffered can neither win nor even point to the neighborhood in which victory might be located. For in his view the neighborhood of victory lies in exactly the opposite direction: the transcendence of color through love.

Yet the tragic fact is that love is not the answer to hate—not in the world of politics, at any rate. Color is indeed a political rather than a human or a personal reality and if politics (which is to say power) has made it into a human and personal reality, then only politics (which is to say power) can unmake it once again. But the way of politics is slow and bitter, and as impatience on the one side is matched by a setting of the jaw on the other, we move closer and closer to an explosion and blood may yet run in the streets.

Will this madness in which we are all caught never find a resting-place? Is there never to be an end to it? In thinking about the Jews I have often wondered whether their survival as a distinct group was worth one hair on the head of a single infant. Did the Jews have to survive so that six million innocent people should one day be burned in the ovens of Auschwitz? It is a terrible question and no one, not God himself, could ever answer it to my satisfaction. And when I think about the Negroes in America and about the image of integration as a state in which the Negroes would take their rightful place as another of the protected minorities in a pluralistic society, I wonder whether they really believe in their hearts that such a state can actually be attained, and if so *why* they should wish to survive as a distinct group. I think I know why the Jews once wished to survive (though I am less certain as to why we still do): they not only believed that God had given them no choice, but they were tied to a memory of past glory and a dream of imminent redemption. What does the American Negro have that might correspond to this? His past is a stigma, his color is a stigma, and his vision of the future is the hope of erasing the stigma by making color irrelevant, by making it disappear as a fact of consciousness.

I share this hope, but I cannot see how it will ever be realized unless color does *in fact* disappear: and that means not integration, it means assimilation, it means—let the brutal word come out—miscegenation. The Black Muslims, like their racist counterparts in the white world, accuse the "so-called Negro leaders" of secretly pursuing miscegenation as a goal. The racists are wrong, but I wish they were right, for I believe that the wholesale merger of the two races is the most desirable alternative for everyone concerned. I am not claiming that this alternative can be pursued programmatically or that it is immediately feasible as a solution; obviously there are even greater barriers to its achievement than to the achievement of integration. What I am saying, however, is that in my opinion the Negro problem can be solved in this country in no other way.

I have told the story of my own twisted feelings about Negroes here, and of how they conflict with the moral convictions I have since developed, in order to assert that such feelings must be acknowledged as honestly as possible so that they can be controlled and ultimately disregarded in favor of the convictions. It is *wrong* for a man to suffer because of the color of his skin. Beside that clichéd proposition of liberal thought, what argument can stand and be respected? If the arguments are the arguments of feeling, they must be made to yield; and one's own soul is not the worst place to begin working a huge social transformation. Not so long ago, it used to be asked of white liberals, "Would you like your sister to marry one?" When I was a boy and my sister was still unmarried I would certainly have said no to that question. But now I am a man, my sister is already married, and I have daughters. If I were to be asked today whether I would like a daughter of mine "to marry one," I would have to answer: "No, I wouldn't *like* it at all. I would rail and rave and rant and tear my hair. And then I hope I would have the courage to curse myself for raving and ranting, and to give her my blessing. How dare I withhold it at the behest of the child I once was and against the man I now have a duty to be?"

[1963]